GENERATIONAL GOALKEEPING

A GRASSROOTS ROADMAP FOR AGES U8 – WORLD CLASS

Senior Edition: U16 – U18

By

Paul D. Blodgett, M.Ed.

Paul Blodgett Goalkeeper Training School, LLC

This curriculum is written as a template for the chronological development of goalkeepers from ages U8 – U18; to the author's knowledge, no other such document exists outside of individual club organizations. It is an effort to homogenize the approach to training and developing keepers so that a consistency might be established. This series is a grassroots approach to training the position. The desire is that a true Goalkeeper Culture may be established in an effort to catapult the position to its rightful position – the forefront.

Author's Note

This series of volumes has been years in the making. That being said, multiple changes have occurred in the position and in the game during its writing. Because of these rapid changes, some new terminologies, techniques and tactical developments might vary relative to today's game.

Please take into consideration that the changes in the position and the game are ongoing and will continue to evolve.

Due to the massive amount of information contained within this body of work, the manuscript has been broken down into six separate volumes, as described below:

Three complete volumes containing all of the information:

- Youth Edition: Ages U8 & U10
- Junior Edition: Ages U12 & U14
- Senior Edition: Ages U16 – U18

Three additional volumes containing Lesson Plans only:

- Youth Edition: Ages U8 & U10
- Junior Edition: Ages U12 & U14
- Senior Edition: Ages U16 – U18

Once a complete volume in any age group is acquired, the remaining volumes containing the Lesson Plans only, can be purchased to complete the series.

Foreword

I met Paul Blodgett in 1976 when I had just graduated from Springfield College in Springfield, MA., and where Paul had just received his Master's Degree in Education. I got to know Paul after scoring a few goals against his adult soccer team in the Massachusetts Amateur Soccer League. After observing his goalkeeping performance in that game, where he made 40 saves out of 45 shots on goal, I convinced him to transfer to my team. Keeping in mind that he had never trained as a goalkeeper or played soccer before that game, it was obvious to me that he was a natural talent in the goal.

Since that game in 1976, Paul Blodgett has been a student and teacher of the game, perfecting his craft in many soccer environments. He coached 5 years at Agawam High School in Massachusetts, over 20 years at Rutgers University in New Jersey (Men's Program) and 14 years at The College of New Jersey (Women's Program). Coach Blodgett continues to train in the New Jersey Youth Soccer Olympic Development Program (boys and girls) and continues to work with youth and college goalkeepers throughout New Jersey through his Goalkeeper Training School.

Coach Blodgett has created an easy-to-read instructional guide for coaches of goalkeepers. The book is truly a "Roadmap to Developing the Next Generation of Goalkeepers". The content exemplifies Paul's unique ability to paint clear pictures for goalkeepers of all ages in his training sessions. This curriculum is an important resource for goalkeeper trainers at all levels. As the former US Youth Soccer National Director of Coaching Education and USSF National Staff Coach, I strongly endorse Coach Blodgett's book and recommend its use by youth and senior soccer coaches.

Sincerely,

Tom Goodman, M.Ed.

Dedications

Father and Mother

Dr. Robert N. Blodgett, Sr. (1921 – 1981)

And

Elizabeth Marie (Musto) Blodgett (1924 – 1998)

I dedicate this book to my mother and father; thank you for giving me life and providing me the with the opportunities to experience all it has to offer. My love to you both is eternal.

Schyler Herman

Schyler Herman was a goalkeeper I met through Players Development Academy (PDA) in NJ, where she played for the PDA Crew. Driving from her hometown of Saylorsburg, PA to PDA in NJ, she rode with her family well over an hour each way for training.

She was as driven and dedicated a player as I have seen in my career. She had no fear, was a superb athlete, and possessed all the faculties needed to take her to whatever level she desired to play. On top of all of these things, she was a joy to coach and to be around; she made those around her better due to her personality and character.

At the age of 14, she was a rising young star who started at Pleasant Valley High School as a freshman. During the season, Schyler's parents started noticing that she was suffering from unusually deep bruises which rose above those normally associated with goalkeeper battle wounds.

During an intense game on September 29, 2017, Schyler came in contact with another player, and a deep hematoma formed. Her parents took her to the emergency room the next day. The X-rays came out negative for a fracture, but by the end of the day, blood work suggested Schyler had leukemia. She was rushed to The Children's Hospital in Philadelphia for immediate treatment because her blood levels were so critical.

On October 2nd, 2017, Schyler was diagnosed with pre-B acute lymphoblastic leukemia, the most common type of leukemia in children, according to the National Institutes of Health. Pre-B acute lymphoblastic leukemia is where the bone marrow makes too many immature white blood cells, and thus her battle against the disease began.

On June 18th, 2018, Schyler received CAR T-cell immunotherapy which was supposed to eliminate her ALL leukemia. Instead, her leukemia mutated into AML leukemia which is a more aggressive form, and it mutated from her original chemo-resistant cancer.

On October 29th, Schyler suffered a brain bleed due to AML Leukemia and passed away on October 31st, 2018 laying in her mother's arms.

Schyler lived for soccer – she trained constantly to one day be the best female keeper ever. She never gave up this dream even when suffering through the worst of her chemo. She stayed positive every day fully expecting to be between the pipes again.

I visited Schyler, as well as Mike and Sherrie Herman, her very loving and supportive parents, at CHOP in Philadelphia several times. Her will to beat the disease that was overcoming her was one of the most moving experiences in my life. I miss her greatly but I feel her spirit to be alive and well.

Schyler Herman

03/20/2003 - 10/31/2018

SchylerStrong Foundation Inc: https://www.schylerstrong.com

Ricky Zinter

Richard "Ricky" Zinter was one of a kind and lived by his motto of "You're responsible for your own happiness". He was born on Feb 1, 1981, and grew up in Penfield NY, a suburb of Rochester.

He played soccer (mostly as a goalkeeper), lacrosse (defense), and hockey (forward) all through high school. He started playing these sports in Penfield when he was about 5 and also for 3 years in Japan during high school, where he won several soccer awards. He still holds the New York State, Section 5 record of a 0.18 GAA, set in 1998.

Ricky attended Rutgers University, where his most memorable moment was defeating UConn, the defending national champion, in the NCAA tournament his junior year. He always had the great support of his parents, Rick Zinter and Maria Reitano Zinter.

But it was not all soccer-related, as Ricky was an avid snow skier and outdoors enthusiast. A year after college he transferred to Denver, where he applied his computer skills at work and continued his soccer, hockey, and skiing activities outside of work. It was skiing when he met Sarah Robbins, his future wife.

It was on June 20, 2015, that Ricky died in a white-water rafting accident. A tribute to the positive impact he had on people's lives is that three of his high school teammates hold a fundraiser for a college scholarship in his name. The attendance and money raised, even years after his passing at the annual "Round Fore Ricky", is a testament to his lasting and future impact on others.

Ricky was known for his infectious smile and as someone who brought happiness and brightness to everyone he touched. His smile lit up the room and people just loved to be around him. He was always generous with giving his time to young kids, teaching them skiing and soccer. Ricky had a listening ear and cared deeply about his friends and family. It was his zest for life and all of the thrills and challenges that it brought to him that were fulfilling. Ricky's spirit is strongly felt to this day. I loved training him and just being around him. He is greatly missed.

Round Fore Ricky: https://www.facebook.com/roundforericky; www.roundforericky.com

Erica Keil

Erica Keil grew up in Wayne, New Jersey where she played for TSF Academy and DePaul Catholic High School. At TSF, she went through the program starting at U12 all the way to the W League team. At DePaul Catholic, she was a four-year starter and achieved All-County and All-State selections, as well as being captain. For college, Erica chose to go to Virginia Wesleyan University where she was a three-year starter, an All ODAC selection, and an All-Region selection. She finished her career leading the Marlins to the NCAA three times and an ODAC regular season title in 2012.

Keil put up her cleats and started coaching as a graduate assistant at Wesley College where she also completed a Master's Degree in Athletic Leadership with an emphasis on coaching. At Wesley, she helped lead the team to their first ECAC appearance. After Wesley, she joined the coaching staff at North Carolina

Wesleyan College as an assistant coach. At NCWC she coached an All-Conference goalkeeper and helped her team make it to the playoffs in 2016 and 2017. Stints at Yeshiva University and LIU Brooklyn followed, along with The College of New Jersey. At TCNJ she was part of the Atlantic Region Staff of the Year, coached the Conference Goalkeeper of the Year, who was also selected as an All-American, and helped the team to a NCAA National Runner-Up and NJAC Conference Championship season. She also coached at Frostburg Women's Soccer which reached their first D2 NCAA tournament and were regular season Conference Champions.

Off the field, Erica has fought through various health battles including diagnoses of Granulamotis with Polyangiitis and atypical Trigeminal neuralgia. In 2020, Erica and her family started the Keilstrong Foundation where they use parts of Erica's story to raise money for various charities. Most recently they raised over $5,000 for the Vasculitis Foundation. Her parents, Eric and Nancy, are two rocks that have given her the foundation to fight and survive.

I have worked with Erica since she was a young keeper. A very dedicated athlete who absolutely loves the position, she worked very hard at her craft which led her to play, and excel, at the collegiate level. Erica has a great love for soccer, which is obvious in her career choice to stay involved with the game. Personally, it brings me great joy and satisfaction to teach and mentor such a passionate individual, who then goes on to have success.

Erica's battles with her health are both courageous and uplifting. Every time an issue arises, she faces the situation head-on and with the fight and confidence that she will conquer whatever comes her way. To say that I admire such a character is an understatement. Erica is a continual inspiration to me. I thoroughly enjoy her friendship, her knowledge, her passion for life, and her love of the game.

KeilStrong Foundation: https://www.facebook.com/KeilStronFdn

Acknowledgments

A project that is as comprehensive as this one was, cannot be accomplished without the help and guidance from many people on many different fronts. It is literally impossible for me to name everyone in my life and career who has influenced me to become the person and teacher that I am today. That being said, I would like to acknowledge several people that were influential in completing this project.

Bob Reasso – Bob, one of my greatest and dearest friends, was the one responsible for me getting into the game. We met in graduate school at Springfield College, Bob wanted to pursue soccer as a career, and I just pursuing my Masters to become a physical education teacher. He rose to the elite in soccer coaching and his career is legendary. Bob took me under his wing and presented me with the ensuing opportunities for my career as a goalkeeper coach. I followed along with Bob in his college coaching career at Nasson College in Maine and then at Rutgers University in New Brunswick, NJ. He was instrumental in me learning the game and he gave me the freedom to develop my goalkeeping expertise as I saw fit. I will always be thankful to Bob for helping me to find my passion and then providing me with the opportunities to pursue that passion.

Tom Goodman – This curriculum project was initiated by my great friend Tom Goodman. Tom is a national and internationally renowned clinician and teacher of the game; formerly the US Youth Soccer National Director of Coaching Education and USSF National Staff Coach. Tom's past curriculum work in youth soccer development led him to research developmental curriculums for goalkeepers, and he found that there were none on a national scale. Tom was my inspiration and guide to work on and complete this document. I thank him for the rock behind this body of work – it would not exist or have been completed without him. Tom is responsible for me being the teacher within the game that I am today.

Lubos Ancin – Lubos Ancin, who has risen to the positions of Associate Head Coach/Goalkeeper Coach of the highly successful Rutgers Women's Soccer Program, as well as, the Goalkeeper Director of PDA (Players Development Academy) Girls' Soccer, is and has been vital in my development of planning and implementing training sessions. A dear friend, whom I trained as a college and professional keeper, returned to New Jersey after his professional playing career to help fulfill a dream of ours in working together as a very strong team of educators and mentors of the position. Lubos' requisites for training attitude of working hard, listening and apply, and being a good human being, are cornerstones of all of our training sessions and are reasons for our successes in developing keepers. I consider Lubos one of the premier developers of goalkeepers in the country.

Tim Janes – A former goalkeeper student of mine, Tim took on the role of editing this body of work – no small task due to the intricacies and details of the writing overall and of the lesson plans in particular. One will note the detail in each lesson plan which is a reflection of my teaching method, making the editing a challenging endeavor. Going beyond just editing details, Tim also edited for content by making contributions that added fullness and clarity. I would have been dead in the water without Tim's help.

Bob Blodgett, Jr, brother; Jare' Cardinal, sister – My life is fulfilled because of my two wonderful siblings, whom I love dearly; always, always, always there…

Kathleen Marcy – who gave incredible support during the long and arduous time of writing this curriculum.

John J. Foster (Fos) – my oldest friend (since, 6 years old) whom I consider **as** family; a tremendous sounding board and supporter, who has always kept me on a forward path.

Jake Fredericks – A dear friend, confidant, and mentor; I am blessed with his friendship.

Table of Contents

Notables and Influentials

Karina LeBlanc (KK) – When it comes to people who have been influential in my life as a person and as a coach, KK is right there at the top of the list. One of the most dynamic and personable people I have ever met; KK came into my life at a point when my coaching career needed to be resurrected; we developed a mutual relationship of love and respect that stands strong to this day.

Taken from her website (www.karinaleblanc.com), some of her athletic accomplishments are: She's the longest-serving women's professional soccer player in Canada; played in 5 FIFA World Cups; was a Bronze Medalist in the London Olympics; won 2 Pan Am Gold Medals and is in the Canada Soccer Hall of Fame.

After her illustrious playing career, KK went on to have success in business as Head of Women's Football for CONCACAF and is presently the President and GM of the Portland Thorns. She Heads her own Foundation, KARINA LEBLANC FOUNDATION, which gives girls the verve and strength to be whom they are meant to be.

KK was instrumental in helping me reinstate my purpose as a coach, teacher, and mentor of the position.

Lubos Ancin – Lubos is one of the most influential people, not only in my coaching career but also in my life. An exemplary man who cares deeply about the position, the game, his family, and his friends. My life is greatly enhanced by his presence. He is an exceptional teacher and innovator in the advancement of goalkeeping. (See more about Lubos in "Acknowledgements".)

Tim Howard/Tim Mulqueen (Mulch) – Arguably the best player/mentor relationship in the history of the goalkeeper position in US Soccer. Tim is considered the G.O.A.T of US Keepers, which I support, because of his historic success as a professional and National Team keeper, as well as, his incredible knowledge and teaching ability to keepers of all ages.

In addition to Tim Howard's phenomenal playing career, he has notably expressed dealing with Turrets Syndrome throughout his life. Tim has created a foundation in support of Turrets; please follow his Foundation: www.timhowardfoundation.org

Mulch was Tim's mentor, and I had the good fortune of being a mentor to Mulch. Personally, the dynamic played out by them asking me to be a Director at their Goalkeeper Camp in Florida – one of the best coaching and learning experiences I have had in my career. Mulch's knowledge and experience are second to none, having not only worked with Tim but also most of the National team GK's from Tony Meola onward. Tim's ability to take his world-class experiences and present them to the keepers in such a way for all of them to understand and learn was very valuable.

Mulch's honors include being a member of St. Joseph's Metuchen High School Athletic Hall of Fame, St. Joseph's University Soccer Hall of Fame, and Rutgers University Athletic Hall of Fame.

To say I became a better coach because of my experiences with both of them is an understatement. I was honored when Mulch introduced me as "The Godfather of Goalkeeping"! My ultimate respect remains for both.

JD Martin – One of the absolute gifts that come as a result of coaching and mentoring individuals is establishing life-long, meaningful relationships with people who impact one's life – JD Martin is one of those people. An exceptional human being, JD is one of my closest friends to this day. He is arguably the most technical goalkeeper with whom I've had the opportunity to work. JD is a natural leader, who has been successful in every endeavor that he has taken on. A staunch family man, JD is a fiery competitor who attacks challenges with vigor. I consider it an honor to have one of my former goalkeepers as a confidant and a mentor in return.

JD is featured on the cover of this book when he was a GK at North Brunswick High School.

Casey Murphy – Blodge and I traveled to work at Tim Howard's Goalkeeping Camp in 2016. I was 20 years old. This was my first-time coaching, and what better mentor to have with me than Coach Blodge?

I joke and call Coach Blodge the "Grandfather of Goalkeeping". His coaching experience is beyond compare and his knowledge of goalkeeping turned me into such a student of the game at such a young age. I started working with Blodge when I was just 14-15 years old and even though I had so much to learn, he didn't make it feel overwhelming. For Blodge it was a process, and he kept us on the right path to proper technique and a good attitude.

Blodge's group sessions were super-efficient. Whether it was a small group of 2-3 GK's or a bigger group of 7-8 keepers, he always made it a point to educate each individual goalkeeper to fit their individual skill level and physical ability.

Ryan Hayward – Ryan is a great friend and consultant. He is a former Regional Goalkeeper for TCNJ Men's Soccer and was the Goalkeeper Coach at The College of New Jersey for over a decade. Ryan went on to be the Second Assistant/Goalkeeper Coach for Princeton Men's Soccer.

Not long after making the jump to full-time coaching, Ryan met me, and we developed a personal and professional relationship that lasted for two decades. We spent countless hours together on the field, coaching goalkeepers of all ages and abilities, and we've been great friends ever since. Ryan has a great soccer mind and he help mold me into a more complete teacher of the position.

Ryan credits Paul Blodgett with being the single most influential figure in his development as a soccer and goalkeeper coach, and can't think of anyone in the game who emphasized the importance of addressing the psychological needs of the modern goalkeeper, as well as, Paul.

Agawam High School, Agawam, MA – My coaching career began as the Boy's Junior Varsity and then Varsity Soccer Coach; in 1978, we advanced the program to its first-ever MA State Cup Tournament. We called ourselves "The Steamrollers". My career was off and running...

Rutgers Soccer – My goalkeeper coaching career took off after joining Rutgers Men's Soccer Program under newly hired Head Coach, Bob Reasso in 1981 (previously noted in "Acknowledgments"). It was through my experiences with Bob and Rutgers that I learned the game. Our travels together throughout the US and Europe taught me the passion that is associated with the game and how much soccer (football) is embedded into the culture of the world.

TCNJ, The College of New Jersey – The women's soccer program at TCNJ was started by former Coaches, Joe Russo, and Bob Turner; it developed into one of the most storied college programs in the history of women's collegiate soccer; Joe and T came to me to join their program after I left Rutgers. This gave me the opportunity of working with some of the best women goalkeepers to come out of NJ. It was a fantastic coaching/teaching experience for me to be able to mold the keepers into the team system and it proudly help me develop 5 GK All-Americans in a row.

TCNJWS Coaching Staff pictured clockwise starting from the bottom: Katie Lindacher, Joe Russo, Bob Turner, Paul Blodgett.

UGKA, The United Goalkeeping Alliance – founded by Erik Eisenhut out of the Pittsburgh, PA area, is the best platform for goalkeeper education and an all-around collection of passionate GK coaches with whom I have been associated. I joined the Alliance and am now on the Board of Directors. The assistance of the Board and the Alliance as a whole, has been very instrumental in the publishing and aiding the distribution of this curriculum. If you are a goalkeeper or a goalkeeper coach, I strongly urge you to become a member of the UGKA in order to take advantage of the multiple programs that UGKA has to offer. Many thanks to the Board of Directors for their help in making this document a reality: Erik Eisenhut, Mike Kappas, Andreas Papakostas, Mackenzie Pinto, Chad Prickett, Brett Rosenberger, Rick Stainton, Ryan Godda Thompson, and Paul Blodgett. (www.unitedgkalliance.com)

MGTS, Modern Goalkeeper Training Systems – founded by John Plaugic from New Jersey, MGTS one of the premiere goalkeeper training companies in the country; I am on the staff at MGTS as one of the Directors of Goalkeeper Development; John has supported my role at MGTS, not only as a staff member for teaching goalkeepers, but also for mentoring the staff on becoming better teachers of the position. Staff: Elvir Prasovic, Jim "Harry" Harrison, Matt Broomall, Brett Axelrod, Mackenzie Hanna, Nick Linebaugh, Erica Keil and Tiago Capela. (www.moderngoalkeepertraining.com)

Introduction

Training the goalkeeper in the game of soccer requires being knowledgeable not only about the position but also about the game itself. The evolution of the game and the resulting changes within it have mostly centered around the goalkeeper position. Within the position, the metamorphosis is a constant one with new, modern techniques becoming the norm. The proper training and development of goalkeepers is essential to the success of any team, club, or organization. You, as a goalkeeper coach, need to be fully prepared to bring the best training environment to the keepers on your team and your organization.

The position needs consistent, specialized training that follows a logical progression throughout the ages of development. One of the problems – and a major concern – about teaching the position is that there is no consistent training protocol. Many trainers seem to have their own approaches. Goalkeepers who cross-train with multiple coaches are taught completely different things. There are GK curriculums that have been prepared for certain organizations; however, one does not exist on a scale that offers a common-sense approach for coaches (regardless of their knowledge and experience) who desire to teach and train goalkeepers.

There is a difference between training keepers and actually teaching them, the latter of which will give individuals the best chance of reaching their potential, whatever level that may be. It is understood that many coaches do not fully grasp the nuances of the position: how it should be trained, how to incorporate keepers into team training, and how to deal with the mental development of the players. The pathway to becoming a player who is technically proficient, tactically astute, and mentally strong is difficult. This position is a time-honored one; it involves years of guided development by the coach, dedication by the player, and support by the organization. Every player develops at a different rate. Flexibility, tolerance, and positivity are valuable teaching tools. This curriculum will offer guidance to reinforce these principles.

Being able to develop keepers requires creating a **Goalkeeper Culture** within the club; this culture needs to be consistent throughout, and it must constantly adapt to modern trends of the game. The days of pushing GK training off to a side area and not including the keeper in the team training are waning and should disappear. All clubs and organizations must offer a professional environment for their keepers. How to develop a **Goalkeeper Culture** will be discussed in a chapter within this book.

The purpose of this curriculum is to provide an age-appropriate, chronological guide to coaches who train for the position within their organization. It is based on over 45 years of coaching experience within the game; it is a collaboration of thoughts and ideas shared by many goalkeepers and team coaches. I have worked with goalkeepers of all ages, from U8 up through world-class keepers who have represented their countries. I trained keepers at the collegiate level for decades with the Rutgers University Men's team and TCNJ (The College of New Jersey) Women's Soccer program. As the Technical Director for the Boys/Girls Goalkeepers with the NJYS/ODP (New Jersey Youth Soccer/Olympic Development Program) and as the owner of my own Goalkeeper School in New Jersey, I have had the opportunity to work with and develop thousands of keepers. I have also had the chance to influence how the position is taught and trained.

This curriculum consolidates the goalkeeper training approach into one that simplifies the training methods, creates consistency in how the position is trained, and is adaptable to changes within the game.

Goalkeeper Coaching Philosophy

The success of teaching the goalkeeper position is dependent upon the athletes understanding of why they are performing certain tasks, not just in doing those tasks. If players understand why they are doing something, they will be more likely to integrate those points into their repertoire. We need to get away from keepers just being reactive; they must start thinking more. Learning and understanding the game (tactics) is essential in being able to play the position and the game successfully. Teach players, don't just dictate to them.

Technical mastery is a cornerstone of the curriculum. Our Teaching Method will be discussed fully. It is based on 45 years of trial and error, and it has proven to be successful for goalkeepers at all levels. Learning the fundamentals is imperative. The position and the game are evolving quickly, but mastering the basics is still the foundation for growth and success. Once basics are learned, then alternative methods can be introduced.

Tactical applications are incorporated into training and development. Functional training – goalkeeper training that has a purpose within the game – is particularly important. It helps prepare keepers for situations that will occur. Incorporating keepers in team training is a valuable part of development for both the individual GK and the team as a whole. Coordination between the head coach and the GK coaching staff will help make training sessions more purposeful.

Major emphasis is placed on the mental development of the keeper, helping them to deal with the stresses of handling the position. The best coaching/teaching approach is by creating a positive learning environment – this instills confidence. Confidence levels can make or break a keeper. Having and maintaining confidence throughout the stresses of the position is always a challenge for both the keeper and the coach. Positive reinforcement is a far better approach to this reinforcement. Correcting a GK's technical mistakes and tactical decisions positively will result in quicker growth and development; this will build up mentality and confidence instead of tearing it down. This requires a conscious effort on the part of the coach. The coach must define the important moments of attack, transition, and defense.

Repetitive training has its purpose but training that involves multi-tasking and staying in the moment holds greater value. Activities that have keepers going from one moment into the next are good mental preparations for matches. Teaching keepers to stay within each moment of activities prepares them for the same types of scenarios in the game.

The game itself requires goalkeepers to read situations, make decisions, communicate, and execute; it also requires keepers to accept consequences as a result of making poor or improper decisions. Coaches cannot expect keepers to make better decisions if they have not been prepared for those situations in training.

The consistency of the training approach by the staff is critical to the success of developing the goalkeepers and developing the goalkeeper culture throughout the club. That being said, goalkeeper coaches take on a tremendous responsibility to properly train, develop, and mentor the keepers within their respective organizations. This is a position that takes great patience both in learning by the keepers and teaching by the staff.

Goalkeeper Coaching Expectations

Following are the expectations for goalkeeper coaches, which will result in a better chance for success in not only helping the GK's reach their potential but also in establishing a goalkeeper culture that will be respected.

1. Image:
   a. Coaches need to be professional in appearance and actions
   b. Shirts should be tucked in
   c. Gear (kit, boots, gloves) should be well-maintained as an example for the keepers
   d. A good image will garner respect
2. Professionalism:
   a. Knowledgeable
   b. Punctual
   c. Being prepared, organized
   d. Having written, well-planned lesson plans with proper progressions
   e. Exhibit proper behavior
   f. Discipline
   g. Adaptability
3. Communication:
   a. Possess excellent communication skills
   b. Able to produce a fun and educational training environment
4. Establish a positive teaching/learning environment
5. Be a mentor:
   a. Be trustworthy and honest in answering questions and in evaluations
   b. Take the time to understand the keepers
   c. Develop relationships with not only the keepers but with their parents
   d. Be open to parent's questions and concerns
   e. Be accessible
   f. Be prompt in returning messages
6. Have a well-organized database of the keepers and lines of communication

Teaching Method

To have a successful GK developmental curriculum, a well-planned, consistent training program, and teaching method need to be implemented. Following is a teaching method that has been devised over decades of teaching the position at all levels, from grassroots to world-class. It has been supplemented with study and research from clinics, seminars, symposiums, videos, match analysis, and on-site observations of some of the best training in the world. This teaching method has proven to be successful in helping GKs develop technically, tactically, and mentally.

COACHING CONSIDERATIONS

Technically:

- Develop the fundamentals
- Teach the proper techniques at the appropriate ages
- Teach progressions
- Don't progress to a higher level until the previous level is mastered
- Skill development should:
    - o Be taught correctly and consistently, resulting in mastery
    - o Help improve athleticism
    - o Aid in injury prevention
- It is important to master the technique so keepers:
    - o Don't have to think about technique during games
    - o Can then concentrate on the game

Tactically:

- Teach GK's from behind the goal
- Teach within the game
- Help GKs read situations

- Evaluate their decisions:
  - Important that GK's make decisions and stay with them once made
  - Results of the decision will determine if it were correct or not
- GK's need to:
  - Observe
  - Communicate
  - Execute
- GK's need to watch and study the game whether it be live or on TV/video:
  - At least 45 minutes/week
- Encourage questions and dialogue
- Keepers need to learn the game and understand tactics
- Keepers need to understand and help implement their team's tactics; use them as the eyes in the back of the field
- **Match Analysis:**
  - One of the best tools to advance a keeper's development
  - Coaches need to go to games and offer a Match Analysis
  - Have a dialogue with keepers after each half
  - Go over the different situations that occurred
  - Encourage the keeper to offer answers to questions instead of telling the answers
- GK training should mirror the game so keepers can apply their tools in live situations

Mentally:

- The GK position is a time-honored position – it takes years to master
- Be patient in teaching it
- Be a mentor
- Understand that the position is a tough one to learn
- Encourage keepers to take risks as part of the learning process
- Encourage keepers to get out of their comfort zones
- **Must allow GK's to make mistakes – they are a great learning tool**
- Important to create a positive learning environment:
  - Constructive criticism – never destructive criticism
  - Be supportive
- Have keepers train like a pro:
  - Create and maintain a professional training environment
  - Keep the training area organized
  - Tell keepers whether reps are by time or number
- **Confidence:**
  - A keystone to the position
  - Is fragile, especially to younger, developing keepers
  - Build it – don't destroy it
  - Learn how to rebuild it, if it does take a hit

KEYS TO TEACHING THE POSITION

Teaching Technique

1. Be a teacher:

A GK coach needs to be a teacher, not just a trainer, especially during the developmental stages. Sessions should be well prepared. Coaches should anticipate that something may not go as planned and be able to adjust, if necessary. Keep the sessions simple and try not to cover too much at one time. If a particular technique needs more time to be learned, then take the time. When presenting an activity, coaches should make sure that the keepers understand what is to be accomplished and what the coach is looking for.

A useful method is:

- o Explain the activity
- o Demonstrate the activity
- o Re-explain the activity
- o Ask if there are any questions

2. Observation:

"The most important principle of coaching is observation." – Tom Goodman

The key to being a good coach and teacher is observation. It is important to pay attention to details. Keen observation is absolutely essential in helping keepers learn the proper techniques; they need to know when something is being done correctly or incorrectly, especially in the developing stages of GK's. Through careful observation on the part of the coach, the minute details can be addressed.

Coaching moments will occur – be observant when they arise and make good use of them as a teaching point.

The use of **Guided Discovery** is a very useful tool in these situations:

- o First, coaches need to recognize a teaching moment
- o When it occurs, ask questions that guide the keeper to the answer:
  - ▪ Don't just give the answer
- o Allow the keeper to think, respond, and then direct another question if necessary

Don't just tell keepers what to do, help them to understand WHY to do something. Generally, once players understand why something should be done a certain way, they will be more likely to do it; just telling them what to do may not be as successful.

Keepers shouldn't just react to a situation; instead, they should:

- o Read the situation
- o Decide what to do (Decision Making)
- o Communicate what needs to be done
- o Execute

3. Slow things down! Quality, NOT Quantity!

It is essential, especially when teaching the younger ages and beginners, to slow things down. The quality of repetitions far outweighs the number of repetitions. Slowing things down allows the keeper to feel the technique; it is easier to point out and understand mistakes, as well. When learning a skill, it is important to teach the nerves to fire in a consistent manner – this leads to mastery; this can only be achieved by slowing things down and through quality repetitions.

Rapid-fire training is not good for mastering skills. In fact, during development, it can cause GK's to master mistakes. Once the technique is learned, then speed can be implemented.

Rapid-fire training is good, however, for developing reactions and can be useful in GK-specific fitness training.

4. Use of keywords while GK's are performing activity:

When training techniques, it can be helpful to use repetitive words that become associated with an activity. These words can be injected throughout the activity as key points of concentration to help the GK when learning skills. These words can also be helpful as remembrance tools when a GK is coming back after an injury or a period off and is working to regain form.

Some examples:

- o "Eyes" – maintaining eye contact with the ball throughout the catch
- o "Set" – being sure the GK is set for the shot
- o "Communicate" – reminding GK to use proper words at the proper time
- o "Body behind the ball" – staying fluid after a catch; finishing the catch in a balanced, athletic form
- o "Feel the finish" – having GK's feel the catch

5. Feel the finish!

When training goalkeepers during the developmental and learning stages, it is important for them to feel how they are finishing a particular catch or skill. This is an excellent technique when learning something new. As mentioned earlier, this requires slowing down the training and allowing the keepers to actually feel how they are finishing the catch. Generally, if the finish is correct, then the things that lead up to the finish will be correct.

When beginning keepers are learning a catching technique, have them look into the ball (like they are looking into a crystal ball – this engages the eyes throughout the catch) and hold the finish for the count of "One thousand one." Then have the GK's put themselves through a mental checklist after the finish:

- o "Are my feet the right distance apart?"
- o "Is my body balanced?"
- o "Is my body behind the ball?"
- o "Is my finish correct and in an athletic form?"
- o "Are my eyes looking into the ball?"

Having the keepers do a mental checklist after a catch also:

- o Slows down the finish
- o Helps GK's to feel the correct finish
- o Let's mastery come more quickly (as well as quicker recovery from a layoff)

A coaching phrase that is helpful and can be used to reinforce these principles is: "Start in an athletic position, finish in an athletic position."

6. Training the eyes!

A major reason why keepers may not have good hands and are continually spilling the ball is that the eyes are not engaged throughout the whole catch. This must be stressed when teaching keepers how to catch a ball, especially younger keepers who are trying to develop their hands.

"Look into the ball after it is in the hands." This phrase takes developing hand/eye coordination to a different level. In many cases, coaches tell keepers to: "Look at the ball."; "See the ball in the hands." Taking it further by looking into the ball after it's in the hands, forces the eyes to maintain contact with the ball a little bit longer and really engages them throughout the catch. It also slows down the catch, which, as mentioned previously, aids in mastery.

This teaching technique is also valuable in helping keepers when coming back after an injury or layoff. The eyes are the first things to go, but with this training, they will be the first things to come back.

7. Teach in sequences – training the mind:

The GK position involves moving from one task to another. The body must be trained to move fluidly from one action to another. The mind must also be trained to do the same. GK's minds need to prepare for a task, complete the task, and then move on to the next task.

This can be trained in practice sessions by creating a **sequential activity** where:

- o The GK moves from one task to another
- o The GK stays within each task within the sequence (staying in the moment)
- o The GK completes the task before going on to the next one

Following is an example of such a sequential activity that is used in a training session:

1. Keeper uses footwork to move into a position
2. Keeper prepares to receive the ball with the feet
3. Keeper communicates to receive the ball
4. Keeper collects the ball with the feet using a certain technique
5. Keeper communicates on the distribution
6. Keeper distributes the ball out to a target
7. Keeper uses a footwork pattern into another position
8. Keeper handles a type of shot
9. Keeper communicates on the distribution
10. Keeper distributes the ball to a target

The activity above, as simple as it seems, involves 10 different tasks within the whole sequence. **Coaches need to observe:**

- o Did the keeper stay within each moment of the sequence?
- o Was each task executed properly?
- o Was each task finished properly?
- o Was the whole sequence performed properly?

If one of the tasks was not performed correctly or completely, then the sequence will not be complete:

- o This involves staying in the moment and must be trained
- o As a coach it is important to teach keepers to stay within the moment and to complete each segment of the task
- o This prepares the minds of keepers to adapt to game situations which are constantly moving and flowing

8. Importance of Rhythm Work:

Rhythm Work is sequence training that combines different movement patterns (Foot-work), touches with the feet, handling, and distribution. These skills can be put together into any grouping. This type of training is designed to get keepers into a rhythm before jumping into team training or live situations. This is a great warm-up activity. It is also excellent if the GK coach has only a limited time to prepare keepers for work with the team.

Set-up:

- o Utilize equipment (cones, ladders, hurdles)
- o Use of various **Foot-work** patterns
- o Use any form of **foot skills**
- o Incorporate different types of services
- o Vary the forms of handling
- o Not a rapid-fire type of activity, although all **Foot-work** should be performed as fast as possible
- o Designed for repetitive movement and touches

9. COMMUNICATION!

Be sure that GK's incorporate communication into all aspects of training. GK's need to make communication an integral part of their training, so it becomes natural during the game.

Examples:

- o Demand the ball when played to the feet
- o Communicate when distributing the ball to a field player
- o Calling for the ball when going to collect it
- o Commanding the defense to clear a ball

10. Competition!

Goalkeepers love and need to compete; create a training environment that includes a competition of some form within the session:

- o Should have a quality training partner whenever possible to push them and compete against them
- o Teams should have a minimum of two GKs so that there is always competition for the position
- o Create competitive games so that keepers can go against each other:
  - Shadow
  - GK Wars
  - Shooting games
  - Kicking games

11. Use of video:

Video replay of technical training can be extremely valuable to help keepers understand what they are doing correctly or incorrectly. Many keepers respond to visual cues more so than verbal ones.

12. The value of training with a partner:

"One of the best ways to learn something is to teach it!" – Paul Blodgett

Training with a partner can be a good way for GKs to learn something better or quicker. When training with partners, encourage the keepers to watch, evaluate, and help each other during training. Encourage keepers to observe and critique a training partner's performance, offering praise or constructive criticism. This develops leadership, camaraderie, and communication skills. Carefully observing others perform the same tasks that the GKs themselves are performing reinforces the learning process.

13. 1v1 versus partner/small group training:

1v1 training can be a good teaching method when:

- o Training a new GK to understand or learn the coach's teaching method
- o Correcting improper technique
- o Conditioning

Small group or partner training adds the variables of:

- o Competition
- o Multi-tasking
- o Creating more complex training scenarios
- o Dealing with different forms of services

Conclusion

The above **Teaching Method** is a good template for helping GKs to learn and master the position. A coach's personality and energy are just as valuable. Training should demand hard work and intent. The coach needs to establish a challenging training environment.

Keepers need to understand that when crossing the line onto the field of training, it is time to get down to it and focus on training. Stepping back over the line to get off the field is the time to relax and have a few laughs. This creates professionalism in training.

It is important to pick out moments in training and coaching to offer life-learning lessons. Be a teacher, not just a coach. Observe teachable moments – position related or life-related – and use them to present valuable lessons. This is when one becomes a mentor, the next level beyond being a coach and a teacher. This is when relationships are established that can have life-long effects for both the keeper and the coach.

Introduction to the Lesson Plans

The session plans that are included in this curriculum are a collaboration of input from several outstanding coaches with whom I have been able to work.

Many of these plans can be interchanged between the various age groups, though age and the level of technical ability will dictate what should or should not be used. It should be noted that these training sessions are just templates and suggestions on how to develop a progressive curriculum; personal knowledge and experience on behalf of the GK coach will influence what each coach may desire to include or not include.

The lesson plans are described in great detail and should be of value to even a novice GK coach. GK coaches with greater experience may find the details and coaching points helpful in guiding their GKs to reach technical mastery.

It should be noted that the evolution of the goalkeeper in today's soccer environment is constant. Modern techniques are being introduced regularly. As a result, what is taught and how it is taught is changing, as well.

These session plans reflect over 40 years of experience training goalkeepers of all ages and levels. What remains constant is paying attention to detail, making sure GKs master each level before being pushed to the next, and coaching and teaching in a positive environment.

Detailed written lesson plans are designed for five different age groups:

- Age groups:
    - U8
    - U10
    - U12
    - U14
    - U16 – U18
- There are 10 training sessions per age group

Sessions/Plans consist of:

- Subject matter covered in the session
- Techniques referenced in each session:
    - Refer to the **Technique Used in Training Session Section** in the **Addendum** to see the full detail of each technique covered in each session
- **Set Up** (diagrams)
- **Dynamic Warm-up** suggestions:
    - Dynamic warm-up can be adjusted to benefit the time/space of the training area or session subject
- **Activities per Set Up:**
    - Approximate time allotment for each activity
    - Coaches should be flexible with the time allotment – time depends upon:
        - Length of time available for the training session

- Number of GK's attending the session
- If a coach needs to slow down the activity so that proper execution is taking place
- **Coaching Points per Set Up**:
  o When making coaching points:
    - Don't over coach
    - Slow down the presentation of each point so GKs can fully understand
    - Choose the right moments to make the points
    - Use of **Guided Questions**

Additional Information:

- Do not hurry up the session just to get all of the activities in the session completed
- Cover as much as one can
- Allow time at the end of each session for game-like/shooting activities
- Sessions do not necessarily have to be followed in any particular order, but it is recommended for the youngest groups so that a logical progression in technical development can be followed
- Coaches should use discretion on advancing onto the next session within each age group depending on:
  o How learning is progressing (don't hurry the learning process)
  o Developing technique correctly (if GK's are struggling with particular techniques – repeating sessions is fine)
- These sessions are templates – they are suggestions on the subject matter to be covered; coaches can use them as models and develop their plans, methods, and progressions
- Coaches need to remember that training should be based on the quality of repetitions, NOT the quantity of repetitions
- Stress that each component of a particular activity be completed correctly before going on to the next component of the activity, this includes the use of proper communication when/where appropriate
- Progressions have a purpose, no part of a progression should be ignored

Equipment required:

- Balls (appropriate size per age group)
- Cones
- Pinnies
- Goals are important, although many activities can be performed without goals
- Appropriate space:
  o Availability of the 18yd box is important

Author's Note:

It is suggested that the curriculum for the U8 & U10 sessions be closely followed. The mastery of these steps will be the foundations for the growth and development of the later stages.

The U12 – U16-U18 sessions can be interchanged in any way that the GK coach wishes. Tactical applications start to become important at 12 years and up; coaches should attempt to coordinate technical work to align with team tactics, so the keepers may maximize the benefits.

Please note that technical ability varies greatly within each age group due to the growth and development of the keepers.

Quality over quantity remains the norm.

Player Development and Training Sessions
The U16 – U18 Age Group (Grades 9 – 12)

This age group marks a critical period in a GK's growth and development, not only as a keeper but also as a player. A keeper should now be fully committed to playing the position and should delve into it to its fullest. This is the age where attrition usually occurs due to bad experiences in the game, including lack of playing time or disappointment in coaching and/or mentoring. The importance of quality coaching is essential. The players are interested in team development and success; a good coaching/training environment will nurture this interest. Keepers need to hone skills to the point where they perform them correctly and naturally. The U14 skills must be mastered in order to be successful in this age group. Mastering the skills allows GK's to concentrate on the game and the situations that occur within the game. Speed of play, speed of thought, organization, leadership, and communication are key components for development. Competition, whether it be in games or with a training partner becomes important. Creating relationships with teammates, especially the defensive unit will result in good team building and team spirit.

The **Principles** of play are presented and coached through the thirds of the field and must be infused in every aspect of training.

Principles of Play

Attacking Principles	Defensive Principles
Penetration	Recovery (Immediate Chase)
Support	Pressure
Mobility	Cover
Width	Balance
Depth (Length)	Compactness
Improvisation (deception, creativity)	Counter Attack

Role of the Coach

The coach within this age group must not only be knowledgeable, but also possess an engaging personality that will result in respect on the part of the keepers. The coach as a mentor is of the utmost value. Trust along with a positive training environment will help keepers be more successful. Coaches need to understand that they can develop confidence or destroy it quickly with the wrong approach; knowing that every keeper is different and they may have to adjust their approach accordingly. What works for one may not work for another.

Training sessions should be competitive and more intense – constantly changing so that there is a freshness to them. Although technical work is always necessary, training should now include more game-like situations. A close association with the head coach is necessary and training sessions should coincide with the theme of the day for the team's session. At times, a goalkeeper coach may have only 15 – 30 minutes on certain training days to get keepers ready to join the team which calls for efficient preparation. Coaches need to pay attention to technical detail and fine tune all aspects of the skills necessary to play the position. They also need to be able to think on their feet and adjust to quick changes in training schedules. A good coaching practice during team training is for the coach to set up behind the goal to observe and reinforce concepts. However, it is a good and useful practice for the GK coach to roam around the field to observe tactics from a different perspective and see how the GK is observing situations and reacting to them.

It can never be underestimated how important the relationship is between the GK coach and the GK. Life lasting associations can occur due to what is established during this age group.

License Recommendations

- U.S. Soccer Grassroots 11v11 License
- U.S. Soccer C/B or A (Youth) License
- United Soccer Coaches Level 1 – Level 3 and Advanced GK Diplomas

The U16 – U18 Player Characteristics

Mental/Psychological (cognitive)

- Improved learning through years of playing soccer…experience
- Thinking like an adult in the adult environment…more players, larger field
- Make decisions to help the "team" succeed
- Improved ability to sequence thought, coordinate actions, and perform more complex tasks…can anticipate possible outcomes based on the recognition of visual cues
- Ability to use more abstract thought to meet the demands of the game
- Understanding attacking principles, as well as defensive principles so they can anticipate developing situations
- Use more of their teammates to solve game problems
- Training must replicate the game

Physical (psychomotor)

- Continue to gain a tremendous amount of physical strength, endurance, and power
- **Flexibility training is key to prevention of injury; this cannot be stressed enough!**
- More confident with physical technical demands; incorporating explosive power
- Goalkeeping skills are becoming refined incorporating explosive power
- GK's learn to cover a 4 – 5yd goal quickly and efficiently
- Children continue to be in growth spurts
- Overuse injuries occur when age appropriate development is ignored
- Height in boys ranges between 5'7" – 6' and weight ranges between 130 – 185lbs
- Height in girls averages 5'4" and weight ranges between 115 – 120lbs

Socially (psychosocial)

- Gender differences are more apparent
- Spend more time with their friends and less time with their parents
- Some have the responsibility of a job outside of school
- Taking more responsibility for their actions
- Making good decisions
- Learning from experiences as to what is right and wrong

- Values impact their ethical and moral behavior on and off the field

What to Teach U16 – U18 Players (Game Components)

Technique (skills)

- **Foot-work** should be fast and clean in all directions
- Refining technique under the pressures of the game (opponents, time, and space)
- Paying attention to details in all aspects of skill training
- Be held to a higher standard; learning to recognize and correct own mistakes
- Increase technical speed
- Extension diving to cover upper and lower 90's
- Setting into the appropriate stance depending upon distance the GK is from the ball
  - o Long range distance (12yds and out); **Modern Set Position**
  - o Close-range distance (GK getting to within 6 – 12yds of the ball); **Close Range Stance**
  - o 2 – 3yd distance; **Containment Stance**
  - o 1yd/point blank distance; **K-save Stance**
- Driven balls with both feet to various targets (with & without pressure)
- Clearances to targets
- Throwing with distance and accuracy
- Deflections becoming more important due to the speed and weight of shots
- Parrying the ball with a purpose (direction); learning to put the ball into safe

  areas

- Recovery; same direction and opposite direction (spin recovery)
- Dealing with balls in crowded spaces and pressure situations
- Reading crosses with various spins and wind conditions
- Punching and tipping
- Owning the ball on collapses/dives
  - o Traditional 3 hand control (ground 3rd hand)
  - o European style lower hand/arm extended owning the ball with upper hand, chest and ground
- Playing live rebounds

Psychology

- Psychology becomes a major focus
- Displaying professionalism
- Positive approach to stresses of the game
  - o Handling the "controllable" and the "uncontrollable"
    - Teammates
    - Coaches
    - Referees

- Fans
- Parents
- Weather
- Field conditions, etc.

- Dealing with various forms of reinforcement from coaching staff (positive or negative); accepting criticism
  o Mental toughness
  o Dealing with mistakes
  o Controlling emotions
  o Not showing weaknesses mentally

- Self-motivation; practice on own; setting and attaining goals

- Being accountable for one's actions

- Being a motivator for the team and the other GK's

- Understanding and dealing with the pressures in training and games

- Developing a winning attitude; strive for success

- Focusing for 90 minutes

- Understanding the different levels of concentration within the game
  o Levels of high concentration
  o Levels of lower concentration
  o **Never levels of no concentration**

- Importance of playing games within one's mind during training
  o i.e. When giving up a rebound during the session, get up and get set as if another shot is coming, even if one is not
  o Preparing one's mind for what is coming next by creating a continuation of the action (playing the game, not just doing the activity)

- Realizing that the GK is always on stage; people love to watch GK's train and play therefore GK's need to perform and act accordingly

- **Communication skills**
  o Simple clear and concise commands
    - **"KEEPER!"** not "Keep"; two syllables create more power in the voice
    - **"AWAY!"**
    - **"Drop!"; "Push up!"; "Stay attached!"; "Slide left!"; "Touch your mark!"**
  o Complement the defense when they do well
  o Hold the defense accountable when they breakdown or miss an assignment

Fitness (conditioning)

- Focuses on being soccer fit; can handle and deal with the length and pace of the training and match environment

- Have a consistent and complete warm-up routine

- Realizing they shouldn't train hard every day; periodization

- GK specific fitness training concentrating on short bursts and quick recovery; interval training that should mirror actions in the game
  o Longer sprints are of no purpose
  o Need to become quick, powerful, and explosive over 4 – 5 yards

- Nutrition & Proper diet – pre-game, post-game, tournaments, etc.; hydration routines
- Prevention and care of injuries is very important
- Importance of rest/recovery

Tactics (decisions)

- Focus on team tactics; play as a team of 11 players; how the various lines of players (keeper, backs, midfield players, and forwards) connect to attack and defend successfully
- Watch and read about the position and the game; learn and understand the game
- Control the defensive unit; not only the back 3, 4, or 5 defenders, but the defensive MF's, as well
- Be willing to experiment with positioning and decisions in practice and scrimmages to learn strengths and limitations
  o How far to go off the line on crosses, etc.
- Owning the 6yd box
- **Positioning and angles**
  o Being comfortable with playing well outside the 18yd box; staying connected with the team as it moves up and back
  o Understanding distance off the goal line depending upon the distance of the shot
  o The significant 3 Zones within the 18yd box to aid in positioning (See Addendum)

Rules

- Standard Laws of the Game
- Gamesmanship…Playing within the rules of the game and the behavior of the officials

US Youth Soccer U16 – U18 Modifications to The Game

- Playing numbers
  o 11v11 (with goalkeepers)
- Field Dimensions
  o Length
    ▪ 110 – 120 yards
  o Width
    ▪ 60 – 75 yards
- Goal Dimensions
  o Height
    ▪ 8 feet
  o Width
    ▪ 24 feet
- Duration
  o Two periods of 40 – 45 minutes
- Ball
  o Number 5
- Offside
  o Yes

Practice & Game Considerations

- Practice Length
    o 90 minutes
- Practice/Game Ratio
    o 4 practices/1 game
- Limit number of hard sessions/week (once)
- Importance of rhythm work in training sessions
- Play games and compete in training sessions

U16 – U18 Training Session #1
Distribution/Handling

Techniques used in this session

- **Chop Step**
- **2 Touch Passing**
- **1 Touch Passing**
- **Inside of the Foot Pass (IOF)**
- **Laced Ball along the Ground**
- **Modern Set Position**
- **Chest Down/Basket Catch**
- **Front Smother Catch**
- **Controlled Collapse Left/Right**
- **Low-ball Deflections**
- **Mid-ball Deflections**

The key for Training Session

- ^ = cone (^1 – cone 1)
- X = Times (2X – 2 times)

Stage 1

Dynamic Warm-Up

Set Up

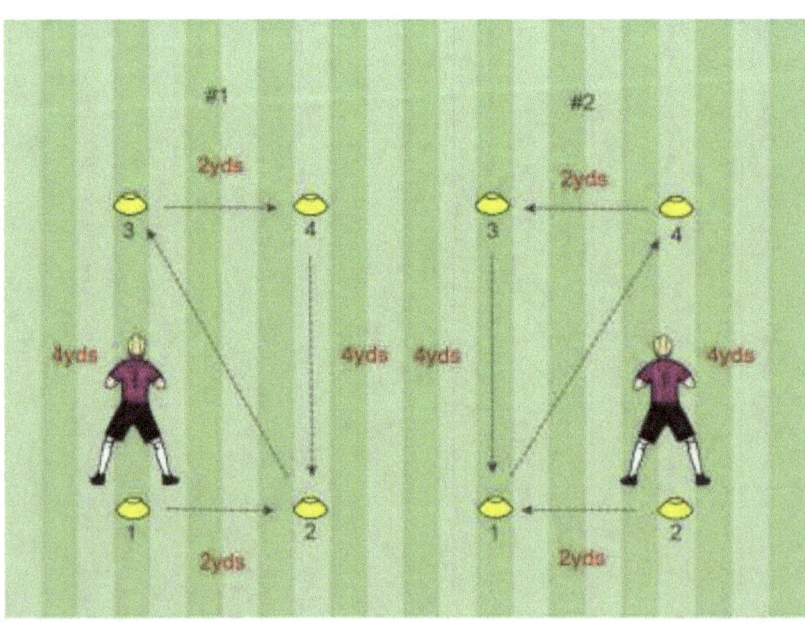

- Place ^1, ^2, ^3 & ^4 in a rectangle
- ^1/^2 & ^3/^4 are placed 2yds apart
- ^1/^3 & ^2/^4 are placed 4yds apart
- GK starts behind ^1

Activity 1 (5 – 8mins)

- GK starts in **Modern Set Position** directly behind ^1 facing forward (towards ^3)
- GK quickly shuffles to the right to ^2
- GK then performs a dynamic motion diagonally across to ^3
- GK then shuffles to the right to ^4
- GK backpedals to ^2
- GK stays at ^2 & reverses the process
- GK quickly shuffles to the left to ^1
- GK then performs the same dynamic movement diagonally across to ^4
- GK then shuffles to the left to ^3
- GK backpedals to ^1
- GK stays at ^1 & repeats the process but does a different dynamic movement
- Dynamic motions
    - Jog
    - High knees
    - Butt kicks
    - Skipping & forward arm circles
    - Skipping & arm circles backward
    - Skipping & swinging arms across the chest
    - Open the gate
    - Close the gate
    - Lunges (lunging forward with one foot at a time – alternate feet)
    - Straight leg sweeps (bend forward & sweep the ground with both hands, take 3 small steps & do it again, etc.)
    - Twist body with elbows touching opposite knee
    - Side shuffle to ^ facing inward
    - Side shuffle to ^ again facing inward
    - Carioca to ^ facing inward
    - Carioca to ^ again facing inward
    - Sprint to ^
- Water break with additional static stretching

Coaching Points

- Reinforce proper execution of various movements
- Players shouldn't rush through these activities
- Movements should be executed deliberately, stressing the quality of each movement

Stage 2

Distribution with the Feet

Set Up 1

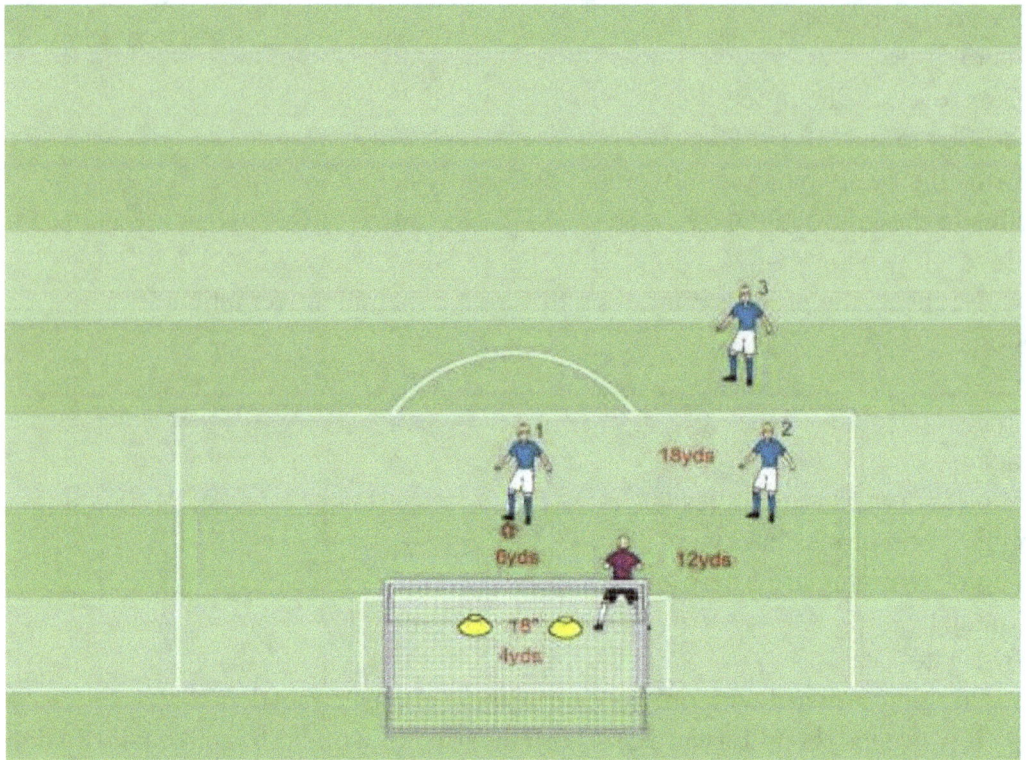

- Use of regular size goal
- Place 2 ^'s in the middle of the goal; 4yds off the line & 18" from each other
- Server 1 starts with balls at feet 6yds from the ^'s
- Server 2 stands to the right of the goal, 12yds off the goal line & midway between the six yd box & 18 yd-box lines
- Server 3 stands to the right of the goal, 18yds off the goal line & midway between the D & the corner of the 18yd box
- GK starts in **Modern Set Position** just to the right of the ^'s

Modern Set Position

Photos Courtesy of Matt Broomall & Modern Goalkeeper Training Systems, LLC

Inside of the Foot Pass (IOF)

Photo Courtesy of Matt Broomall

Laced Ball on the Ground

Photo Courtesy of Matt Broomall & Modern Goalkeeper Training Systems, LLC

Activity 1 (8mins)

- GK asks for the ball to be passed back from Server 1 using proper communication ("Yes & Server 1's name!")
- GK uses **2 Touches** (any foot combination) to pass the ball back to Server 1
- GK then uses **Chop Step Foot-work** to move left through the ^'s
- GK resets outside opposite ^ then backpedals a few steps towards the goal line to open some space from Server 1
- GK again asks for the ball to be played back from Server 1 using proper communication
- Server 1 passes the ball back to the GK's left foot
- GK uses **Inside of Left Foot** to lightly touch the ball diagonally across on an angle towards Server 2
- GK then takes a 2nd touch to **Distribute** the ball with an **Inside of the Foot Pass (IOF)** (using the right foot) to Server 2 using proper communication ("Yes & Server 2's name!")
- Server 2 receives the ball & passes it back across to Server 1
- GK resets to the right of the ^'s
- GK again asks for the ball to be passed back from Server 1 using proper communication ("Yes & Server 1's name!")
- GK uses **2 Touches** (any foot combination) to pass the ball back to Server 1
- GK then uses **Chop Step Foot-work** to move left through the ^'s
- GK resets outside opposite ^ then backpedals a few steps towards the goal line to open some space from Server 1
- GK again asks for the ball to be played back using proper communication

- Server 1 passes the ball back to the GK's left foot
- GK uses **Inside of Left Foot** to touch the ball diagonally across on an angle towards Server 3
- GK then takes a 2nd touch to **Lace the Ball** across the ground (using the right foot) to Server 3 using proper communication ("Yes & Server 3's name!")
- Server 3 receives the ball & passes it back across to Server 1
- GK resets to the right of the ^'s
- Repeat 5X
- GK's rotate and repeat activity

Coaching Points

- GK's always start in the **Modern Set Position**
- GK's use proper communication when asking for the ball or when **Distributing** the ball
- GK's feet are slightly bouncing when receiving a ball to the feet
- All touches are clean & in the proper direction
- GK's **Foot-work** is quick & clean
- GK's use correct foot on diagonal touch
- GK's diagonal touch is positive & on an angle towards target, NOT negative towards the goal
- GK's **Distribution** is accurate and hit with proper weight

Set Up 2

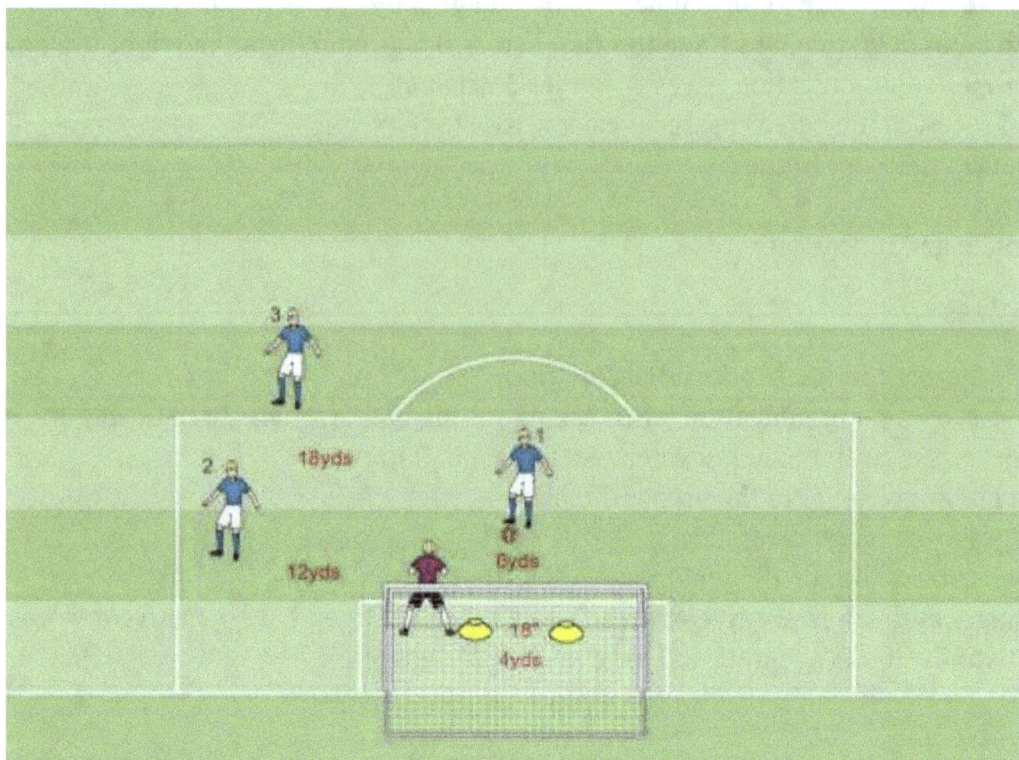

- Use of regular size goal
- Place 2 ^'s in the middle of the goal; 4yds off the line & 18" from each other
- Server 1 starts with balls at feet 6yds from the ^'s
- Server 2 stands to the left of the goal, 12yds off the goal line & midway between the 6yd box & 18yd box lines
- Server 3 stands to the left of the goal, 18yds off the goal line & midway between the "D" & the corner of the 18yd box
- GK starts in **Modern Set Position** just to the left of the ^'s

Activity 1 (8mins)

- GK asks for the ball to be passed back from Server 1 using proper communication ("Yes & Server 1's name!")
- GK uses **1 Touch** (either foot) to pass the ball back to Server 1
- GK then uses **Chop Step Foot-work** to move right through the ^'s
- GK resets outside opposite ^ then backpedals a few steps towards the goal line to open some space from Server 1
- GK again asks for the ball to be played back from Server 1 using proper communication
- Server 1 passes the ball back to the GK's right foot
- GK uses **Inside of Right Foot** to touch the ball diagonally across on an angle towards Server 2
- GK then takes a 2nd touch to **Distribute** the ball with an **Inside of the Foot Pass (IOF)** (using the left foot) to Server 2 using proper communication ("Yes & Server 2's name!")
- Server 2 receives the ball & passes it back across to Server 1
- GK resets to the left of the ^'s
- GK again asks for the ball to be passed back from Server 1 using proper communication ("Yes & Server 1's name!")

- GK uses **1 touch** (either foot) to pass the ball back to Server 1
- GK then uses **Chop Step Foot-work** to move right through the ^'s
- GK resets outside opposite ^ then backpedals a few steps towards the goal line to open some space from Server 1
- GK again asks for the ball to be played back using proper communication
- Server 1 passes the ball back to the GK's right foot
- GK uses the **Inside of Right Foot** to touch the ball diagonally across on an angle towards Server 3
- GK then takes a 2nd touch to **Lace the Ball** across the ground (using the left foot) to Server 3 using proper communication ("Yes & Server 3's name!")
- Server 3 receives the ball & passes it back across to Server 1
- GK resets to the left of the ^'s
- Repeat 5X
- GK's rotate and repeat activity

Coaching Points

- GK's always start in a **Modern Set Position**
- GK's use proper communication when asking for the ball or when **Distributing** the ball
- GK's feet are slightly bouncing when receiving a ball to the feet
- All touches are clean & in the proper direction
- GK's **Foot-work** is quick & clean
- GK's use correct foot on diagonal touch
- GK's diagonal touch is positive & on an angle towards target, NOT negative towards the goal
- GK's **Distribution** is accurate & hit with proper weight

Stage 3

Handling

Set Up 1

- Use of regular goal
- Place 2 ^'s alongside of each other in the middle of the goal, 2yds off the line & 18" from each other
- Server 1 sets up with balls at the feet 6yds in front of the ^'s
- Server 2 sets up 3 – 4yds to the left of Server 1 & 10yds from the GK with ball at feet
- GK starts in **Modern Set Position** just to the left of the ^'s facing Server 1

Chest Down/Basket Catch

Photos Courtesy Erin Guthrie Corsi

Controlled Collapse Right

1 Hand Low-ball Deflection Technique Right

Photos Courtesy of Matt Broomall & Modern Goalkeeper Training Systems, LLC

Bowling

Photo Courtesy of Matt Broomall

Activity 1 (5 – 8mins)

- Play starts with Server 1 striking a low ball to the GK
- GK makes a **Chest Down/Basket Catch** then **Bowls** the ball back to Server 1 using proper communication ("Yes & Server 1's name!")
- GK waits until Server 1 has control of the ball then quickly goes through the ^'s to the right using **Chop Step Foot-work** & resets after the 2nd ^
- Server 1 strikes the ball on the ground to the GK's right so that GK has to make a **Controlled Collapse Save to the Right** or **Deflects** the ball around the post
- If GK collects the ball, GK rolls the ball back to Server 1 from the ground & then recovers quickly to feet, Server 2 hits a driven ball from the ground at or directly around the GK who makes the appropriate save
- After save (&, if possible, **Distribution** back to Server 2), GK resets to the left of the ^'s & repeats the activity
- GK repeats 5X & GK's switch

Coaching Points

- GK's use proper technique on catches

- GK's **Foot-work** through the ^'s is quick & clean
- GK's communicate properly on all **Distributions**
- Servers serve quality balls at the GK

Set Up 2

- Use of regular goal
- Place 2 ^'s alongside of each other in the middle of the goal, 2yds off the line & 18" from each other
- Server 1 sets up with a ball in the hands 6yds in front of the ^'s
- Server 2 sets up 3 – 4yds to the right of Server 1 & 10yds from the GK with ball at feet
- GK starts in **Modern Set Position** just to the right of the ^'s facing Server 1

Diamond/Contour Catch

Photos Courtesy of Matt Broomall & Modern Goalkeeper Training Systems, LLC

Mid-ball Controlled Collapse Left

Photo Courtesy of Matt Broomall

Activity 1 (5 – 8mins)

- Play starts with Server 1 volleying a ball to the GK
- GK makes a **Diamond/Contour Catch** then **Bowls** the ball back to Server 1 using proper communication ("Yes & Server 1's name!")
- As soon as Server 1 settles the ball, GK quickly goes through the ^'s to the right using **Chop Step Foot-work**
- Server 1 strikes a mid-height (knee high) ball to the GK's left so that GK has to make either a **Mid-ball Collapse Save to the Left** or **Deflects** the ball around the post

- If GK collects the ball, GK then rolls the ball back to Server 1 from the ground & then recovers quickly to feet, Server 2 strikes a shot anywhere between the 2nd ^ & the left post on a live shot; GK makes the appropriate save
- After save (&, if possible, **Distribution** back to Server 2), GK resets to the right of the ^'s & repeats activity
- GK repeats 5X & GK's switch

Coaching Points

- GK's use proper technique on catches
- GK's **Foot-work** through the ^'s is quick & clean
- GK's communicate properly on all **Distributions**
- Servers serve quality balls at the GK

<u>Stage 4</u>

Live shooting

Set Up 1

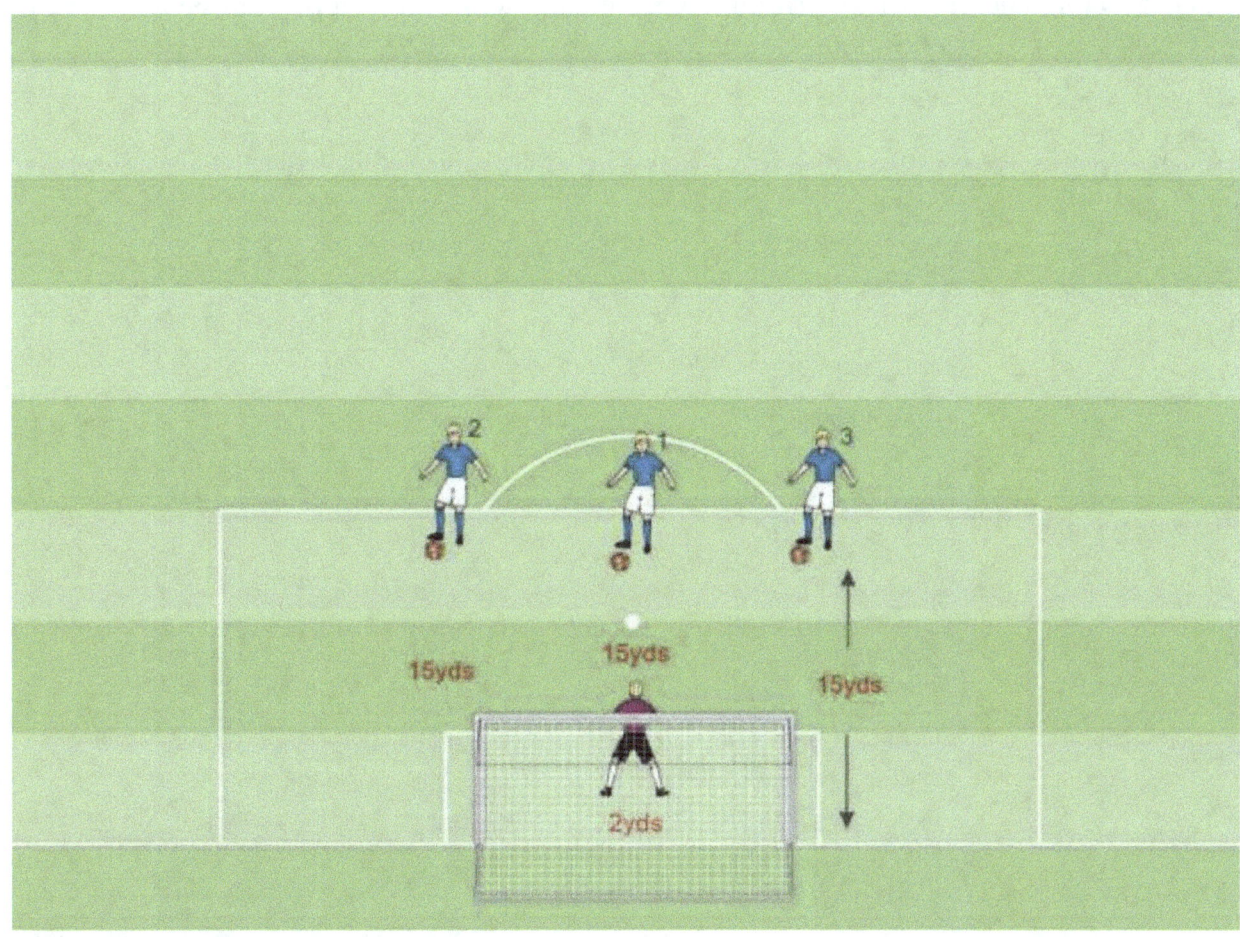

- Use of regular goal
- GK starts in the middle of the goal, 2yds off the line facing Server 1
- Server 1 sets up with balls at feet in the center of the goal & 15yds off the line
- Server 2 sets up with balls at feet just inside the left post & 15yds off the line
- Server 3 sets up with balls at feet just inside the right post & 15yds off the line

Activity 1 (10 – 20mins)

- GK starts in **Modern Set Position** facing Server 1
- Server 1 drives the ball to the GK's hands
- GK catches the ball using the **Diamond/Contour Catch** & **Bowls** the ball back to Server 1 using proper communication
- GK resets facing Server 2
- Server 2 strikes a live shot at the goal; GK attempts to make the save
- GK quickly recovers & resets facing Server 3
- Server 3 strikes a live shot at the goal; GK attempts to make the save
- GK slowly recovers back to the center of the goal to face Server 1
- Repeat activity 5X
- Rotate GK's

Coaching Points

- Servers strike quality services
- GK's use proper technique when making saves & is recovering
- GK's communicate when **Distributing** the ball back to Server on any clean save
- GK's take up proper positioning on each shot

U16 – U18 Training Session #2
Shot Stopping & High balls

Techniques used in this session

- **Shuffle Step**
- **1 Touch Passing**
- **Modern Set Position**
- **Diamond/Contour Catch**
- **One-hand Fist Punching**
- **Recovery**
- **Bowling**

The key for Training Session

- ^ = cone (^1 – cone 1)
- X = Times (2X – 2 times)

Stage 1

Dynamic Warm-up

Set-Up

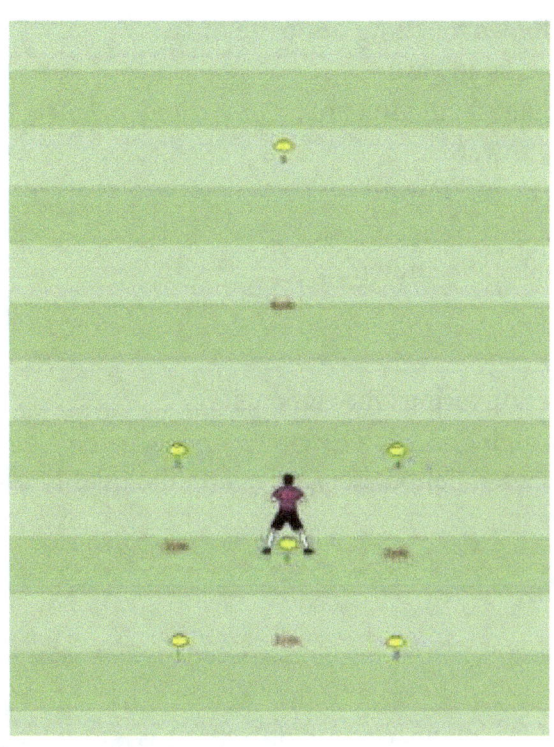

- Make a square out of 4 ^'s, 2yds X 2yds
- Place a 5th ^ right in the middle of the square
- Place a 6th ^ 6yds away from ^5
- GK starts in **Modern Set Position** directly behind ^5

Activity 1 (5 – 8mins)

- GK's hips face forward throughout the foot work inside the square
- GK's **Foot-work** is quick
- **Foot-work** pattern within the square is as follows
    - ^5 to ^3; back to ^5
    - ^5 to ^2; back to ^5
    - ^5 to ^4; back to ^5
    - ^5 to ^1; back to ^5
- GK then performs dynamic movements from ^5 to ^6
- Dynamic motions
    - Jog
    - High knees
    - Butt kicks
    - Skipping & forward arm circles
    - Skipping & arm circles backwards
    - Skipping & swinging arms across the chest
    - Open the gate
    - Close the gate
    - Lunges (lunging forward with one foot at a time – alternate feet)
    - Straight leg sweeps (bend forward & sweep the ground with both hands, take 3 small steps & do it again, etc.)
    - Twist body with elbows touching opposite knee
    - Side shuffle to ^ facing inward
    - Side shuffle to ^ again facing inward
    - Carioca to ^ facing inward
    - Carioca to ^ again facing inward
    - Sprint to ^
- Water break with additional static stretching

Coaching Points

- Reinforce proper execution of various movements
- Players shouldn't rush through these activities
- Movements should be executed deliberately, stressing the quality of each movement

Stage 2

Handling/Foot-work/High Balls

Set Up

- Place ^ down on the field
- GK stands directly behind the ^
- Server 1 sets up 3yds from the ^ & 2 steps to the right of the ^ with ball in hands
- Server 2 sets up 3yds from the ^ & 2 steps to the left of the ^ with ball in hands

Modern Set Position

Diamond/Contour Catch

Photos Courtesy of Matt Broomall & Modern Goalkeeper Training Systems, LLC

High Ball Catching Technique (Diamond/Contour Catch)

Right Knee up Front   **Left Knee Up Front**

Photos Courtesy of Erin Guthrie Corsi

Activity 1 (5mins)

- GK starts in **Modern Set Position** directly behind the ^
- Server 1 says "Go!"
- GK quickly **Shuffles** 1 step to the left of the ^ & sets
- Server 1 **Volleys** ball to GK's hands
- GK makes a **Diamond/Contour Catch** & tosses ball back to Server 1 using proper communication ("Yes & Server 1's name!")
- GK quickly **Shuffles** back behind the ^ & resets
- Server 2 tosses a high ball to the right of the ^
- GK uses quick choppy steps to go for the ball using **High Ball Catching Technique (Diamond/Contour Catch)** & catches ball above the head
  - o GK yells "KEEPER!" before the jump
  - o GK takes off on left foot
  - o GK's right knee goes up on the jump
  - o 1-foot take off; 2-foot landing
  - o GK keeps ball above the head after the landing
- GK tosses ball back to Server 2 using proper communication ("Yes & Server 2's name!")
- GK quickly **Shuffles** back to ^ & resets
- Repeat activity 6X
- Rotate GK's & repeat activity

Coaching Points

- GK shuffle steps are quick & balanced
- GK uses proper **Diamond/Contour Catching Technique** on **Volley** hit to hands & on high ball catch
- GK yells "KEEPER!" before jumping on the **High Ball Catch**
- GK keeps feet chopping until take off (for better timing of the jump)
- GK takes off on left foot
- GK drives right knee upwards
- GK jumps upwards not forwards
- GK catches the ball above & in front of the head (not behind the head)
- GK catches the ball on the way up
- GK lands on both feet
- GK holds the ball above the head after landing on the **High Ball Catch**
- GK tosses ball directly back to the Servers hands
- GK uses proper communication on the **Distribution** back to Server

Activity 2 (5mins)

- GK starts in **Modern Set Position** directly behind the ^
- Server 2 says "Go!"
- GK quickly **Shuffles** 1 step to the right of the ^ & sets
- Server 2 **Volleys** ball to GK's hands
- GK makes a **Diamond/Contour Catch** & tosses ball back to Server 2 using proper communication ("Yes & Server 2's name!")
- GK quickly **Shuffles** back behind the ^ & resets

- Server 1 tosses a high ball to the left of the ^
- GK uses quick choppy steps to go for the ball using **High Ball Catching Technique (Diamond/Contour Catch)** and catches ball above the head
    o GK yells "KEEPER!" before the jump
    o GK takes off on right foot
    o GK's left knee goes up on the jump
    o 1-foot take off; 2-foot landing
    o GK keeps ball above the head after the landing
- GK tosses ball back to Server 1 using proper communication ("Yes & Server 1's name!")
- GK quickly **Shuffles** back to ^ & resets
- Repeat activity 6X
- Rotate GK's & repeat activity

Coaching Points

- GK shuffle steps are quick & balanced
- GK uses proper **Diamond/Contour Catching Technique** on **Volley** hit to hands & on high ball catch
- GK yells "KEEPER!" before jumping on the **High Ball Catch**
- GK keeps feet chopping until take off (for better timing of the jump)
- GK takes off on right foot
- GK drives left knee upwards
- GK jumps upwards not forwards
- GK catches the ball above & in front of the head (not behind the head)
- GK catches the ball on the way up
- GK lands on both feet
- GK holds the ball above the head after landing on the **High Ball Catch**
- GK tosses ball back to Server's hands
- GK uses proper communication on the **Distribution** back to Server

One-fist Punch

Photo Courtesy of Matt Broomall & Modern Goalkeeper Training Systems, LLC

Activity 3 (5mins)

- GK starts in **Modern Set Position** directly behind the ^
- GK quickly **Shuffles** 1 step to the left of the ^ & asks for the ball to be played to the feet from Server 1 using proper communication ("Yes & Server 1's name!")
- Server 1 serves a pass to GK; GK **1 Touches** the ball back to Server 1
- GK quickly **Shuffles** back behind the ^ & resets
- Server 2 tosses a high ball to the right of the ^
- GK uses quick choppy steps to go for the ball & **1 Hand Punches** the ball back to Server 2 using the right hand
    - GK yells "KEEPER!" before the jump
    - GK takes off on left foot
    - GK's right knee goes up on the jump
    - 1-foot take off; 2-foot landing
- GK lightly **1 Hand Punches** the ball back to Server 2
- GK quickly **Shuffles** back to ^ & resets
- Repeat activity 6X
- Rotate GK's & repeat activity

Coaching Points

- GK shuffle steps are quick & balanced
- GK uses proper technique on **1 Touch** back to Server 1
- GK uses proper technique when **1 Hand Punching** the ball back to Server 2
- GK yells "KEEPER!" before jumping
- GK keeps feet chopping until take off (for better timing of the jump)
- GK takes off on left foot
- GK drives right knee upwards
- GK jumps upwards not forwards
- GK lands on both feet

Activity 4 (5mins)

- GK starts in **Modern Set Position** directly behind the ^
- GK quickly **Shuffles** 1 step to the right of the ^ & asks for the ball to be played to the feet from Server 2 using proper communication ("Yes & Server 2's name!")
- Server 2 serves a pass to GK; GK **1 Touches** the ball back to Server 2
- GK quickly **Shuffles** back behind the ^ & resets
- Server 1 tosses a high ball to the left of the ^
- GK uses quick choppy steps to go for the ball & **1 Hand Punches** the ball back to Server 1 using the left hand
    - GK yells "KEEPER!" before the jump
    - GK takes off on right foot
    - GK's left knee goes up on the jump
    - 1-foot take off; 2-foot landing
- GK lightly **1 Hand Punches** the ball back to Server 1
- GK quickly **Shuffles** back to ^ & resets
- Repeat activity 6X

- Rotate GK's & repeat activity

Coaching Points

- GK shuffle steps are quick & balanced
- GK uses proper technique on **1 Touch** back to Server 2
- GK uses proper technique when **1 Hand Punching** the ball back to Server 1
- GK yells "KEEPER!" before jumping
- GK keeps feet chopping until take off (for better timing of the jump)
- GK takes off on right foot
- GK drives left knee upwards
- GK jumps upwards not forwards
- GK lands on both feet

<u>Stage 3</u>

Shot Stopping & High Ball Catching

Set Up 1

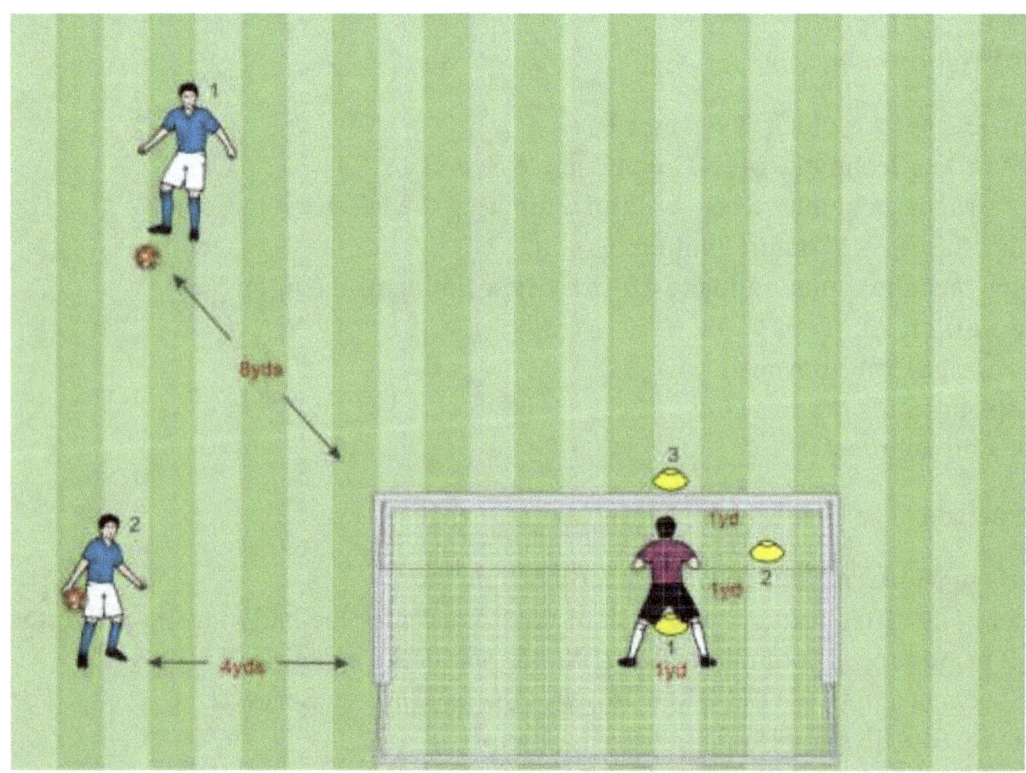

- Use of regular goal
- Place ^1 1yd off the goal line & 1yd to the right of the center of the goal
- Place ^2 to the right of ^1, 1yd away & on a 45-degree angle
- Place ^3 1yd to the left of ^2 (& in front of ^1)
- GK starts behind ^1 in **Modern Set Position** & facing forward
- Server 1 sets up 8yds out from the left goal post with balls at feet
- Server 2 sets up 4yds from the left post with ball in hands

Bowling

Photo Courtesy of Matt Broomall

Activity 1 (8 – 10mins)

- Server 1 says "Go!"
- GK turns towards Server 1 & gets set in proper position for ball being shot from that angle
- Server 1 strikes a shot at goal anywhere between ^1 & the left goal post
- GK makes an appropriate save
    o If the GK collects the ball, GK then **Bowls** the ball back to Server 1 using proper communication ("Yes & Server 1's name!")
- After save, GK **Recovers** quickly back to the ^'s
- GK gets set in the following manner
    o Behind ^1 & ^2 & on the same angle as ^1 & ^2
- Server 2 tosses a long, high ball in the direction of the GK
- Toss can be
    o At the GK
    o Behind the GK
    o Off the GK's line
- GK reads the flight of the ball
    o Yells "KEEPER!" when makes decision to go for it
    o Jumps off left foot
    o Drives right knee upwards
    o Collects the ball with a **High Ball Technique (Diamond/Contour Catch)**
    o **Punches** the ball using 1 or 2 hands
    o Lands on 2 feet
- If GK collects the ball, then distributes the ball back to Server 2 using proper communication ("Yes & Server 2's name!")
- GK goes back to ^1, resets & repeats activity
- Repeat activity 6X
- Rotate GK's

Coaching Points

- GK uses proper techniques in handling the shot & **High Ball Catching**

- GK calls "KEEPER!" or "AWAY!" early & when the decision is made to go for the ball, or not
- GK takes off on proper foot
- Proper knee goes up
- Server's services are spot on
- Proper positioning in goal for a deeper angled cross or corner kick
  - Rule of Thumb
    - Middle of goal or one step back from the middle of the goal
    - One step off the line
    - Body angled on a 45-degree angle towards the ball
- Proper positioning in goal for cross coming from a higher angle up field
  - Rule of Thumb
    - Favoring the near post (a shot can be taken)
    - Body opened on a 45-degree angle towards the ball
    - GK is ready for either a shot or a cross
- **Decision making on High Balls**
  - When the cross is struck, GK's need to hold their ground & read the flight of the ball before attacking it
  - How to go for the ball depends upon its flight pattern
    - In-swinger ball (ball curving inward to the goal)
    - Out-swinger ball (ball curving outward away from the goal)
    - A floater ball with lots of back spin (ball will rise upwards more)
    - Low, hard driven ball with little spin (ball will come into the area low, hard & fast)
    - **What is the effect of the wind on each of these kicks?**
  - Is the ball coming towards the 6yd box or going outside of it? Stay or go?
  - What is the quickness/speed of the GK?
  - How tall is the GK?
  - What is the GK's range?
  - What is the pathway to the ball like?
    - Crowded (punch or get set for a shot) or is there an open lane (go collect the ball)?

Set Up 2

- Use of regular goal
- Place ^1 1yd off the goal line & 1yd to the left of the center of the goal
- Place ^2 to the left of ^1, 1yd away & on a 45-degree angle
- Place ^3 1yd to the right of ^2 (& in front of ^1)
- GK starts behind ^1 in **Modern Set Position** & facing forward
- Server 1 sets up 8yds out from the right goal post with balls at feet
- Server 2 sets up 4yds from the right post with ball in hands

Activity 2 (8 – 10mins)

- GK starts in **Modern Set Position** behind ^1 & facing forward
- Server 1 says "Go!"
- GK turns towards Server 1 & gets set in proper position for ball being shot from that angle
- Server 1 strikes a shot at goal anywhere between ^1 & the right goal post
- GK makes an appropriate save
    - o If the GK collects the ball, GK then **Bowls** the ball back to Server 1 using proper communication ("Yes & Server 1's name!")
- After save, GK **Recovers** quickly back to the ^'s
- GK gets set in the following manner
    - o Behind ^1 & ^2 & on the same angle as ^1 & ^2
- Server 2 tosses a long, high ball in the direction of the GK
- Toss can be
    - o At the GK
    - o Behind the GK
    - o Off the GK's line
- GK reads the flight of the ball

- o Yells "KEEPER!" when makes decision to go for it
- o Jumps off right foot
- o Drives left knee upwards
- o Collects the ball with a **High Ball Technique (Diamond/Contour Catch)**
- o **Punches** the ball using 1 or 2 hands
- o Lands on 2 feet
- If GK collects the ball, then **Distributes** the ball back to Server 2 using proper communication
- GK goes back to ^1, resets & repeats activity
- Repeat activity 6X
- Rotate GK's

Coaching Points

- GK uses proper techniques in handling the shot & **High Ball Catching**
- GK calls "KEEPER!" or "AWAY!" early & when decision is made to go for the ball, or not
- GK takes off on proper foot
- Proper knee goes up
- Server's services are spot on
- Proper positioning in goal for a deeper angled cross or corner kick
    - o Rule of Thumb
        - ▪ Middle of goal or one step back from the middle of the goal
        - ▪ One step off the line
        - ▪ Body angled on a 45-degree angle towards the ball
- Proper positioning in goal for cross coming from a higher angle up field
    - o Rule of Thumb
        - ▪ Favoring the near post (a shot can be taken)
        - ▪ Body opened on a 45-degree angle towards the ball
        - ▪ GK is ready for either a shot or a cross
- **Decision-making on High Balls**
    - o When the cross is struck, GK's need to hold their ground & read the flight of the ball before attacking it
    - o How to go for the ball depends upon its flight pattern
        - ▪ In-swinger ball (ball curving inward to the goal)
        - ▪ Out-swinger ball (ball curving outward away from the goal)
        - ▪ A floater ball with lots of back spin (ball will rise upwards more)
        - ▪ Low, hard driven ball with little spin (ball will come into the area low, hard & fast)
        - ▪ **What is the effect of the wind on each of these kicks?**
    - o Is the ball coming towards the 6yd box or going outside of it? Stay or go
    - o What is the quickness/speed of the GK?
    - o How tall is the GK?
    - o What is the GK's range?
    - o What is the pathway to the ball like?
        - ▪ Crowded (**Punch** or get set for a shot) or is there an open lane (go collect the ball)?

Stage 4

Live Crosses & Live Shooting

Set-Up

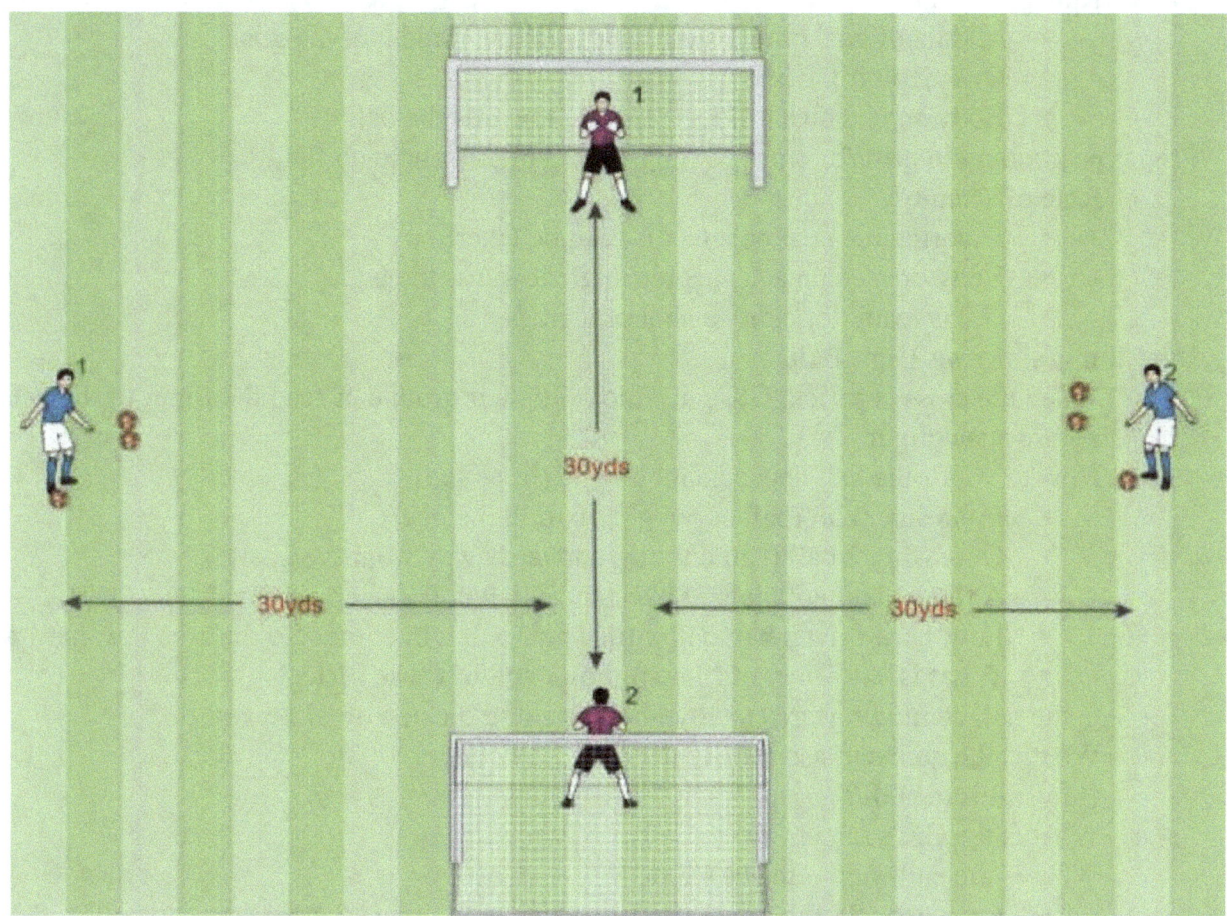

- Use of 2 regular goals set 30yds from each other GK's in each goal
- Server 1 sets up with balls 30yds on one side line & between the 2 goals
- Server 2 sets up with balls 30yds on the other side line & between the 2 goals

Activity 1 (10 – 20mis)

- Server 1 starts by driving a cross randomly to either GK1 or GK2
- The GK collects the cross
- After collecting the cross, the GK puts the ball down & shoots at the opposite goal & attempts to score
- GK's can keep score against each other
- Server 2 then repeats the activity from the other side
- Alternate services until each GK has collected 6 crosses
- Alternate GK's & repeat activity
- Can do a round-robin competition if have enough GK's

Coaching Points

- Both GKs should be communicating on every cross
  - o GK collecting the cross – "KEEPER!"

  o GK not collecting the ball – "AWAY!"
- Proper execution of **High Ball Catching Technique (Diamond/Contour Catch)**
- Servers serve in quality crosses
- Proper positioning in goal for a deeper angled cross or corner kick
  - Rule of Thumb
    - Middle of goal or one step back from the middle of the goal
    - One step off the line
    - Body angled on a 45-degree angle towards the ball
- Proper positioning in goal for cross coming from a higher angle up field
  - Rule of Thumb
    - Favoring the near post (a shot can be taken)
    - Body opened on a 45-degree angle towards the ball
    - GK is ready for either a shot or a cross
- **Decision making on High Balls**
  - When the cross is struck, GK's need to hold their ground & read the flight of the ball before attacking it
  - How to go for the ball depends upon its flight pattern
    - In-swinger ball (ball curving inward to the goal)
    - Out-swinger ball (ball curving outward away from the goal)
    - A floater ball with lots of back spin (ball will rise upwards more)
    - Low, hard-driven ball with little spin (ball will come into the area low, hard & fast)
    - **What is the effect of the wind on each of these kicks?**
  - Is the ball coming towards the 6yd box or going outside of it? Stay or go?
  - What is the quickness/speed of the GK?
  - How tall is the GK?
  - What is the GK's range?
  - What is the pathway to the ball like?
    - Crowded (**Punch** or get set for a shot) or is there an open lane (go collect the ball)?

U16 – U18 Training Session #3
Cut back Saves/Over Hand Deflections

Techniques used in this session

- **Volleys**
- **Controlled Collapse Catch left & right**
- **Diamond/Contour Catch**
- **Modern Set Position**
- **Close Range Set Position**
- **Cut Back Position**
- **Low-ball Deflections**
- **Mid-ball Deflections**
- **Recovery**
- **High-ball Deflections (away from or to the side of the goal)**

The key for Training Session

- ^ = cone (^1 – cone 1)
- X = Times (2X – 2 times)

Stage 1

Dynamic Warm-up

Set-Up

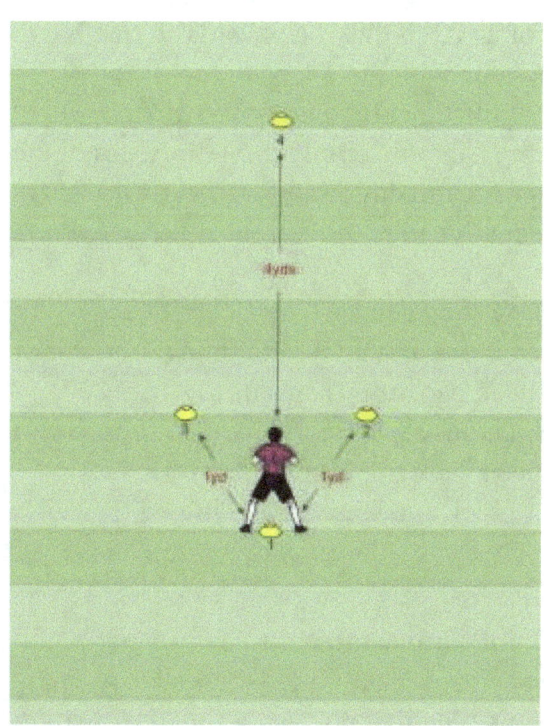

- Place 3 ^'s in a V shape, 1yd apart
- Place a 4th ^ 4yds away from ^2 & ^3
- ^1 is the starting ^; ^4 is the ending ^

- All starting **Foot-work** will be fast feet (quick feet) forward to ^3 & back to start; then fast feet forward to ^4 & back to start
- All of the dynamic movements will then be performed between ^1 & ^4
- GK's will jog back to start at ^1
- All movements will be done 1X or 2X each (depending on amount of time available for the whole session)

Activity 1 (5 – 8mins)

- Dynamic movements between ^1 & ^4 are (order can be varied or modified)
    - Jog up & jog back
    - High knees up & jog back
    - Butt kicks up & jog back
    - Skipping & forward arm circles
    - Skipping & arm circles backwards
    - Skipping & swinging arms across the chest
    - Open the gate & jog back
    - Close the gate & jog back
    - Inside up & jog back ("Inside" is performed in the following way)
        - While keeping the back upright & straight, dangle both arms down in front of the body towards feet
        - Pull one foot up & in so that hand touches the arch of the inside of that foot; do the same with the opposite foot
        - Performed while quickly jogging forward
    - Outside up & jog back ("Outside" is performed in the following way)
        - Dangle arms straight down at the sides
        - Pull one foot up & slightly backwards so that hand touches the outside of the foot & then do the same with the opposite foot
        - Performed while quickly jogging forward
    - Facing sideways at ^1, get into **Modern Set Position**; quick shuffle to ^4 & jog back; do the same in the opposite direction
    - Same as above except dynamic movement is carioca; do it facing both ways
    - Lunges up & jog back
    - Straight leg sweeps & jog back
    - GK sprints to ^2 & circles around it with quick foot work in a counter-clockwise fashion; back pedals with speed back to ^1; sprints to ^4
    - GK sprints to ^3 & circles around it with quick foot work in a clockwise fashion; then backpedals with speed back to ^1; sprints to ^4
- Take 2 minutes for a water break and static stretching on their own

Coaching Points

- Reinforce proper execution of various movements
- Players shouldn't rush through these activities
- Movements should be executed deliberately, stressing the quality of each movement

Stage 2

Handling Rhythm Work

Set Up 1

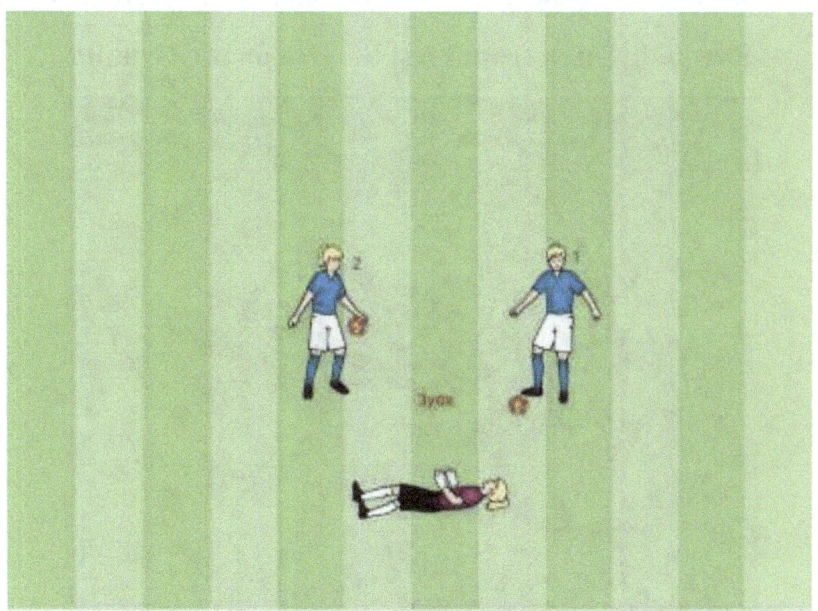

Picture of starting Position for this Activity

Photo Courtesy of Matt Broomall & Modern Goalkeeper Training Systems, LLC

- GK sets up by lying on the ground on the right side
  - Left leg extended laterally
  - Right leg bent at knee & tucked under left leg
  - Only part of body touching the ground are the legs up to the right hip

- o Body is cocked on a 45-degree angle upward with chest, head & hands facing towards the Servers
- o Hands in **Set Position**
- Server 1 sets up with ball at the feet, 3yds away from the GK & slightly to the GK's right
- Server 2 sets up with ball in the hands, 3yds away from the GK & slightly to the GK's left

Low-ball Catch from First Service on the Ground

Catching Form from Second Service (From the Volley)

Photos Courtesy of Matt Broomall & Modern Goalkeeper Training Systems, LLC

Activity 1 (3 – 4mins)

- GK starts in position described above
- Server 1 strikes a low ball on the ground to the GK's right (but close to the body)
- GK collapses upper body to the ground & catches the ball using **Controlled Collapsing Technique to the Right**
- GK **Distributes** the ball **directly** back to Server 1 by rolling it on the ground releasing the ball with the upper (left) hand to give the ball a top-spin release
- GK communicates on the **Distribution** to Server 1 ("Yes & Server 1's name!")
- GK then raises the body back up into the cocked position
- Server 2 **Volleys** a ball to the GK who collects it using a **Diamond/Contour Catch**
- GK tosses the ball back to Server 2 using proper communication ("Yes & Server 2's name!")
- Repeat activity from both Servers for 45sec
- Rotate GK's & repeat activity

Coaching Points

- GK uses core muscles to cock the body up when lying on side
- Services are accurate
- GK uses proper technique when catching the ground ball and the **Volley**
- GK communicates on all **Distributions** back to the Servers ("Yes & Server's name!")

Set Up 2

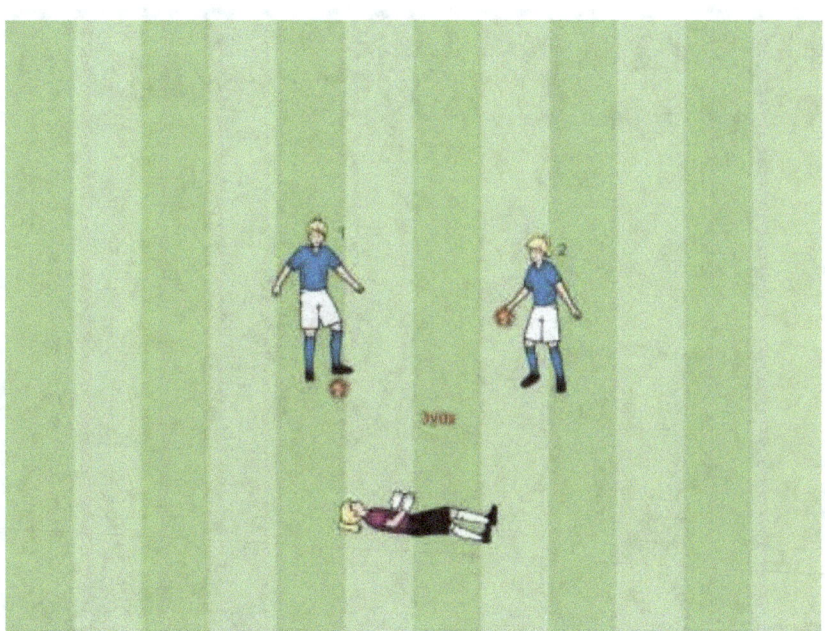

- GK sets up by lying on the ground on left side
    - right leg extended laterally
    - left leg bent at knee & tucked under right leg
    - Only part of body touching the ground are the legs up to the left hip
    - Body is cocked on a 45-degree angle upward with chest, head & hands facing towards the S's
    - Hands in a set position
- Server 1 sets up with ball at the feet, 3yds away from the GK & slightly to the GK's left
- Server 2 sets up with ball in the hands, 3yds away from the GK & slightly to the GK's right

Picture of starting Position for this Activity

Low-ball Catch from First Service on the Ground

Catching Form from Second Service (From the Volley)

Photos Courtesy of Matt Broomall & Modern Goalkeeper Training Systems, LLC

Activity 1 (3 – 4mins)

- GK starts in the position described above
- Server 1 strikes a low ball on the ground to the GK's left (but close to the body)
- GK collapses upper body to the ground & catches the ball using **Controlled Collapsing Technique to the Left**
- GK distributes the ball **directly** back to Server 1 by rolling it on the ground releasing the ball with the upper (right) hand to give the ball a top-spin release
- GK communicates on the **Distribution** to Server 1 ("Yes & Server 1's name!")
- GK then raises the body back up into the cocked position
- Server 2 **Volleys** a ball to the GK who collects it using a **Diamond/Contour Catch**
- GK tosses the ball back to Server 2 using proper communication ("Yes & Server 2's name!")
- Repeat activity from both Servers for 45sec
- Rotate GK's & repeat activity

Coaching Points

- GK uses core muscles to cock the body up when lying on side
- Services are accurate
- GK uses proper technique when catching the ground ball and the **Volley**
- GK communicates on all **Distributions** back to the Servers ("Yes & Server's name!")

Set Up 3

- GK sets up by kneeling facing Server 1
- GK's hands are in set position & the body is slightly bent forward at the waist
- Server1 sets up 2yds away from & facing the GK with ball in hands

Kneeling Starting Position for this Activity

Photos Courtesy of Matt Broomall & Modern Goalkeeper Training Systems, LLC

Activity 1 (2 – 3mins)

- Server 1 starts by tossing the ball slightly outside of the GK's body, at shoulder height & to the GK's right

- GK collects the ball using **Controlled Collapsing Technique to the Right** by bringing the ball down to the ground first before the body hits the ground
    o GK uses the ball to help break the fall
- GK tosses the ball from the ground back to Server 1's hands using proper communication ("Yes & Server 1's name!")
- GK then quickly pops back up to the kneeling position & quickly resets
- Once GK is back into **Set Position**, Server 1 then tosses the ball slightly outside of the GK's body, at shoulder height & to the GK's left
- GK collects the ball using **Controlled Collapsing Technique to the Left** by bringing the ball down to the ground first before the body hits the ground
    o GK uses the ball to help break the fall
- GK tosses the ball from the ground back to Server 1's hands using proper communication ("Yes & Server 1's name!")
- GK then quickly pops back up to the kneeling position & quickly sets
- Repeat 10X to each side
- Rotate GK's & repeat the activity

Coaching Points

- Services are accurate
- GK uses proper technique when catching the tossed ball
- GK brings the ball down to the ground first (after the catch) to help break the fall of the body
- GK communicates on all **Distributions** back to Server 1 ("Yes & Server 1's name!")

Set Up 4

- GK starts on feet & in the **Close Range Set Position** directly facing Server1
- Server 1 starts with ball in hands & 4yds from GK

Close Range Stance/Blocking Stance

Photos Courtesy of Matt Broomall & Modern Goalkeeper Training Systems, LLC

Activity 1 (2 – 3mins)

- Server 1 serves a **Volley** just to the right of the GK (fairly close to the body) & at shoulder height
- GK steps with the right foot towards the ball & collects the ball using the **Controlled Collapse Technique to the Right**, bringing the ball to the ground first to break the fall
- GK tosses the ball back to Server 1 from the ground using proper communication ("Yes & Server 1's name!")
- GK quickly gets back to feet & gets into the **Close Range Set Position**
- Server 1 then serves a **Volley** just to the left of the GK (fairly close to the body) & at shoulder height
- GK steps with the left foot towards the ball & collects the ball using the **Controlled Collapse Technique to the Left**, bringing the ball to the ground first to break the fall
- GK tosses the ball back to Server 1 from the ground using proper communication ("Yes & Server 1's name!")
- GK quickly gets back to feet & gets into the **Close Range Set Position**
- Repeat 10X each side
- GK's rotate & repeat the activity

Coaching Points

- Services are accurate
- GK uses proper technique when catching the tossed ball
- GK brings the ball down to the ground first (after the catch) to help break the fall of the body
- GK communicates on all **Distributions** back to Server 1 ("Yes & Server 1's name!")

Stage 4

Cut Backs/Deflections

Set Up 1

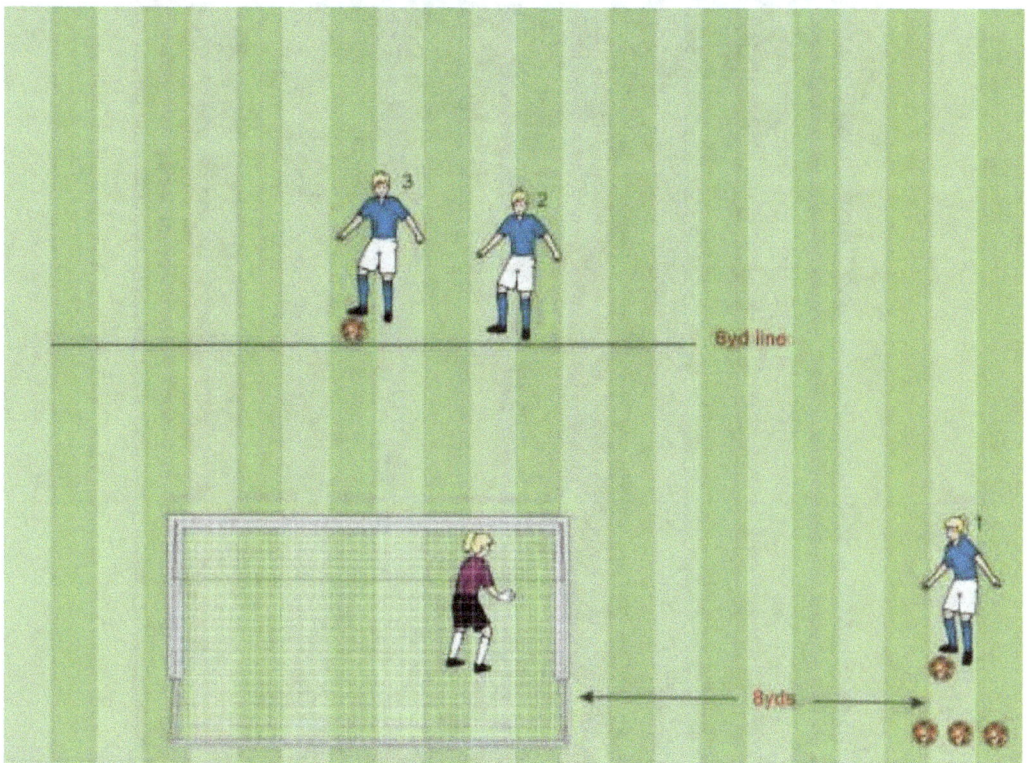

- Use of regular size goal
- Use of 18yd box
- GK sets up in **Cut Back Position** at the near post (right post & closest to Server 1)
- Server 1 sets up on the goal line approximately 8yds from the near post with balls at feet
- Server 2 sets up just outside the 6yd line & 2yds inside the near post (with no ball)
- Server 3 sets up just outside the 6yd box & in the center of the goal with ball in hands

Cut Back Positioning

1 Hand Deflection Technique Left

2 Hand Deflection Technique

Photos Courtesy of Matt Broomall & Modern Goalkeeper Training Systems, LLC

Activity 1 (6 – 8mins)

- GK starts in **Cut Back Position** at the post closest to Server 1
- Server 1 strikes a low ball across the ground to Server 2
- GK quickly moves into proper angle to face Server 2 & in **Close Range Set Position**
- Server 2 strikes the ball on the 1st touch to the target

- GK attempts to make the save
- After the ball is saved, out or in the goal, the GK quickly **Recovers** to the feet
- Server 3 then tosses the ball or throws a low bouncing ball to the GK's left (between the middle of the goal & the far post)
- GK either collects the ball or executes a **Low-ball or Mid-ball Deflection Save (with the left hand)**
    o 2 hand deflection is acceptable, if
        ▪ Ball is coming at a high rate of pace
        ▪ Both hands can get to the ball
- GK goes back to the near post & the activity is repeated
- Repeat 4X – 5X
- Rotate GK's

Coaching Points

- Servers serve quality balls
- Server 3 challenges the GK on the tossed/bouncing ball
- GK is in proper **Cut Back Position** to start
- GK moves quickly into **Close Range Set Position** as the ball is cut back to Server 2
- The GK sets before Server 2 strikes the shot, whether positioned properly or not
- GK's **Recovery** back to feet is quick
- GK makes an effort to save the ball from Server 3, making a decision on whether to catch or deflect
- GK uses proper technique whether **Catching** or **Deflecting** the ball from Server 3
- GK **Deflects** the ball with the left hand (for both the **Low & Mid-ball Deflection**) & puts ball into a safe position
- **2-hand Deflection** is acceptable, if
    o Ball is coming at a high rate of pace
    o Both hands can get to the ball
- **Safe places to deflect the ball**
    o Out-of-bounds
    o Directly down the goal line with enough pace to get the ball out of the 6yd box
    o Angled out towards the corner of the 6yd box
    o **NOT** back into the center of the goal

Set Up 2

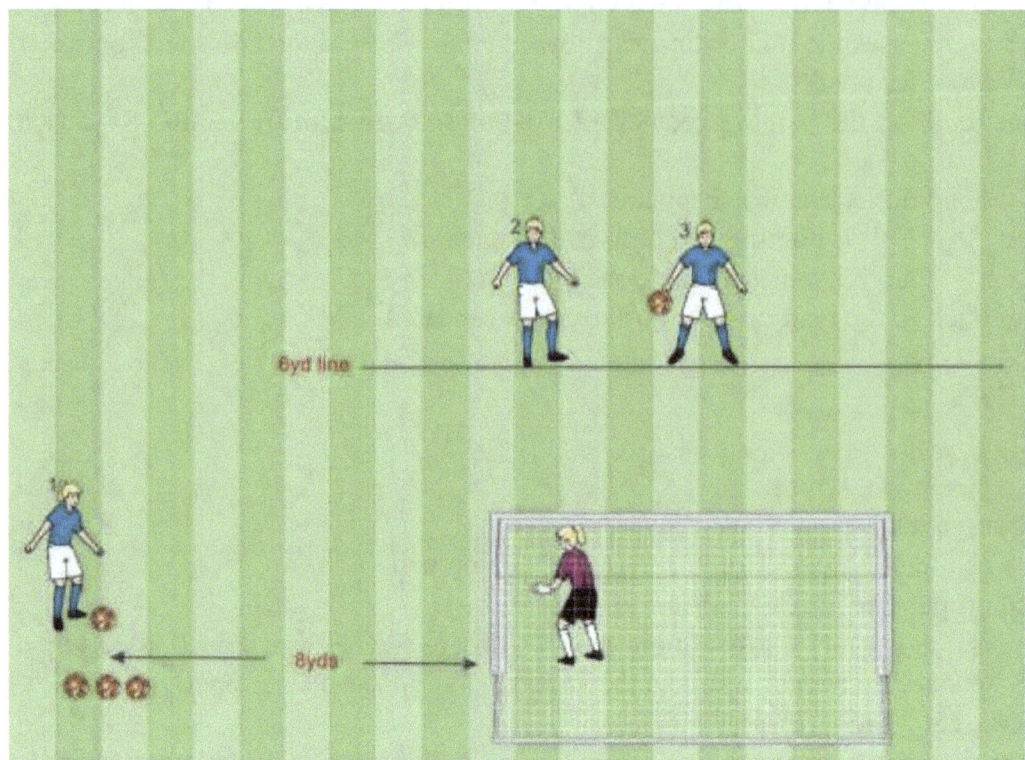

- Use of regular size goal
- Use of 18yd box
- GK sets up in **Cut Back Position** at the near post (left post & closest to Server 1)
- Server 1 sets up on the goal line approximately 8yds from the near post with balls at feet
- Server 2 sets up just outside the 6yd line & 2yds inside the near post (with no ball)
- Server 3 sets up just outside the 6yd box & in the center of the goal with ball in hands

Cut Back Positioning

1 Hand Deflection Technique Left

2 Hand Deflection Technique

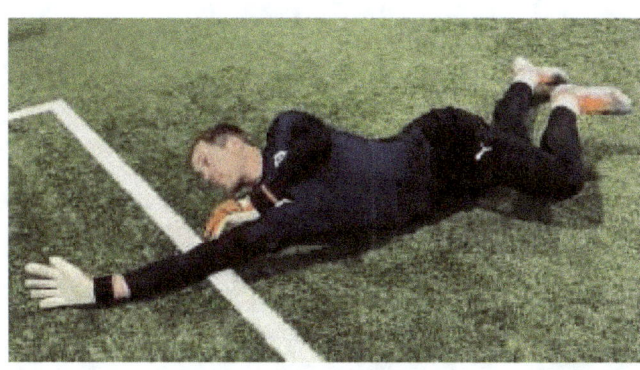

Photos Courtesy of Matt Broomall & Modern Goalkeeper Training Systems, LLC

Activity 1 (6 – 8mins)

- GK starts in **Cut Back Position** at the post closest to Server 1
- Server 1 strikes a low ball across the ground to Server 2
- GK quickly moves into proper angle to face Server 2 & in **Close Range Set Position**
- Server 2 strikes the ball on the 1st touch to the target
- GK attempts to make the save
- After the ball is saved, out or in the goal, the GK quickly **Recovers** to the feet
- Server 3 then tosses the ball or throws a low bouncing ball to the GK's right (between the middle of the goal & the far post)
- GK either collects the ball or executes a **Low-ball or Mid-ball Deflection Save (with the right hand)**
    - ○ **2-hand deflection** is acceptable, if
        - ▪ Ball is coming at a high rate of pace
        - ▪ Both hands can get to the ball
- GK goes back to the near post & the activity is repeated
- Repeat 4X – 5X
- Rotate GK's

Coaching Points

- Servers serve quality balls
- Server 3 challenges the GK on the tossed/bouncing ball
- GK is in proper **Cut Back Position** to start
- GK moves quickly into **Close Range Set Position** as the ball is cut back to Server 2
- The GK sets before Server 2 strikes the shot, whether positioned properly or not
- GK's **Recovery** back to feet is quick
- GK makes an effort to save the ball from Server 3, making a decision on whether to catch or deflect
- GK uses proper technique whether **Catching** or **Deflecting** the ball from Server 3
- GK **Deflects** the ball with the right hand & puts ball into a safe position
- **2-hand deflection** is acceptable, if

- o Ball is coming at a high rate of pace
- o Both hands can get to the ball
- **Safe places to deflect the ball**
  - o Out-of-bounds
  - o Directly down the goal line with enough pace to get the ball out of the 6yd box
  - o Angled out towards the corner of the 6yd box
  - o **NOT** back into the center of the goal

Set Up 3

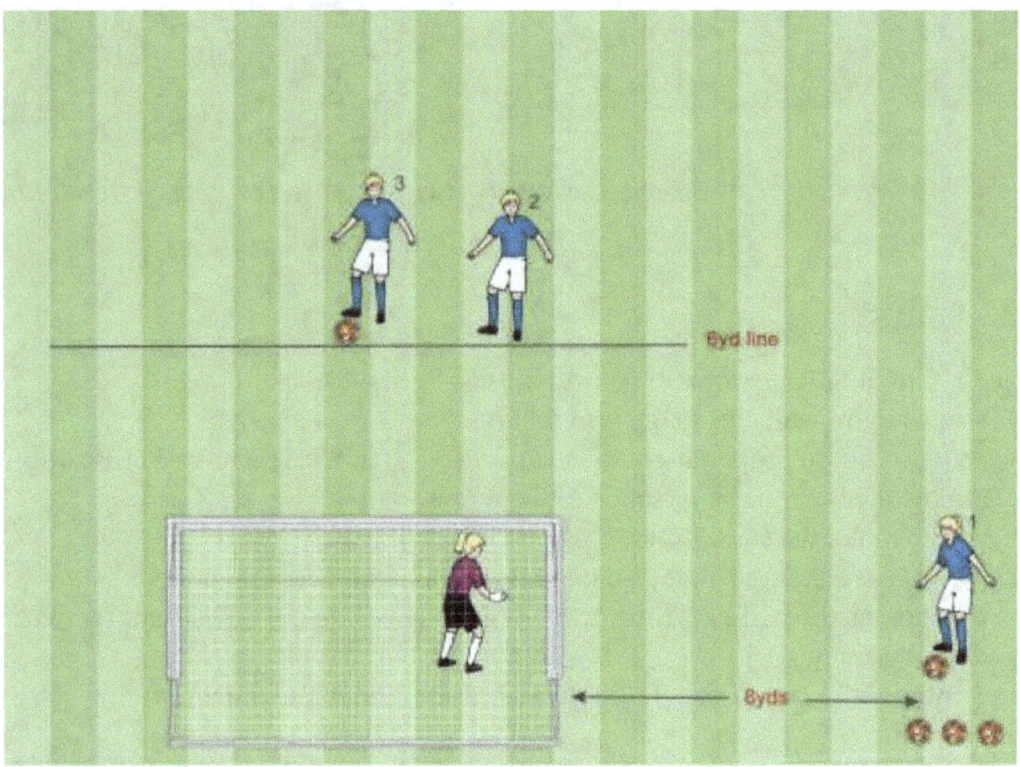

- Use of regular size goal
- Use of 18yd box
- GK sets up in **Cut Back Position** at the near post (right post & closest to Server 1)
- Server 1 sets up on the goal line approximately 8yds from the near post with balls at feet
- Server 2 sets up just outside the 6yd line & 2yds inside the near post (with no ball)
- Server 3 sets up just outside the 6yd box & in the center of the goal with ball in hands

Activity 1 (6 – 8mins)

- GK starts in **Cut Back Position** at the post closest to Server 1
- Server 1 strikes a low ball across the ground to Server 2
- GK quickly moves into proper angle to face Server 2 & in **Close Range Set Position**
- Server 2 strikes the ball on the 1st touch to the target
- GK attempts to make the save
- After the ball is saved, out or in the goal, the GK quickly **Recovers** to the feet
- Server 3 then tosses a high ball or throws a high bouncing ball to the GK's left (between the middle of the goal & the far post)
- GK either collects the ball or executes a **High-ball Deflection Save (with the right hand – upper hand)**

- o **2-hand Deflection** is acceptable, if
  - ▪ Ball is coming at a high rate of pace
  - ▪ Both hands can get to the ball
- GK goes back to the near post & the activity is repeated
- Repeat 4X – 5X
- Rotate GK's

Coaching Points

- Servers serve quality balls
- Server 3 challenges the GK on the tossed/bouncing ball
- GK is in proper **Cut Back Position** to start
- GK moves quickly into **Close Range Set Position** as the ball is cut back to Server 2
- The GK sets before Server 2 strikes the shot, whether positioned properly or not
- GK's **Recovery** back to feet is quick
- GK makes an effort to save the ball from Server 3, making a decision on whether to catch or deflect
- GK uses proper technique whether **Catching** or **Deflecting** the ball from Server 3
- GK **Deflects** the ball with the right (upper hand) & puts ball into a safe position
- The save is a **Deflection** & is redirected; it is not a swat at the ball with the hand
- **2-hand Deflection** is acceptable, if
  - o Ball is coming at a high rate of pace
  - o Both hands can get to the ball
- **Safe places to deflect the ball**
  - o Out-of-bounds
  - o Directly down the goal line with enough pace to get the ball out of the 6yd box
  - o Angled out towards the corner of the 6yd box
  - o **NOT** back into the center of the goal

Set Up 4

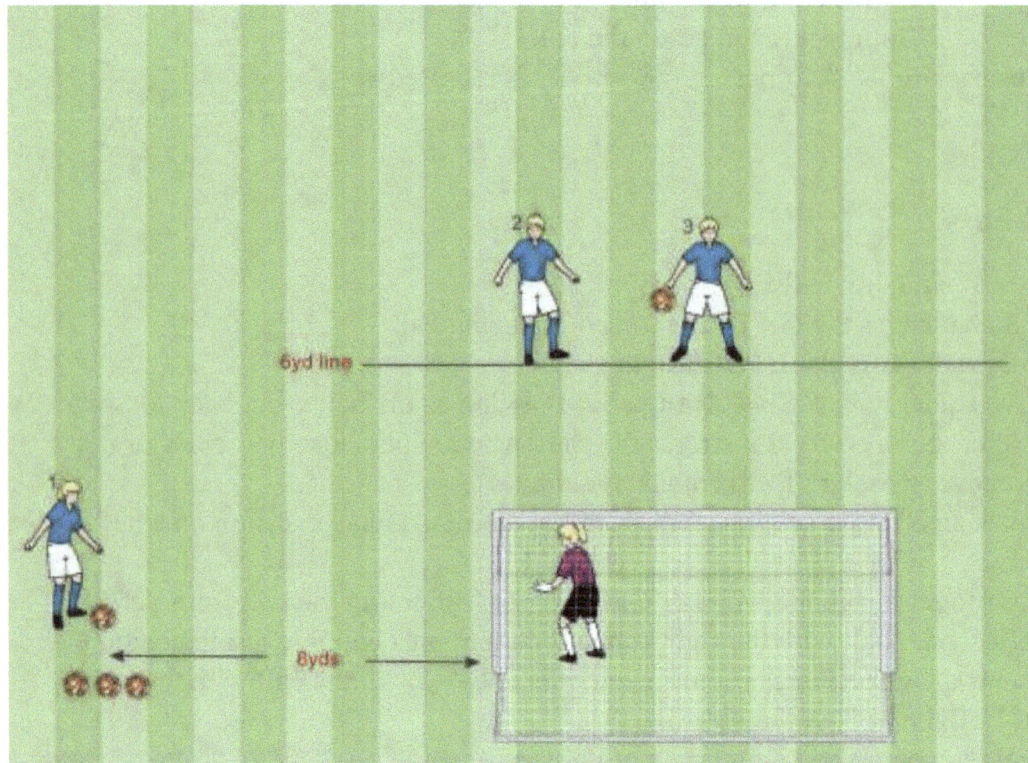

- Use of regular size goal
- Use of 18yd box
- GK sets up in **Cut Back Position** at the near post (left post & closest to Server 1)
- Server 1 sets up on the goal line approximately 8yds from the near post with balls at feet
- Server 2 sets up just outside the 6yd line & 2yds inside the near post (with no ball)
- Server 3 sets up just outside the 6yd box & in the center of the goal with ball in hands

Activity 1 (6 – 8mins)

- GK starts in **Cut Back Position** at the post closest to Server 1
- Server 1 strikes a low ball across the ground to Server 2
- GK quickly moves into proper angle to face Server 2 & in **Close Range Set Position**
- Server 2 strikes the ball on the 1st touch to the target
- GK attempts to make the save
- After the ball is saved, out or in the goal, the GK quickly **Recovers** to the feet
- Server 3 then tosses a high ball or throws a high bouncing ball to the GK's right (between the middle of the goal & the far post)
- GK either collects the ball or executes a **High-ball Deflection Save (with the left – upper hand)**
    o **2-hand Deflection** is acceptable, if
        ▪ Ball is coming at a high rate of pace
        ▪ Both hands can get to the ball
- GK goes back to the near post & the activity is repeated
- Repeat 4X – 5X
- Rotate GK's

Coaching Points

- Servers serve quality balls
- Server 3 challenges the GK on the tossed/bouncing ball
- GK is in proper **Cut Back Position** to start
- GK moves quickly into **Close Range Set Position** as the ball is cut back to Server 2
- The GK sets before Server 2 strikes the shot, whether positioned properly or not
- GK's **Recovery** back to feet is quick
- GK makes an effort to save the ball from Server 3, making a decision on whether to catch or deflect
- GK uses proper technique whether **Catching** or **Deflecting** the ball from Server 3
- GK deflects the ball with the left (upper) hand & puts ball into a safe position
- The save is a **Deflection** & is redirected; it is not a swat at the ball with the hand
- **2-hand Deflection** is acceptable, if
    o Ball is coming at a high rate of pace
    o Both hands can get to the ball
- **Safe places to deflect the ball**
    o Out-of-bounds
    o Directly down the goal line with enough pace to get the ball out of the 6yd box
    o Angled out towards the corner of the 6yd box
    o **NOT** back into the center of the goal

Stage 5

Live Shooting

Set Up 1

- Use of regular size goal
- Use of 18yd box area
- Server 1 sets up with balls at feet along the end line off the left post & about 10yds away from the post
- Server 2 sets up with balls at feet along the end line off the right post & about 10yds away from the post
- Server 3 sets up just outside of the 6yd box & directly out from the left post
- Server 4 sets up just outside of the 6yd box & directly out from the right post
- Server 5 sets up at the "D" with balls at feet
- GK starts in **Cut Back Position** at the left post
- After a round of shots, GK then sets up in **Cut Back Position** at the right post
- A **variation** can include Server 6 & Server 7 setting up with balls at feet at about 15yds from goal & just inside of Server 2 & Server 3

Activity 1 (10 – 15mins)

- GK starts in **Cut Back Position** at the left post
- Server 1 strikes a cut back ball to either Server 3 or Server 4

- GK moves into position & attempts to save the one time shot from either Server 3 or Server 4 by **Catching** or **Deflecting** the ball
- GK then **Recovers** for a shot from Server 5
- Rebounds are live on Server 5's shot

Variation

- o After Server 5's shot, **GKC** can call out "Server 6!" or "Server 7!" for an additional shot
- o Rebounds are live on either Server 6's or Server 7's shot

- GK then moves over & gets into **Cut Back Position** at the right post
- Server 2 strikes a cut back ball to either Server 3 or Server 4
- GK moves into position & attempts to save the one time shot from either Server 3 or Server 4 by **Catching** or **Deflecting** the ball
- GK then **Recovers** for a shot from Server 5
- Rebounds are live on Server 5's shot

Variation

- o After Server 5's shot, Coach can call out "Server 6!" or "Server 7!" for an additional shot
- o Rebounds are live on either Server 6's or Server 7's shot

- Repeat 3X – 4X at each post
- GK's then rotate & repeat the activity

Coaching Points

- GK sets up in proper **Cut Back Position** to start
- Servers serve quality balls
- GK moves quickly to get into position for each shot
- Server 5 allows GK to get set before shooting
- Server 6 & Server 7 allow GK to get set before shooting
- Rebounds are live on the last shot, wherever taken
- GK uses correct techniques when **Catching** or **Deflecting** the ball

U16 – U18 Training Session #4
Lateral Foot-work Development

Techniques used in this session

- **Modern Set Position**
- **Chop Step Foot-work**
- **Lateral Foot-work**
- **2 Touch Passing**
- **1 Touch Passing**
- **Volley**
- **½ Volley**
- **Driven balls**
- **Diamond/Contour Catch**
- **Front Smother**
- **Bowling**

The key for Training Session

- ^ = cone (^1 – cone 1)
- X = Times (2X – 2 times)

Stage 1

Dynamic Warm-Up

Set-Up

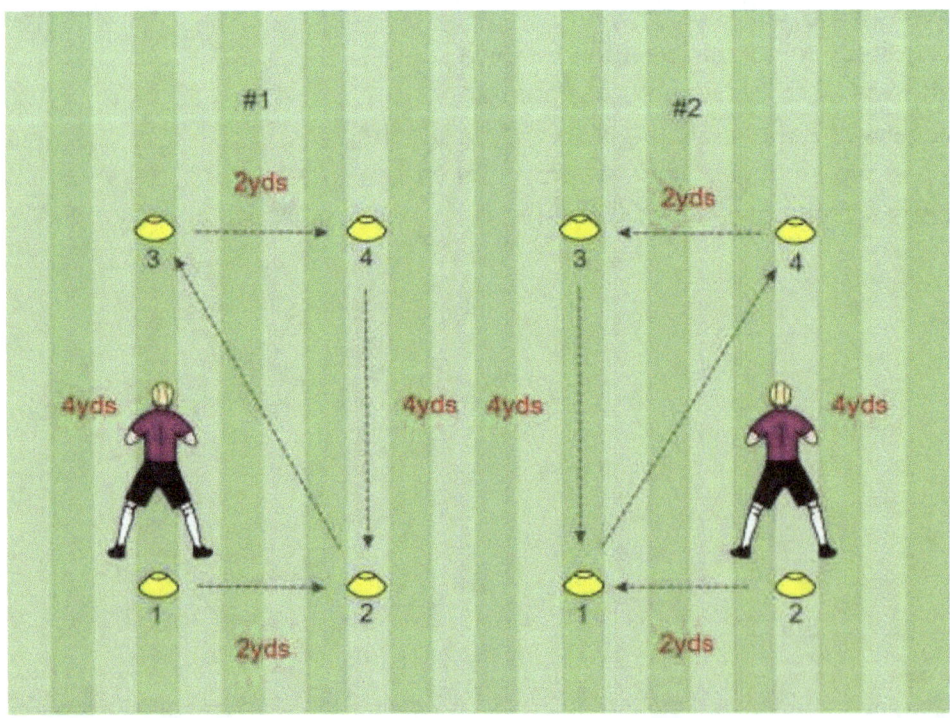

- Place ^1, ^2, ^3 & ^4 in a rectangle
- ^1/^2 & ^3/^4 are placed 2yds apart

- ^1/^3 & ^2/^4 are placed 4yds apart
- GK starts behind ^1

Activity 1 (5 – 8mins)

- GK starts in **Modern Set Position** directly behind ^1 facing forward (towards ^3)
- GK quickly shuffles to the right to ^2
- GK then performs a dynamic motion diagonally across to ^3
- GK then shuffles to the right to ^4
- GK backpedals to ^2
- GK stays at ^2 & reverses the process
- GK quickly shuffles to the left to ^1
- GK then performs the same dynamic motion diagonally across to ^4
- GK then shuffles to the left to ^3
- GK backpedals to ^1
- GK stays at ^1 & repeats the process but doing a different dynamic motion
- Dynamic motions
    - Jog
    - High knees
    - Butt kicks
    - Skipping & forward arm circles
    - Skipping & arm circles backwards
    - Skipping & swinging arms across chest
    - Open the gate
    - Close the gate
    - Lunges (lunging forward with one foot at a time – alternate feet)
    - Straight leg sweeps (bend forward & sweep the ground with both hands, take 3 small steps & do it again, etc.)
    - Twist body with elbows touching opposite knee
    - Side shuffle to ^ facing inward
    - Side shuffle to ^ again facing inward
    - Carioca to ^ facing inward
    - Carioca to ^ again facing inward
    - Sprint to ^
- Water break with additional static stretching

Coaching Points

- Reinforce proper execution of various movements
- Players shouldn't rush through these activities
- Movements should be executed deliberately, stressing the quality of each movement

Stage 2

Lateral Foot-work – Quick Feet/Rhythm Work

Set Up 1

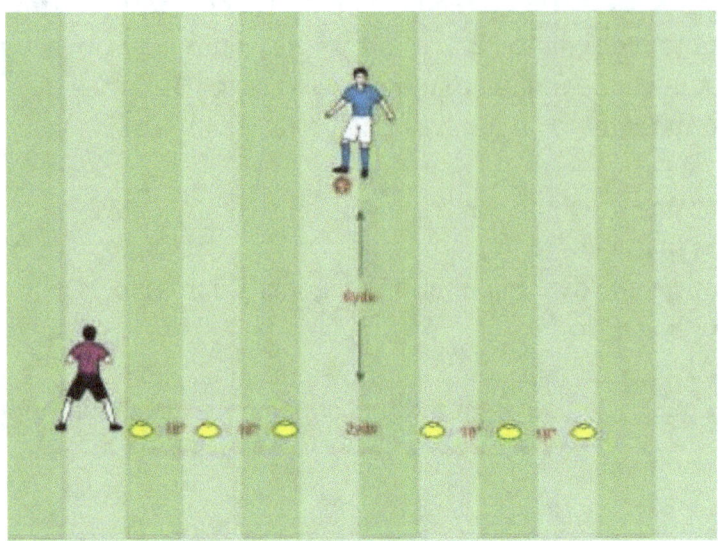

- Place 3 ^'s along-side & 18" away from each other
- Place 3 more ^'s along-side & 18" away from each other & 2yds from the other set of ^'s
- GK sets up in **Modern Set Position** on the left of the ^'s facing Server
- Server sets up in the center of the ^'s & 6yds away with a ball at the feet

Modern Set Position

Photos Courtesy of Matt Broomall & Modern Goalkeeper Training Systems, LLC

Inside of the Foot Pass (IOF)

Photo Courtesy of Matt Broomall

Activity 1 (3 – 5mins)

- GK starts the activity by using **Chop Step Foot-work** through the 3 ^'s moving to the right (moving quickly)
- After the 3rd ^, GK stops into **Modern Set Position**, and asks for the ball to the feet from Server using proper communication ("Yes & Server's name!")
- Server passes the ball to the GK
- GK uses **2 Touches** (using any combination with the feet) to pass the ball back to Server
- GK then steps back behind the ^'s & jogs to the other side
- GK sets up in **Modern Set Position** on the right of the ^'s facing Server
- GK starts the activity by using **Chop Step Foot-work** through the 3 ^'s moving to the left (moving quickly)
- After the 3rd ^, GK stops into **Modern Set Position**, asks for the ball from Server using proper communication ("Yes & Server's name!")
- Server passes the ball to the GK
- GK uses **2 Touches** (using any combination with the feet) to pass the ball back to Server
- GK then steps back behind the ^'s & jogs to the beginning position at the left of the ^'s
- Repeat 4X each side
- Rotate GK's & repeat activity

Coaching Points

- The **Foot-work** is fast & clean
- Proper communication is used when asking for the ball to the feet
- Server does not pass the ball to the GK until proper communication is used by GK
- Server serves quality passes
- GK's **2 Touch Passing** is clean & accurate
- GK uses various touches with the feet; not using the same foot every time

Set Up 2

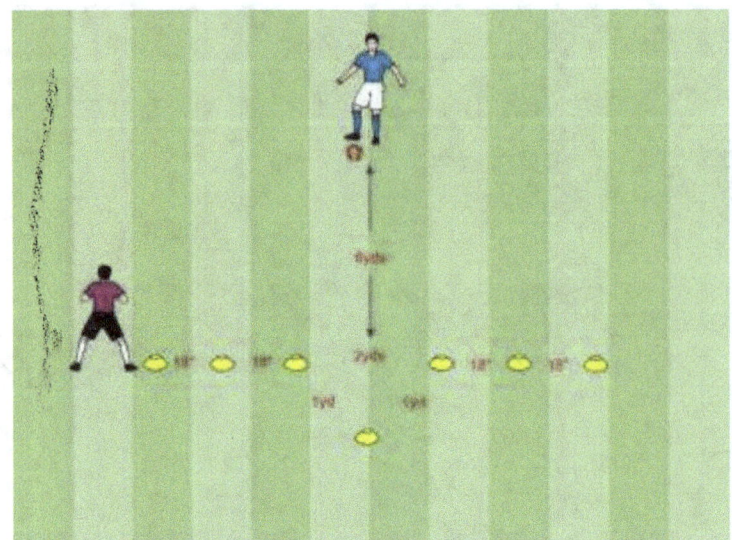

- Place 3 ^'s along-side & 18" away from each other
- Place 3 more ^'s along-side & 18" away from each other & 2yds from the other set of ^'s
- Place a final ^ 1yd back from the 2yds space making a triangle
- GK sets up in **Modern Set Position** on the left of the ^'s facing Server
- Server sets up in the center of the ^'s & 6yds away with a ball at the feet

Activity 1 (3 – 5mins)

- GK starts the activity by using **Chop Step Foot-work** through the 3 ^'s moving to the right (moving quickly)
- After the 3rd ^, the GK quickly backpedals around the back ^ & quickly steps forward between the 2 middle ^'s
- GK asks for the ball to the feet from Server using proper communication ("Yes & Server's name!")
- GK then **1 Touches** the ball back to Server using either foot
- GK then steps back behind the ^'s & jogs to the other side
- GK sets up in **Modern Set Position** on the right of the ^'s facing Server
- GK starts the activity by using **Chop Step Foot-work** through the 3 ^'s moving to the left (moving quickly)
- After the 3rd ^, the GK quickly backpedals around the back ^ & quickly steps forward between the 2-middle ^'s
- GK asks for the ball to the feet from Server using proper communication ("Yes & Server's name!")
- GK then **1 Touches** the ball back to Server using either foot
- GK then steps back behind the ^'s & jogs to the beginning position at the left of the ^'s
- Repeat 4X each side
- Rotate GK's & repeat activity

Coaching Points

- The **Foot-work** is fast & clean
- Proper communication is used when asking for the ball to the feet
- Server does not pass the ball to the GK until proper communication is used by GK
- Server serves quality passes

- GK's **1 Touch Passing** is clean & accurate
- GK does not use the same foot every time

Set Up 3

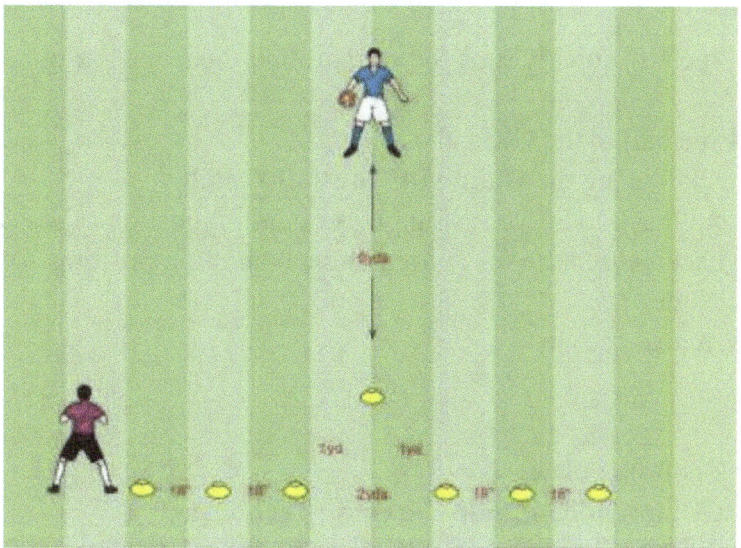

- Place 3 ^'s along-side & 18" away from each other
- Place 3 more ^'s along-side & 18" away from each other & 2yds from the other set of ^'s
- Place a final ^ 1yd in front of the 2yds space making a triangle
- GK sets up in **Modern Set Position** on the left of the ^'s facing Server
- Server sets up in the center of the ^'s & 6yds away with a ball in the hands

Diamond/Contour Catch

Photo Courtesy of Matt Broomall

Activity 1 (3 – 5mins)

- GK starts the activity by using **Chop Step Foot-work** through the 3 ^'s moving to the right (moving quickly)
- After the 3rd ^, the GK quickly runs forward around the front ^ & quickly steps backward between the 2 middle ^'s
- Server **Volleys** the ball to the GK's chest
- GK collects the ball using the **Diamond/Contour Catch**

82

- GK tosses the ball back to Server using proper communication ("Yes & Server's name!")
- GK then steps back behind the ^'s & jogs to the other side
- GK sets up in **Modern Set Position** on the right of the ^'s facing Server
- GK starts the activity by using **Chop Step Foot-work** through the 3 ^'s moving to the left (moving quickly)
- After the 3rd ^, the GK quickly runs forward around the front ^ & quickly steps backward between the 2 middle ^'s
- Server **Volleys** the ball to the GK's chest
- GK collects the ball using the **Diamond/Contour Catch**
- GK tosses the ball back to Server using proper communication ("Yes & Server's name!")
- GK then steps back behind the ^'s & jogs to the beginning position at the left of the ^'s
- Repeat 4X each side
- Rotate GK's & repeat activity

Coaching Points

- The **Foot-work** is fast & clean
- GK uses proper **Diamond/Contour Catching Technique**
- Proper communication is used when GK **Distributes** ball back to Server
- Server makes sure that the GK is set before serving the ball
- Server serves quality **Volleys**

Stage 3

No Collapse Drill

Set Up 1

- Use of regular goal
- Place 6 ^'s side by side, 18" away from each other with a 2yd gap between the two middle ^'s & 1yd off the goal line
- Server sets up with ball in hands 6yds from the center of the goal

- GK sets up just outside the far left ^ facing Server

Front Smother Catch

Photo Courtesy Erin Guthrie Corsi

Activity 1 (6 – 8mins)

- GK initiates activity by using quick **Chop Step Foot-work** moving to the right through the ^'s (GK leads with the right foot)
- GK stops at the 2yd gap & gets into **Modern Set Position**
- Server **Volleys** the ball anywhere between the 2-center ^'s that are placed 2yds apart
- GK collects the ball using **Diamond/Contour Catch** but **MUST** stay up on feet for all catches
    - o GK is **NOT** allowed to collapse side-ways for any shot struck between the 2yd gap (**No Collapse Drill**)
- GK is allowed to use a **Front Smother Catch** if ball comes in low & hard
- GK tosses the ball back to Server using proper communication ("Yes & Server's name!")
- GK jogs to opposite side of the goal & sets up next to the far right ^
- GK initiates activity by using quick **Chop Step Foot-work** moving to the left through the ^'s (GK leads with the left foot)
- GK stops at the 2yd gap & gets into **Modern Set Position**
- Server ½ **Volleys** the ball anywhere between the 2-center ^'s that are placed 2yds apart
- GK collects the ball using **Diamond/Contour Catch** but MUST stay up on feet for all catches
    - o GK is **NOT** allowed to collapse side-ways for any shot struck between the 2yd gap (**No Collapse Drill**)
- GK is allowed to use a **Front Smother Catch** if ball comes in low & hard
- GK tosses the ball back to Server using proper communication ("Yes & Server's name!")
- GK jogs to opposite side of the goal & again sets up next to the far left ^
- Repeat activity 6X on both sides
- Rotate GK's & repeat activity

Coaching Points

- GK's **Foot-work** is quick & clean
- Server serves quality **Volleys & ½ Volleys**
- GK's **Diamond/Contour Catching Technique** is proper
- GK communicates on **Distribution** back to Server
- GK does not collapse between the 2-center ^'s
- GK must use quick **Lateral Foot-work** to stay on feet

Set Up 2

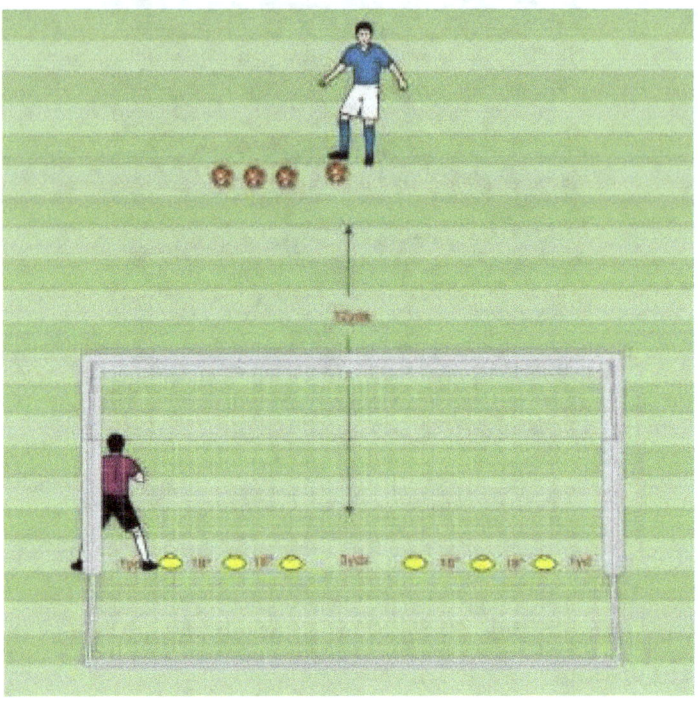

- Use of regular goal
- Place 6 ^'s side by side, 18" away from each other with a 3yd gap between the two middle ^'s & 1yd off the goal line
- Server sets up with ball at feet 12yds from the center of the goal
- GK sets up just outside the far left ^ facing Server

Bowling

Photo Courtesy of Matt Broomall

Activity 1 (8 – 10mins)

- GK initiates activity by using quick **Chop Step Foot-work** moving to the right through the ^'s (GK leads with the right foot)
- GK stops at the 3yd gap & gets into **Modern Set Position**
- Server strikes a **Driven Ball** anywhere between the 2-center ^'s that are placed 3yds apart
- GK collects the ball using **Diamond/Contour Catch** but MUST stay up on feet for all catches
    o GK is **NOT** allowed to collapse side-ways for any shot struck between the 3yd gap (**No Collapse Drill**)
- GK is allowed to use a **Front Smother Catch** if ball comes in low & hard
- GK **Bowls** the ball back to Server using proper communication ("Yes & Server's name!")
- GK jogs to opposite side of the goal & sets up next to the far right ^
- GK initiates activity by using quick **Chop Step Foot-work** moving to the left through the ^'s (GK leads with the left foot)
- GK stops at the 3yd gap & gets into **Modern Set Position**
- Server strikes a **Driven Ball** anywhere between the 2-center ^'s that are placed 3yds apart
- GK collects the ball using **Diamond/Contour Catch** but MUST stay up on feet for all catches
    o GK is **NOT** allowed to collapse side-ways for any shot struck between the 3yd gap (**No Collapse Drill**)
- GK is allowed to use a **Front Smother Catch** if ball comes in low & hard
- GK **Bowls** the ball back to Server using proper communication ("Yes & Server's name!")
- Repeat activity 6X on both sides
- Rotate GK's & repeat activity

Coaching Points

- GK's **Foot-work** is quick & clean
- Server serves quality **Driven Balls**
- GK's **Diamond/Contour Catching Technique** is proper
- GK's **Distribution** is proper & accurate
- GK communicates on **Distribution** back to Server
- GK does not collapse between the 2-center ^'s
- GK must use quick **Lateral Foot-work** to stay on feet

Set Up 3

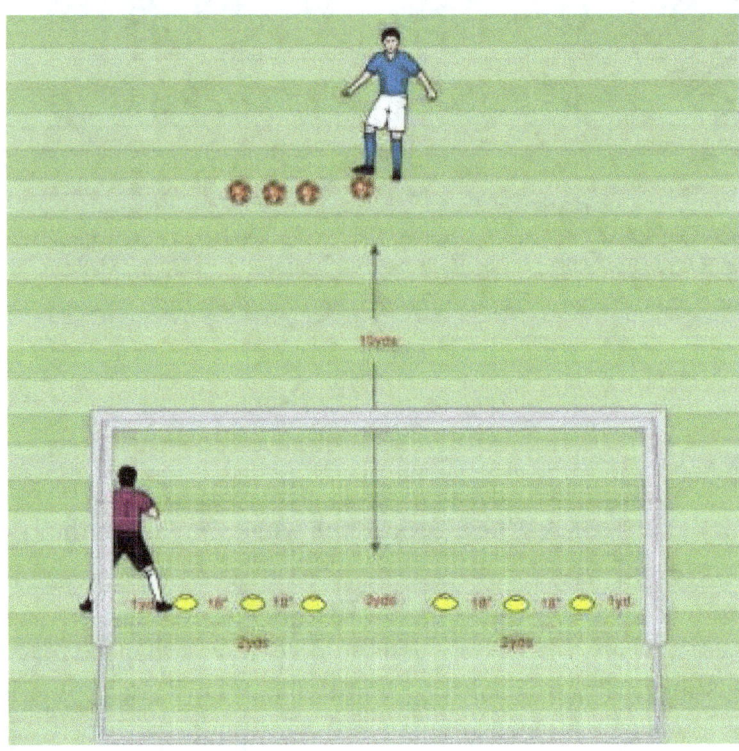

- Use of regular goal
- Place 6 ^'s side by side, 18" away from each other with a 3yd gap between the two middle ^'s & 2yds off the goal line
- Server sets up with ball at feet 15yds from the center of the goal
- GK sets up just outside the far left ^ facing Server

Activity 1 (8 – 10mins)

- GK initiates activity by using quick **Chop Step Foot-work** moving to the right through the ^'s (GK leads with the right foot)
- GK stops at the 3yd gap & gets into **Modern Set Position**
- Server strikes a **Driven Ball** anywhere between the 2-center ^'s that are placed 3yds apart
- GK collects the ball using **Diamond/Contour Catch** but MUST stay up on feet for all catches
  - o GK is **NOT** allowed to collapse side-ways for any shot struck between the 3yd gap (**No Collapse Drill**)
- GK is allowed to use a **Front Smother Catch** if ball comes in low & hard
- GK **Bowls** the ball back to Server using proper communication ("Yes & Server's name!")
- GK jogs to opposite side of the goal & sets up next to the far right ^

- GK initiates activity by using quick **Chop Step Foot-work** moving to the left through the ^'s (GK leads with the left foot)
- GK stops at the 3yd gap & gets into **Modern Set Position**
- Server strikes a **Driven Ball** anywhere between the 2-center ^'s that are placed 3yds apart
- GK collects the ball using **Diamond/Contour Catch** but MUST stay up on feet for all catches
  - GK is **NOT** allowed to collapse side-ways for any shot struck between the 3yd gap (**No Collapse Drill**)
- GK is allowed to use a **Front Smother Catch** if ball comes in low & hard
- GK **Bowls** the ball back to Server using proper communication ("Yes & Server's name!")
- Repeat activity 6X on both sides
- Rotate GK's & repeat activity

Coaching Points

- GK's **Foot-work** is quick & clean
- Server serves quality **Driven Balls**
- GK's **Diamond/Contour Catching Technique** is proper
- GK's **Distribution** is proper & accurate
- GK communicates on **Distribution** back to Server
- GK does not collapse between the 2-center ^'s
- GK must use quick **Lateral Foot-work** to stay on feet

Stage 4

Live Shooting

Set Up 1

- Use of regular goal
- Server sets up with ball at feet inside the "D" (arc)

- GK sets up in the middle of the goal about 2yds off the line & facing towards the left corner flag

Activity 1 (10 – 15mins)

- Server initiates the activity by yelling "GO!"
- GK quickly turns to face the Server & gets into **Modern Set Position**
- Server touches the ball then strikes a shot anywhere on goal
- GK attempts to make the save using any catch needed but attempts to stay on the feet as long as possible while going for the ball
- If GK collects the ball, GK then **Bowls** the ball back to Server using proper communication ("Yes & Server's name!")
- If GK deflects the ball back towards Server, Server can go for a rebound shot
- If GK deflects the ball away from Server but it is still inbounds, GK gets into proper **Set Position** as if ready to receive a 2nd shot on goal
- GK again sets up in the middle of the goal about 2yds off the line but facing towards the right corner flag
- Server yells "GO!"
- GK quickly turns to face the S & gets into **Modern Set Position**
- Server touches the ball then strikes a shot anywhere on goal
- GK attempts to make the save using any catch needed but attempts to stay on the feet as long as possible while going for the ball
- If GK collects the ball, GK then **Bowls** the ball back to Server using proper communication ("Yes & Server's name!")
- If GK deflects the ball back towards Server, Server can go for a rebound shot
- If GK deflects the ball away from Server but it is still inbounds, GK gets into proper **Set Position** as if ready to receive a 2nd shot on goal
- Repeat activity 6X on both sides
- Rotate GK's & repeat activity

Coaching Points

- GK's quickly turn on Server's command of "GO!"
- Server does not hit a dead ball but touches the ball first & then hits a rolling ball
- GK's go for every shot on goal
- GK's attempt to stay on the feet as long as possible while going for the shot
- GK's **Distribution** is proper & accurate
- GK's communicate on **Distribution** back to Server
- If GK gives up a rebound, they get up quickly & get ready for a possible 2nd shot on goal
- GK's use quick **Lateral Foot-work** to stay on feet

U16 – U18 Training Session #5
High Ball Foot-work/Handling

Techniques Used in this Session

- **Foot-work: Fast Feet (Quick Feet)**
- **2 Touch Passing**
- **Volley (using the Inside of the Foot & Laces)**
- **½ Volley**
- **Hands Low Catch**
- **Bowling**
- **Overhand Throw**
- **High Ball Catching Technique**
- **Diamond/Contour Catch**

The key for Training Session

- ^ = cone (^1 – cone 1)
- X = Times (2X – 2 times)

Stage 1

Dynamic Warm-up

Set up

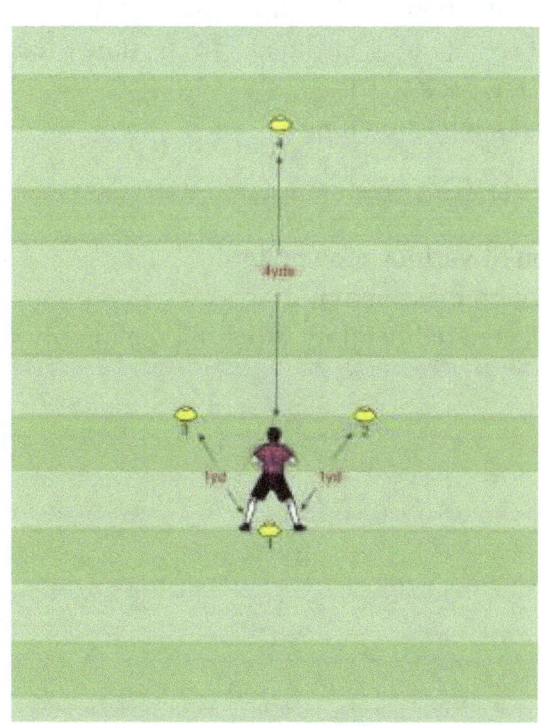

- Place 3 ^'s in a V shape, as shown above; ^2 & ^3 are at a 45-degree angle from ^1 & placed 1yd away
- Place ^4 4yds in front of ^2 & ^3
- ^1 is the starting ^; ^4 is the ending ^

- All starting **Foot-work** is **Fast Feet (Quick Feet)** forward to ^2 & back to start – then **Fast Feet** forward to ^3 & back to start
- All of the dynamic movements are performed between ^1 & ^4
- GK's jog back to start (^1)
- All movements done 1X or 2X each (depending on amount of time available for the whole session)

Activity 1 (5-8mins)

- Dynamic Movements from ^1 to ^4
  - Jog to ^4; jog back to ^1
  - High knees to ^4; jog back to ^1
  - Butt kicks to ^4; jog back to ^1
  - Skipping & forward arm circles to ^4; jog back to ^1
  - Skipping & arm circles backwards to ^4; jog back to ^1
  - Skipping & swinging arms across the chest to ^4; jog back to ^1
  - Open the gate to ^4; jog back to ^1
  - Close the gate to ^4; jog back to ^1
  - Lunges (lunging forward with one foot at a time – alternate feet) to ^4; jog back to ^1
  - Straight leg sweeps (bend forward & sweep the ground with both hands, take 3 small steps & do it again, etc.) to ^4; jog back to ^1
  - Twist body with elbows touching opposite knee to ^4; jog back to ^1
  - Side shuffle to ^4 facing in one direction; jog back to ^1
  - Side shuffle to ^4 facing in opposite direction; jog back to ^1
  - Carioca to ^4 facing in one direction; jog back to ^1
  - Carioca to ^4 facing in opposite direction; jog back to ^1
  - Quick feet forward to ^2; quick backpedal to ^1; quick feet forward to ^3; quick backpedal to ^1; sprint to ^4; jog back to ^1; 2X
- Water break with additional static stretching

Coaching Points

- Reinforce proper execution of various movements
- Players shouldn't rush through these activities
- Movements should be executed deliberately, stressing the quality of each movement

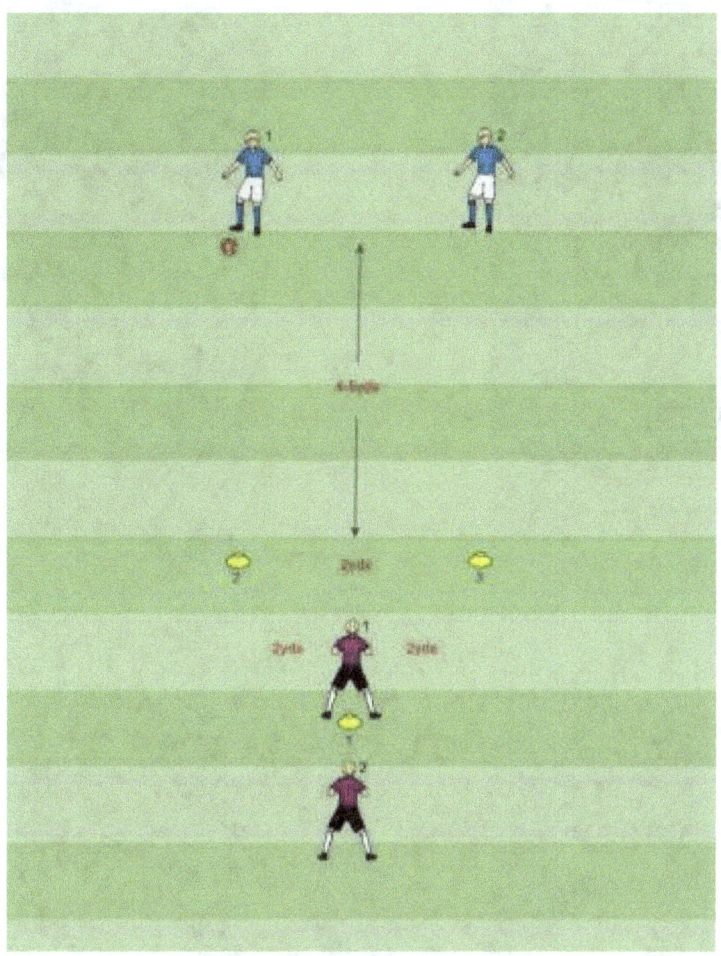

Stage 2

Foot-work/Handling Progression

Set Up 1

- Set up 3 ^'s in a 2yd equilateral triangle
- ^1 is the starting ^; ^2 is to the left; ^3 is to the right
- GK1 starts in **Modern Set Position** straddling ^1
- GK2 lines up behind GK1
- Server 1 & Server 2 set up opposite ^2 & ^3; 4 – 5yds away
- Server 1 starts with the ball at the feet (1 ball only)

Modern Set Position

Hands Low Catch

Photos Courtesy of Matt Broomall & Modern Goalkeeper Training Systems, LLC

Activity 1 (5mins)

- GK1 initiates the activity by moving forward to the center of ^2 & ^3 by using **Fast Feet Foot-work**
- Once GK1 is between ^2 & ^3; GK1 asks for the ball to be played back as a back pass from Server 1 using proper communication ("Yes & Server 1's name!")

- GK1 **2 Touches** the ball across to Server 2 then gets into **Modern Set Position** facing Server 2
- Server 2 strikes a low ball to GK1 who collects the ball using a **Hands Low Catch**
- GK1 **Bowls** the ball back to Server 1 using proper communication ("Yes & Server 1's name!")
- GK1 then backs off & gets behind GK2 who repeats the activity
- Once GK2 is between ^2 & ^3; GK2 asks for the ball to be played back as a back pass from Server 1 using proper communication ("Yes & Server 1's name!")
- GK2 **2 Touches** the ball across to Server 2 then gets into **Modern Set Position** facing Server 2
- Server 2 strikes a low ball to GK2 who collects the ball using a **Hands Low Catch**
- After the **Hands Low Catch** from Server 2, GK2 **Bowls** the ball back to Server 2 who will start with the back pass on the 2nd repetition to GK1
- GK1 again moves forward to the center of ^2 & ^3 by using **Fast Feet Foot-work**
- Once GK1 is between ^2 & ^3; GK1 asks for the ball to be played back as a back pass from Server 2 using proper communication ("Yes & Server 2's name!")
- GK1 **2 Touches** the ball across to Server 1 then gets into **Modern Set Position** facing Server 1
- Server 1 strikes a low ball to GK1 who collects the ball using a **Hands Low Catch**
- GK1 **Bowls** the ball back to Server 2 using proper communication ("Yes & Server 2's name!")
- GK1 then backs off & gets behind GK2 who repeats the activity
- Once GK2 is between ^2 & ^3; GK2 asks for the ball to be played back as a back pass from Server 2 using proper communication ("Yes & Server 2's name!")
- GK2 **2 Touches** the ball across to Server 1 then gets into **Modern Set Position** facing Server 1
- Server 2 strikes a low ball to GK2 who collects the ball using a **Hands Low Catch**
- After the **Hands Low Catch** from Server 2, GK2 **Bowls** the ball back to Server 1 who will start with the back pass on the next repetition to GK1
- Repeat activity 4X to each side
- GK's rotate in & out & the whole activity is repeated

Coaching Points

- GK's **Foot-work** is **Fast Feet up & down**; feet stay spread at shoulder's width; NOT in front of one another
- GK's eyes stay focused on the ball during **Foot-work**; not on the ground
- Server's services are accurate & at proper pace
- When receiving the ball to the feet, the GK's are in a 2-foot bounce stance, not stationary
- GK's foot touches & passes are accurate & at proper pace
- GK's technique on the **Hands Low Catch** is correct
- GK's use proper communication when receiving the back pass & when **Distributing** the ball
- GK's **Distribute** the ball to the proper Server to make sure that the proper serving order is maintained

Set Up 2

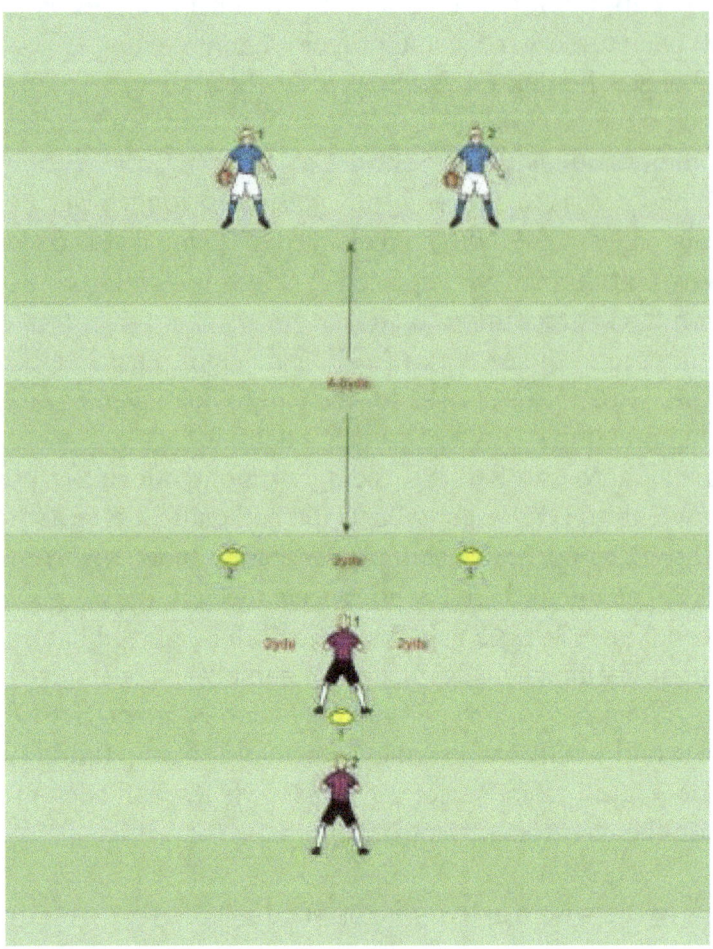

- The **Set Up** for **Activity 2** is the same as in **Activity 1** except Server 1 & Server 2 now have the ball in their hands

Volley

Diamond/Contour Catch

Photos Courtesy of Matt Broomall & Modern Goalkeeper Training Systems, LLC

Right Knee up Front   ## Left Knee Up Front

Photos Courtesy of Erin Guthrie Corsi

Activity 2 (5mins)

- GK1 initiates the activity by moving forward to the center of ^2 & ^3 by using **Fast Feet Foot-work**
- Once GK1 is between ^2 & ^3; GK1 asks for the ball to be tossed to the right foot from Server 1 using proper communication ("Yes & Server 1's name!")
- GK1 **Volleys** the ball back to Server 1 using the **Inside of the Foot** then gets into **Modern Set Position** facing Server 2
- Server 2 **Volleys** the ball to the chest/face of GK1
- GK1 collects the ball using the **Diamond/Contour Catch**
- GK1 tosses the ball back to Server 2 using proper communication ("Yes & Server 2's name!")
- GK1 then quickly backpedals behind ^1
- GK1 generates a quick up & down foot movement (in place) & waits for Server 2 to serve a high ball to the right of ^3
- GK1 yells "KEEPER!" & collects the ball using the **High Ball Catching Technique (Diamond/Contour Catch)** driving the right knee upwards
- GK1 lands on 2 feet, tosses the ball back to Server 2 using proper communication ("Yes & Server 2's name!")
- GK1 goes back behind GK2 who is now set over ^1
- GK2 repeats the same activity
- The 2nd repetition starting with GK1 is now the opposite
  - Receives a toss to the left foot for the **Volley** back to Server 2
  - Receives the high ball toss from Server 1 to the left of ^2
- GK's repeat the activity 4X to each side
- GK's rotate in & out; whole activity is repeated

Coaching Points

- GK's **Foot-work** is **Fast Feet up & down**; feet stay spread at shoulder's width; NOT in front of one another
- GK's eyes stay focused on the ball during **Foot-work**; not at the ground
- Server's services are accurate & at proper pace
- When receiving the ball to the feet, the GK's are in a 2-foot bounce stance, not stationary
- GK's foot touches & passes are accurate & at proper pace
- GK's technique on the **Diamond/Contour Catch** is correct
- GK generates up/down foot movement before going for the high ball
- GK's technique on the **High Ball Catch** is correct
- GK's call "KEEPER!" when they **make the decision** to go for the ball
- GK's go up with the correct knee when going for the high ball
  - Right knee goes up when going to the right
  - Left knee goes up when going to the left
- GK's land on both feet
- GK's use proper communication when receiving the back pass & when **Distributing** the ball

Set Up 3

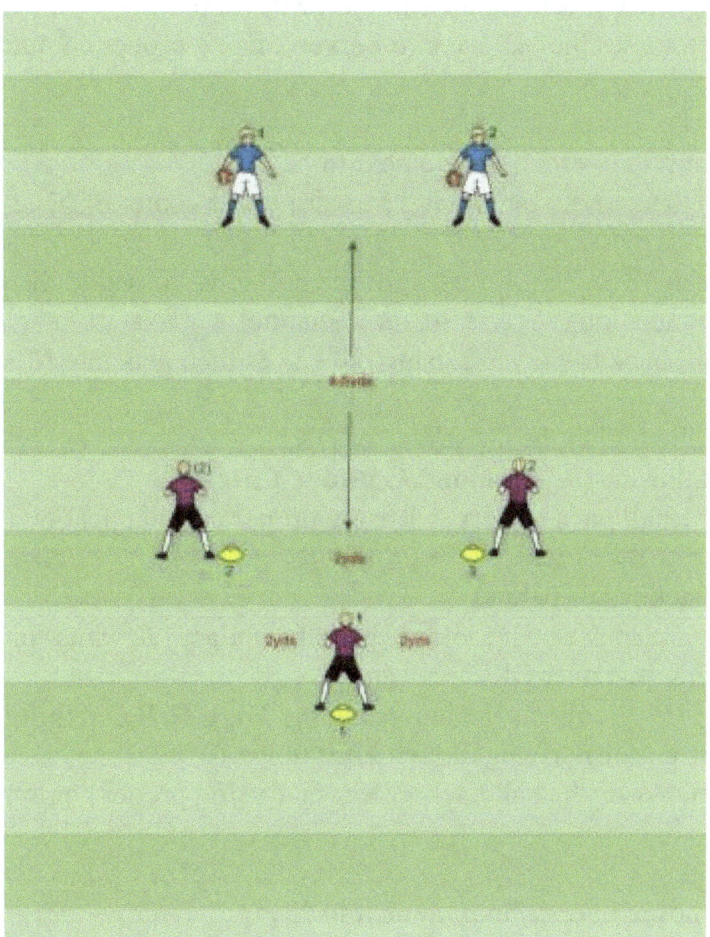

- Set up 3 ^'s in a 2yd equilateral triangle
- ^1 is the starting ^; ^2 is to the left; ^3 is to the right
- GK1 starts in **Modern Set Position** straddling ^1
- GK2 lines up right next to ^3
- Server 1 & Server 2 set up opposite ^2 & ^3; 4 – 5yds away
- Server 1 & Server 2 have the ball in their hands

Activity 1 (5mins)

- GK1 initiates the activity by moving forward to the center of ^2 & ^3 by using **Fast Feet Footwork**
- Once GK1 is between ^2 & ^3; GK1 asks for the ball to be tossed to the right foot from Server 1 using proper communication ("Yes & Server 1's name!")
- GK1 **Volleys** the ball back to Server 1 using the **Laces** then gets into **Modern Set Position** facing Server 2
- Server 2 ½ **Volleys** the ball to the chest/face of GK1
- GK1 collects the ball using the **Diamond/Contour Catch**
- GK1 **Distributes** the ball back to Server 2 using proper communication ("Yes & Server 2's name!")
- GK1 then quickly backpedals behind ^1
- GK1 generates a quick up & down foot movement (in place) & waits for Server 2 to serve a high ball to the right of ^3 & just over GK2's head

- GK1 yells "KEEPER!" & collects the ball using the **High Ball Catching Technique (Diamond/Contour Catch)** driving the right knee upwards
- GK1 lands on 2 feet, tosses the ball back to Server 2 using proper communication ("Yes & Server 2's name!")
- GK1 goes back to ^1
- GK2 now quickly moves over & lines up next to ^2
- GK1 again initiates the activity by moving forward to the center of ^2 & ^3 by using **Fast Feet Foot-work**
- Once GK1 is between ^2 & ^3; GK1 asks for the ball to be tossed to the left foot from Server 2 using proper communication ("Yes & Server 2's name!")
- GK1 **Volleys** the ball back to Server 2 using the **Laces** then gets into **Modern Set Position** facing Server 1
- Server 1 ½ **Volleys** the ball to the chest/face of GK1
- GK1 collects the ball using the **Diamond/Contour Catch**
- GK1 **Distributes** the ball back to Server 1 using proper communication ("Yes & Server 1's name!")
- GK1 then quickly backpedals behind ^1
- GK1 generates a quick up & down foot movement (in place) & waits for Server 1 to serve a high ball to the left of ^2 & just over GK2's head
- GK1 yells "KEEPER!" & collects the ball using the **High Ball Catching Technique (Diamond/Contour Catch)** driving the left knee upwards
- GK1 lands on 2 feet, tosses the ball back to Server 1 using proper communication ("Yes & Server 1's name!")
- GK1 goes back to ^1
- GK2 then quickly moves over & lines up next to ^3
- GK's repeat the activity 4X to each side
- GK's rotate in & out; whole activity is repeated

Coaching Points

- GK's **Foot-work** is **Fast Feet up & down**; feet stay spread at shoulder's width; NOT in front of one another
- GK's eyes stay focused on the ball during **Foot-work**; not at the ground
- Server's services are accurate & at proper pace
- When receiving the ball to the feet, the GK's are in a 2-foot bounce stance, not stationary
- GK's foot touches & passes are accurate & at proper pace
- GK's technique on the **Diamond/Contour Catch** is correct
- GK generates up/down foot movement before going for the high ball
- GK's technique on the **High Ball Catch** is correct
- GK's call "KEEPER!" when they **make the decision** to go for the ball
- GK's go up with the correct knee when going for the high ball
  - o Right knee goes up when going to the right
  - o Left knee goes up when going to the left
- GK lands on both feet
- GK's use proper communication when receiving the back pass & when **Distributing** the ball

Stage 3

Handling Various Forms of Crosses

Set Up 1

- Use of full-size goal with 3 ^'s placed along-side of each other
- ^1 placed 2yds inside of post & 2yds off of goal line
- ^2 placed 4 yds inside near post (middle of goal) and 2yds off goal line
- ^3 placed 2yds from back post and 2yds off goal line
- GK sets up at near post facing Server 1
- Server 1 sets up 4 yds out-side of the near post & in line with the ^'s (2yds off the end line)
- Server 2 sets up along-side Server 1 but 2 is farther out from Server 1
- Server 1 & Server 2 start with a ball in hands

Crossing Stance

Overhand (Windmill) Throw

Photos Courtesy of Matt Broomall & Modern Goalkeeper Training Systems, LLC

Activity 1 (5 – 10mins)

- GK starts in **Modern Set Position** facing Server 1
- Server 1 says "Go!"
- GK turns & uses quick **Foot-work** to move clockwise around ^1 (while keeping the chest & shoulders square to Server 1) & gets back into original spot in **Modern Set Position** for a service from Server 1
- Server 1 **Volleys** the ball to GK's chest/face
- GK catches the ball using proper **Diamond/Contour Catch**
- GK tosses the ball back to Server 1 using proper communication ("Yes & Server 1's name!") & resets for a crossing situation again from Server 1
    - o **Crossing Stance** – GK stands on a 45-degree angle from the goal line & tilted (facing) towards the direction from where the ball is coming
- Server 1 then tosses a high ball out between ^1 & ^2
- GK turns, runs & catches high ball using proper **High Ball Catching Technique (Diamond/Contour Catch)**, jumping off left foot & bringing right knee up for protection/balance/thrust
- GK lands on 2 feet, finds Server 1 & **Overhand Throws** the ball back to Server 1 using proper communication ("Yes & Server 1's name!")
- GK then back pedals between ^1 & ^2 to the goal line, resets into **Crossing Set Position**
- Server 2 now throws a high ball between ^2 & ^3
- GK turns, runs & catches high ball using proper **High Ball Catching Technique (Diamond/Contour Catch)**, jumping off left foot & bringing right knee up for protection/balance/thrust

- GK lands on 2 feet, finds Server 2 & **Overhand Throws** the ball back to Server 2 using proper communication ("Yes & Server 2's name!")
- GK then backpedals between ^2 & ^3 to the goal line, resets into **Crossing Set Position**
- Server 1 throws a longer high ball past ^3
- GK turns, runs & catches high ball using proper **High Ball Catching Technique (Diamond/Contour Catch)**, jumping off left foot & bringing right knee up for protection/balance/thrust
- GK lands on 2 feet, finds Server 1 & **Overhand Throws** the ball back to Server 1 using proper communication ("Yes & Server 1's name!")
- Repeat activity 4X – 6X
- Rotate GK's & repeat activity

Coaching Points

- Server 1 & Server 2 serve proper high balls so that GK's are able to go & catch them
- GK's yell "KEEPER!" when decision is made to go for the ball
- GK's use proper **High Ball Catching Technique** for catching high balls
- GK's square their shoulders to the ball when making the catch
- GK's communicate properly when **Distributing** the ball ("Yes & Server's name!")
- GK's reset at starting point after every rep

Set Up 2

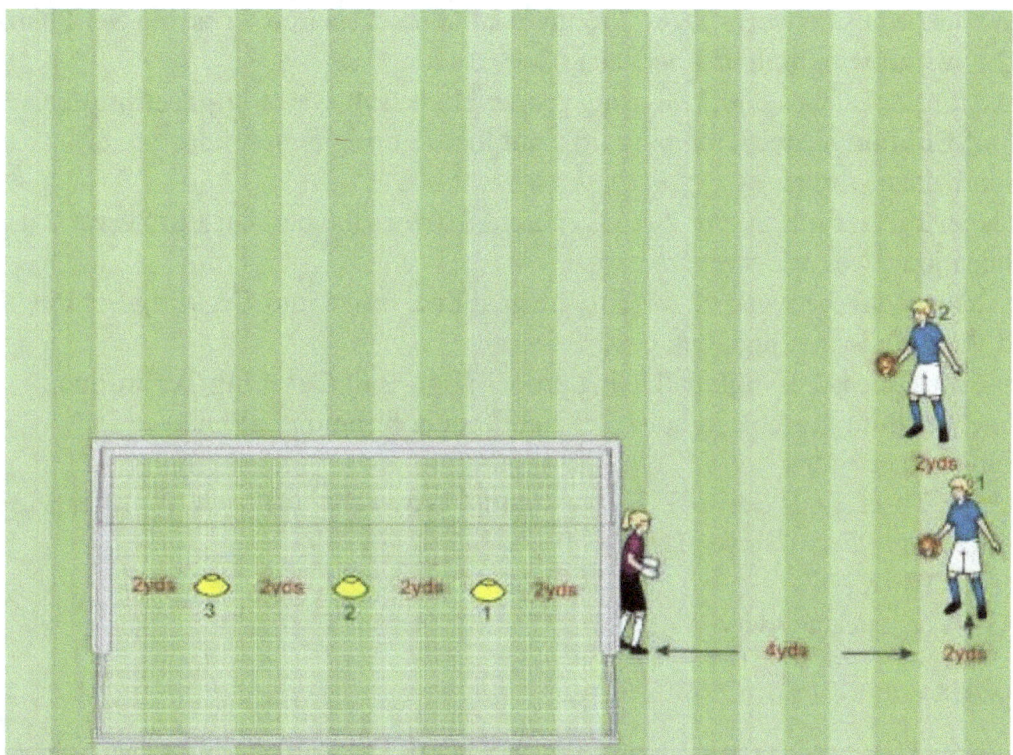

- Set up is the reverse of **Set Up 1** in Stage 3
- Use of full-size goal with 3^'s placed along-side of each other
- ^1 placed 2yds inside of post & 2yds off of goal line
- ^2 placed 4yds inside near post (middle of goal) and 2yds off goal line
- ^3 placed 2yds from back post and 2yds off goal line
- GK sets up at near post facing Server 1

102

- Server 1 sets up 4yds out-side of the near post & in line with the ^'s (2yds off the end line)
- Server 2 sets up along-side Server 1 but 2yds farther out from Server 1
- Server 1 & Server 2 start with a ball in hands

Activity 2 (5 – 10mins)

- GK starts in **Modern Set Position** facing Server 1
- Server 1 says "Go!"
- GK turns & uses quick **Foot-work** to move counter-clockwise around ^1 (while keeping the chest & shoulders square to Server 1) & gets back into original spot in **Set Position** for a service from Server 1
- Server 1 **Volleys** the ball to GK's chest/face
- GK catches the ball using proper **Diamond/Contour Catch**
- GK tosses the ball back to Server 1 using proper communication ("Yes & Server 1's name!") & resets for a crossing situation again from Server 1
    - o **Crossing Stance** – GK stands on a 45-degree angle from the goal line & tilted (facing) towards the direction from where the ball is coming
- Server 1 then tosses a high ball out between ^1 & ^2
- GK turns, runs & catches high ball using **High Ball Catching Technique (Diamond/Contour Catch)**, jumping off right foot & bringing left knee up for protection/balance/thrust
- GK lands on 2 feet, finds Server 1 & **Overhand Throws** the ball back to Server 1 using proper communication ("Yes & Server 1's name!")
- GK then backpedals between ^1 & ^2 to the goal line, resets into **Crossing Set Position**
- Server 2 now throws a high ball between ^2 & ^3
- GK turns, runs & catches high ball using proper **High Ball Catching Technique (Diamond/Contour Catch)**, jumping off right foot & bringing left knee up for protection/balance/thrust
- GK lands on 2 feet, finds Server 2 & **Overhand Throws** the ball back to Server 2 using proper communication ("Yes & Server 2's name!")
- GK then backpedals between ^2 & ^3 to the goal line, resets into **Crossing Set Position**
- Server 1 throws a longer high ball past ^3
- GK turns, runs & catches high ball using proper **High Ball Catching Technique (Diamond/Contour Catch)**, jumping off right foot & bringing left knee up for protection/balance/thrust
- GK lands on 2 feet, finds Server 1 & **Overhand Throws** the ball back to Server 1 using proper communication ("Yes & Server 1's name!")
- Repeat activity 4X – 6X
- Rotate GK's & repeat activity

Coaching Points

- Server 1 & Server 2 serve proper high balls so that GK's are able to go & catch them
- GK yells "KEEPER!" when decision is made to go for the ball
- GK uses **High Ball Catching Technique** for catching high balls
- GK's square their shoulders to the ball when making the catch
- GK's communicate properly when **Distributing** the ball ("Yes & Server's name!")
- GK's reset at starting place after every rep

Stage 4

High Ball Catching Challenge/Shooting

Set Up 1

- Use of regular size goal & the 18yd box
- Server 1 sets up with several balls at the top of the 18yd box & centrally in front of the goal
- Server 2 sets up outside the right post about 15yds from the goal line; Server 2 acts as an outlet for **Distribution**
- GK1 starts in goal about 2 steps off the goal line
- GK's 2 & 3 line up near the post in a queue

Activity 1 (5 – 15mins)

- Server 1 starts with a ball in the hands
- Server 1 punts the ball very high into the air so that it will come down somewhere between the penalty spot & the goal line
- GK1 must catch the ball with two hands over the head
- **If:**
  - o GK catches the ball cleanly
    - ▪ GK gets **1pt**
    - ▪ GK then will **Distribute** the ball to Server 2 using proper communication ("Yes & Server 2's name!")
    - ▪ GK then sets for a touch/shot from Server 1

- ▪ Rebounds are live on the shot
  - o GK drops or bobbles the ball
    - ▪ GK immediately gets back into goal & gets set for a touch/shot from Server 1
    - ▪ Rebounds are live on the shot
    - ▪ GK owes 5 push-ups for dropping the high ball
- GK1 goes to the end of the line & the next GK steps in
- Repeat the activity
- This can go on for as long as the coach desires

Coaching Points

- All aspects of catching high balls are performed correctly
- GK's yell "KEEPER!" when making the decision to go for high balls

Paul D. Blodgett, M.Ed

U16 – U18 Training Session #6
K-save/Close Range Shots

Techniques used in this Session

- **2 Touch Passing**
- **K-save Stance**
- **Modern Set Position**
- **Close Range Set Position**
- **Cut Back Positioning**
- **Controlled Collapse Catch left & right**
- **Recovery**
- **Bowling**

Key for Training Session

- ^ = cone (^1 – cone 1)
- X = Times (2X – 2 times)

Stage 1

Dynamic Warm-up

Set Up

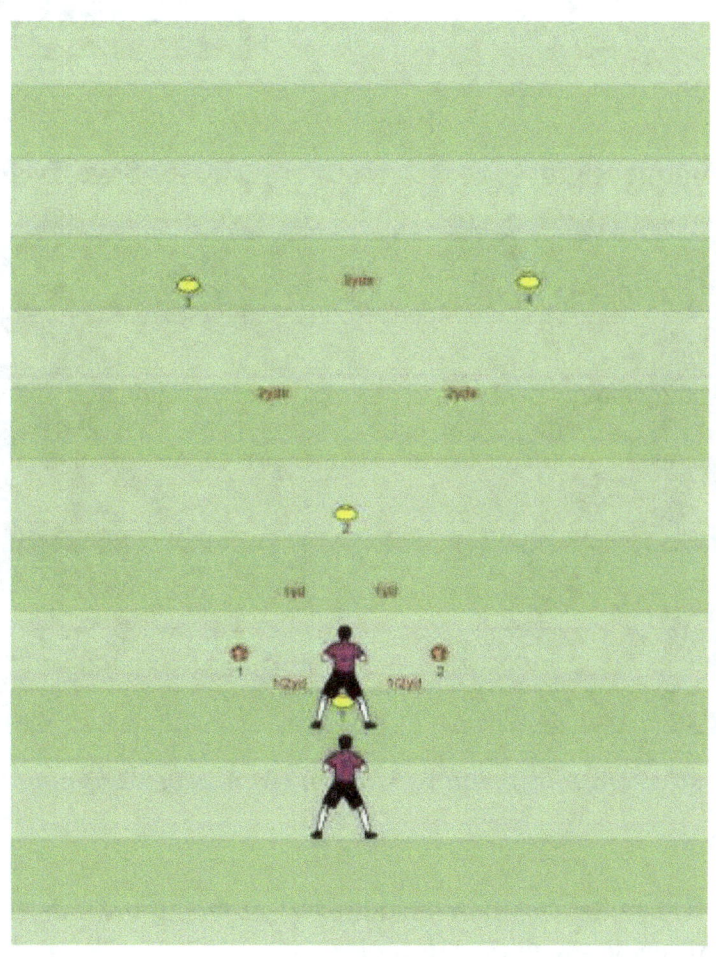

- Place down ^1
- Place ball 1 ½ yd to the left of ^1 & on a 45-degree angle
- Place ball 2 ½ yd to the right of ^1 & on a 45-degree angle
- Place ^2 1yd in front of the balls, directly in line with ^1
- Place ^3 2yds to the left of ^2 & on a 45-degree angle
- Place ^4 2yds to the right of ^2 & on a 45-degree angle
- GK's line up behind ^1 facing forward

Close Range Stance/Blocking Stance

K-Save Technique Right   ### K-Save Technique Left

Photos Courtesy of Matt Broomall & Modern Goalkeeper Training Systems, LLC

Activity 1 (5 – 8mins)

- GK starts in **Close Range Set Position** straddling ^1 & facing towards ^2
- GK steps towards o1 leading with the left foot

- GK drops right knee down at the ball & spreads arms out (left arm high; right arm low) keeping chest forward in the **K-save Stance**
- GK holds this position for 1 second
- GK then gets up quickly & moves to ^2, circles ^2 in a clockwise fashion then does a dynamic move to ^3
- GK then back pedals to ^2 & repeats the same dynamic movement to ^4
- GK then goes to the back of the line
- Next GK in line repeats
- 2nd time through, the GK's go to ball 2
- GK steps towards ball 2 leading with the right foot
- GK drops left knee down at the ball & spreads arms out (right arm high; left arm low) keeping chest forward in the **K-save Stance**
- GK holds this position for 1 second
- GK then gets up quickly & moves to ^2, circles ^2 in a counter-clockwise fashion then does a dynamic move to ^4
- GK then back pedals to ^2 & repeats the same dynamic movement to ^3
- GK then goes to the back of the line
- Next GK in line repeats
- Movements from ^2 to ^3 & ^2 to ^4
    - Jog
    - High knees
    - Butt kicks
    - Skipping & forward arm circles
    - Skipping & arm circles backwards
    - Skipping & swinging arms across the chest
    - Open the gate
    - Close the gate
    - Lunges (lunging forward with one foot at a time – alternate feet)
    - Straight leg sweeps (bend forward & sweep the ground with both hands, take 3 small steps & do it again, etc.)
    - Twist body with elbows touching opposite knee
    - Side shuffle to ^3 & ^4 facing inward
    - Carioca to ^3 & ^4 facing inward
- Water break with additional static stretching

Coaching Points

- When stepping with the lead foot to the ball for the **K-save Stance**, the step is a short step
- The knee is brought down to the heel of the lead foot (so the ball can't go through the legs)
- Chest is square to the attacker
- Arm on knee-up side is angled diagonally upward
- Arm on knee-down side is angled diagonally downward
- GK holds the **K-save Stance** for 1sec & makes any corrections to get the position correct
- Reinforce proper execution of various movements
- Players shouldn't rush through these activities
- Movements should be executed deliberately, stressing the quality of each movement

Stage 2

Left/Right Alternate Collapsing & Recovery

Set Up 1

- Place 4 ball in a diagonal pattern as seen above, approximately 3yds from each other
- Ball 1 placed diagonally to the right of the starting ^
- Ball 2 placed diagonally to the left of ball 1
- Ball 3 placed diagonally to the right of ball 2
- Ball 4 placed diagonally to the left of ball 3 but in line with Server
- Server stands 3yds in front of ball 4 with ball in hands
- GK starts behind the starting ^ in **Modern Set Position**

Modern Set Position

Controlled Collapse Right   **Controlled Collapse Left**

Photos Courtesy of Matt Broomall & Modern Goalkeeper Training Systems, LLC

Activity 1 (8 – 10mins)

- GK starts in the **Modern Set Position** behind the starting ^
- Server says "Go!"
- GK takes 1 or 2 steps leading with the right foot towards ball 1; GK performs a **Controlled Collapse Save to the Right** at ball 1
- GK leaves the ball in the same spot & **Recovers** to both feet
- GK takes 1 or 2 steps leading with the left foot towards ball 2; GK performs a **Controlled Collapse Save to the Left** at ball 2
- GK leaves the ball in the same spot & **Recovers** to both feet

- GK takes 1 or 2 steps leading with the right foot towards ball 3; GK performs a **Controlled Collapse Save to the Right** at ball 3
- GK leaves the ball in the same spot & **Recovers** to both feet
- GK takes 1 or 2 steps leading with the left foot towards ball 4; GK performs a **Controlled Collapse Save to the Left** at ball 4
- GK leaves the ball in the same spot & **Recovers** to both feet
- Server then bounces the ball towards the GK who must catch it in the hands before the 2nd bounce
- GK gives the ball back to Server & goes back to the starting ^
- GK repeats the activity 5X

Coaching Points

- GK leads with the proper foot when stepping to the ball
  - o Right foot when going to the right
  - o Left foot when going to the left
- GK performs correct technique on all collapses
- GK **Recovers** back to feet quickly after each collapse
- On the bounced ball to the hands, GK tries to collect the ball before it bounces twice

Stage 3

K-save/Recovery/2nd Save

Set Up 1

Please note that the following Set Ups in Stage 3 & Stage 4 can be put together at the same time if there are multiple numbers; the activities only require a relatively small amount of space; servers need to be accurate with the services so as not to cross over into the other side of the goal (for safety reasons).

- Use of regular size goal & the 18yd box
- Place ^1 2yds from the right post on a 45-degree angle from the post
- Server 1 sets up with balls at the feet 4yds from the right post down the end line
- Server 2 sets up with balls at feet just outside the right post & about 4yds up from the end line
- GK starts in **Close Range Set Position** straddling ^1 & facing Server 2

Inside of the Foot Pass (IOF)

Photo Courtesy of Matt Broomall

K-Save Technique Right

K-Save Technique Left

Photos Courtesy of Matt Broomall & Modern Goalkeeper Training Systems, LLC

Activity 1 (5 – 8mins)

- GK starts the activity by quickly moving to the right post & asking for the ball to be played to the feet from Server 1 using proper communication ("Yes & Server 1's name!")
- Server 1 passes the ball to the GK

- GK uses **2 Touches** to collect the ball & pass it directly back to Server 1 using any combination of the feet
- GK then turns towards Server 2 who touches a ball away from the feet in the direction of ^1 but not necessarily directly at ^1
- GK takes a quick step to the ball leading with the left foot & performs a **K-save** with the right knee going down
- GK quickly **Recovers** into a **Close Range Set Position** & readies for a possible 2nd shot
- GK goes back & straddles ^1 again & repeats the activity
- Repeat 5X – 6X
- GK's rotate & repeat activity

Coaching Points

- GK begins by straddling ^1 & facing Server 2
- All of GK's **Foot-work** is quick & clean
- GK uses proper communication when asking for the ball to be played to the feet
- Server 1 serves quality balls
- GK's touches with the feet are clean & accurate
- GK reacts to the ball hit by Server 2 & performs a proper **K-save** with the right knee going down
- GK should not take big steps towards the ball but short, quick ones
- GK quickly **Recovers** to feet in anticipation of a rebound shot

Set Up 2 (Same Set Up as in #1 but on the opposite side of the goal)

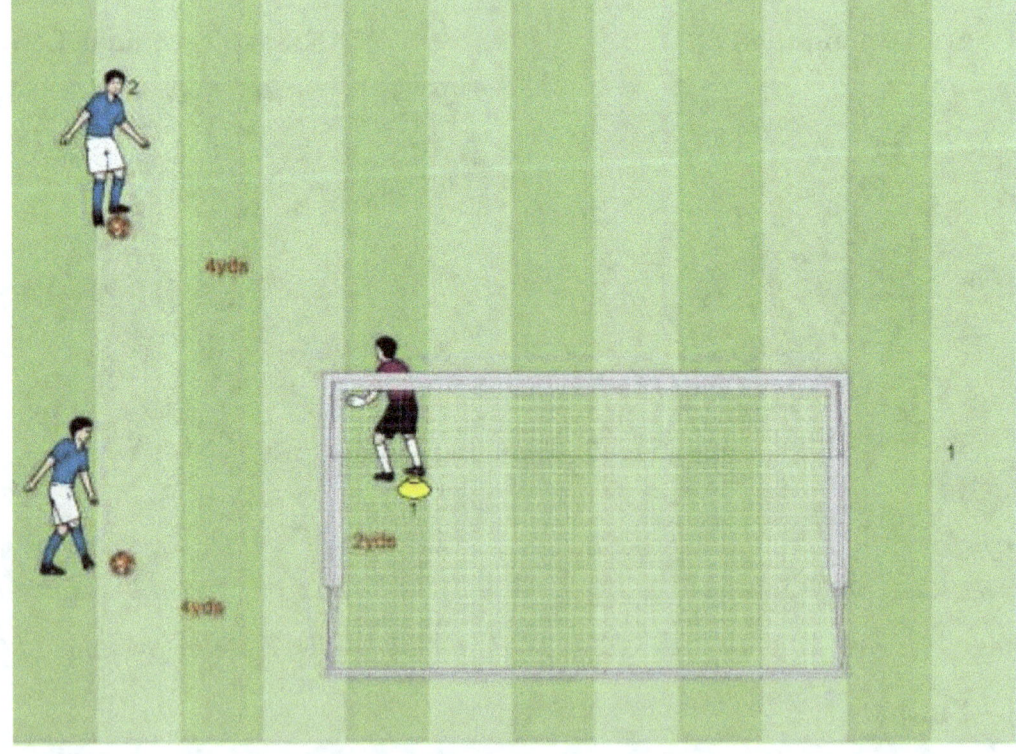

- Use of regular size goal & the 18yd box
- Place ^1 2yds from the left post on a 45-degree angle from the post
- Server 1 sets up with balls at the feet 4yds from the left post down the end line

- Server 2 sets up with balls at feet just outside the left post & about 4yds up from the end line
- GK starts in **Close Range Set Position** straddling ^1 & facing Server 2

Activity 2 (5 – 8mins)

- GK starts the activity by quickly moving to the left post & asking for the ball to be played to the feet from Server 1 using proper communication ("Yes & Server's name!")
- Server 1 passes the ball to the GK
- GK uses **2 Touches** to collect the ball & pass it directly back to Server 1 using any combination of the feet
- GK then turns towards Server 2 who touches a ball away from the feet in the direction of ^1 but not necessarily directly at ^1
- GK takes a quick step to the ball leading with the right foot & performs a **K-save** with the left knee going down
- GK quickly **Recovers** into a **Close Range Set Position** & readies for a possible 2nd shot
- GK goes back & straddles ^1 again & repeats the activity
- Repeat 5X – 6X
- GK's rotate & repeat activity

Coaching Points

- GK begins by straddling ^1 & facing Server 2
- All of GK's **Foot-work** is quick & clean
- GK uses proper communication when asking for the ball to be played to the feet
- Server 1 serves quality balls
- GK's touches with the feet are clean & accurate
- GK reacts to the ball hit by Server 2 & performs a proper **K-save** with the left knee going down
- GK should not take big steps towards the ball but short, quick ones
- GK quickly **Recovers** to feet in anticipation of a rebound shot

Set Up 3

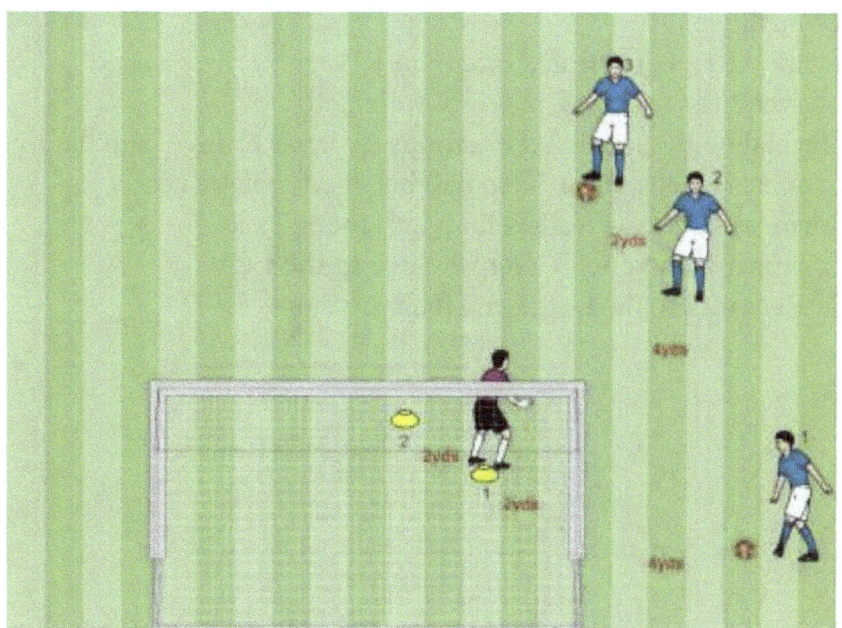

- Use of regular size goal & the 18yd box

114

- Place ^1 2yds from the right post on a 45-degree angle from the post
- Place ^2 on the same line but 2yds from ^1
- Server 1 sets up with balls at the feet 4yds from the right post down the end line
- Server 2 sets up just outside the right post & about 4yds up from the end line
- Server 3 sets up with balls at feet 2yds back of Server 2
- GK starts in **Close Range Set Position** straddling ^1 & facing Server 2

Activity 3 (8 – 10mins)

- GK starts in **Close Range Set Position** straddling over ^1
- Activity begins by Server 1 saying "Go!"
- GK then quickly moves to the right post & asks for a pass to the feet from Server 1 using proper communication ("Yes & Server 1's name!")
- Server 1 passes the ball on the ground to GK
- GK receives the ball & then uses a 2nd touch to lightly pass it towards Server 2 using proper communication (Yes & Server 2's name!")
- As GK passes the ball out to Server 2, GK follows the pass
- Server 2 will take a one-time easy touch towards ^1
- GK moves out to make a **K-save** with the right knee going down
- GK quickly **Recovers** to the feet & gets into the **Close Range Set Position** at ^1
- Server 3 then strikes a low ball towards ^2
- GK makes a **Controlled Collapse Save to the Left**
- GK once again **Recovers** to the feet
- GK then goes back to ^1 for the next repetition
- Repeat 4X – 5X then rotate the GK's

Coaching Points

- GK begins by straddling ^1 & facing Server 2
- All of GK's **Foot-work** is quick & clean
- GK uses proper communication when asking for the ball to be played to the feet
- Server 1 serves quality balls
- GK's touches with the feet are clean & accurate
- GK's pass to Server 2 is accurate & properly weighted
- GK reacts to the ball hit by Server 2 & performs a proper **K-save** with the right knee going down
- GK should not take big steps towards the ball but short, quick ones
- GK quickly **Recovers** to feet & readies for a 2nd rebound shot
- GK performs a proper **Controlled Collapse Save to the Left**
- GK once again **Recovers** to the feet to end the repetition

Set Up 4

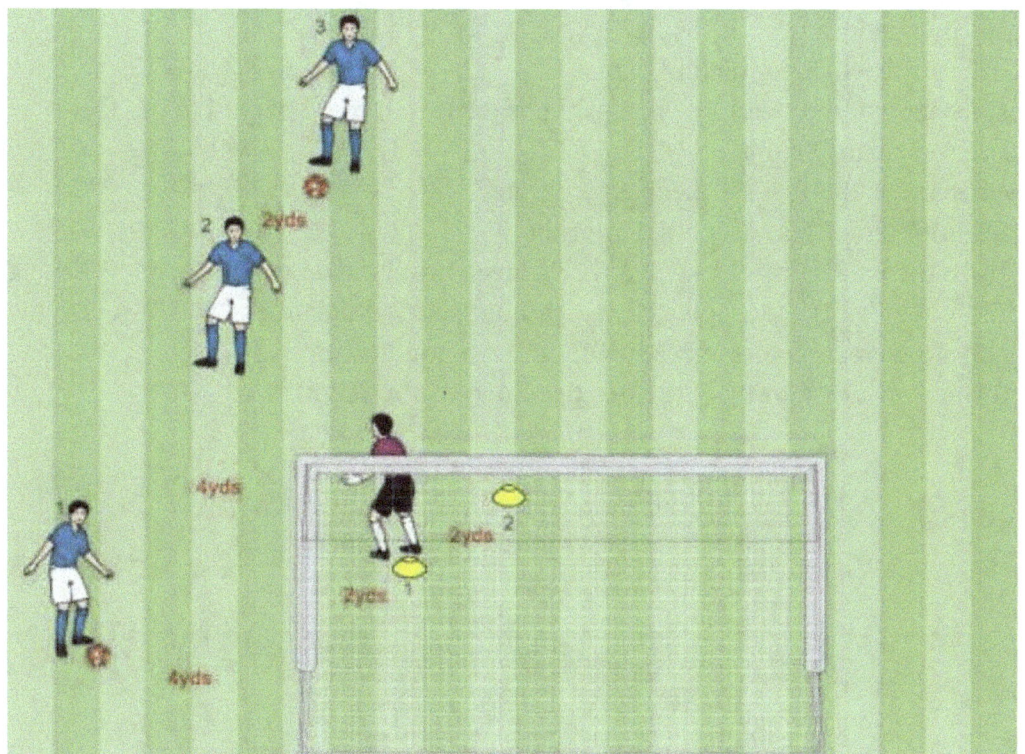

- Use of regular size goal & the 18yd box
- Place ^1 2yds from the left post on a 45-degree angle from the post
- Place ^2 on the same line but 2yds from ^1
- Server 1 sets up with balls at the feet 4yds from the left post down the end line
- Server 2 sets up just outside the left post & about 4yds up from the end line
- Server 3 sets up with balls at feet 2yds back of Server 2
- GK starts in **Close Range Set Position** straddling ^1 & facing Server 2

Activity 4 (8 – 10mins)

- GK starts in **Close Range Set Position** straddling over ^1
- Activity begins by Server 1 saying "Go!"
- GK then quickly moves to the left post & asks for a pass to the feet from Server 1 using proper communication ("Yes & Server 1's name!")
- Server 1 passes the ball on the ground to GK
- GK receives the ball & then uses a 2nd touch to lightly pass it towards Server 2 using proper communication (Yes & Server 2's name!")
- As GK passes the ball out to Server 2, GK follows the pass
- Server 2 will take a one-time easy touch towards ^1
- GK moves out to make a **K-save** with the left knee going down
- GK quickly **Recovers** to the feet & gets into the **Close Range Set Position** at ^1
- Server 3 then strikes a low ball towards ^2
- GK makes a **Controlled Collapse Save to the Right**
- GK once again **Recovers** to the feet to end the repetition
- GK then goes back to ^1 for the next repetition
- Repeat 4X – 5X then rotate the GK's

Coaching Points

- GK begins by straddling ^1 & facing Server 2
- All of GK's **Foot-work** is quick & clean
- GK uses proper communication when asking for the ball to be played to the feet
- Server 1 serves quality balls
- GK's touches with the feet are clean & accurate
- GK's passes to Server 2 are accurate & properly weighted
- GK reacts to the ball hit by Server 2 & performs a proper **K-save** with the left knee going down
- GK should not take big steps towards the ball but short, quick ones
- GK quickly **Recovers** to feet & readies for a 2nd rebound shot
- GK performs a proper **Controlled Collapse Save to the Right**

Stage 4

K-save/Recovery/Live Shot

Set Up 1

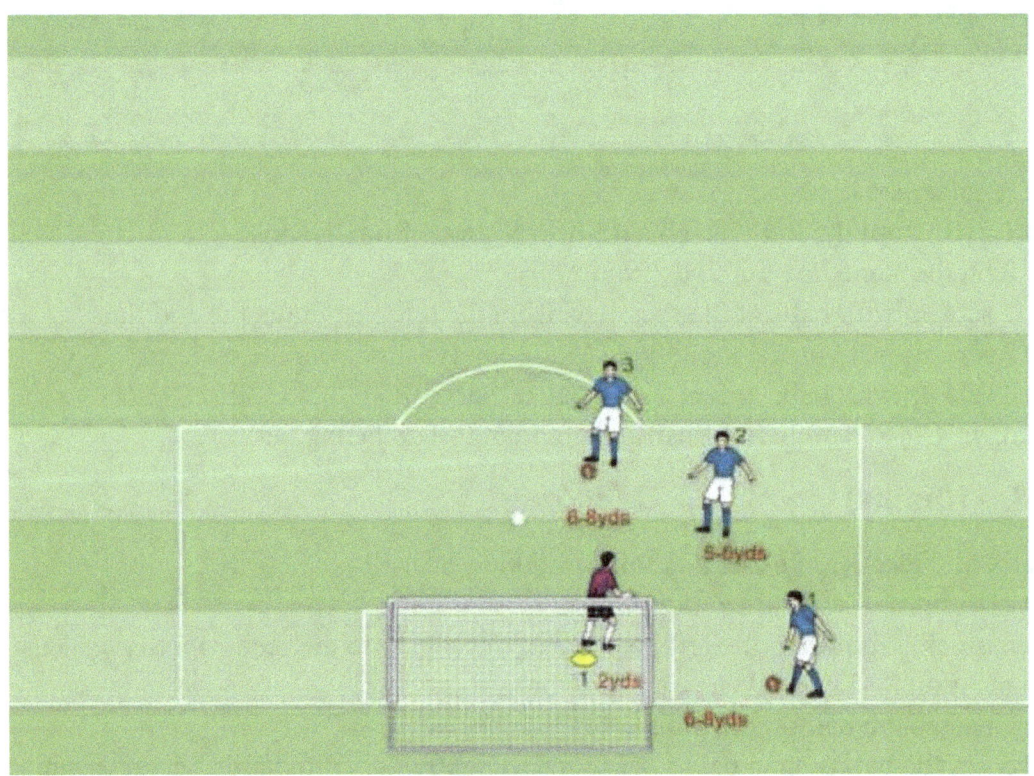

- Use of regular size goal & the 18yd box
- Place ^1 2yds from the right post on a 45-degree angle from the post
- Server 1 sets up with balls at the feet 6yds from the right post down the end line
- Server 2 sets up about 3yds outside the right post & about 4 – 5yds up from the end line
- Server 3 sets up with balls at feet 6 – 8yds directly out from ^1
- GK starts in **Close Range Set Position** straddling ^1 & facing Server 2

Cut Back Positioning

Photo Courtesy of Matt Broomall & Modern Goalkeeper Training Systems, LLC

Bowling

Photo Courtesy of Matt Broomall

Activity 1 (10-15mins)

- GK starts in **Close Range Set Position** straddling over ^1 & facing Server 2
- Server 1 starts the activity by saying "Go!"
- GK then quickly moves to the right post & gets into the **Cut Back Positioning**
- Server 1 strikes a low shot directly at the GK
- GK makes an appropriate **Low-ball Save**
- GK then **Bowls** the ball out to Server 2 using proper communication ("Yes & Server 2's name!")

- o **Ball should be bowled out to Server 2 relatively slowly because the GK needs to chase the distribution out to Server 2**
- GK chases after the ball
- Server 2 hits the ball at the GK on the 1st touch
- GK must get out & make a **K-save** dropping the right knee down
- GK immediately **Recovers** to feet & back pedals behind ^1 & gets into **Close Range Set Position**
- Server 3 strikes a low hard ball to either side of the GK (close to the GK)
- GK makes appropriate **Low-ball Save**
- If GK gives up a rebound-on Server 3's shot, rebound is live for any Server
- GK returns to ^1 & straddles it facing Server 2 & readies for the next repetition
- Repeat 6X then GK's rotate

Coaching Points

- GK begins by straddling ^1 & facing Server 2 in proper **Close Range Set Position**
- All of GK's **Foot-work** is quick & clean
- GK sets up in proper **Cut Back Stance** at the right post
- Server 1 serves quality balls
- GK uses proper technique on the **Low-ball Save**
- GK's **Distribution** to Server 2 is accurate, properly weighted, & done with proper communication ("Yes & Server 2's name!")
- GK quickly follows **Distribution** to Server 2
- GK performs a proper **K-save** with the right knee going down
- GK should not take big steps towards the ball but short, quick ones
- GK quickly **Recovers** to feet & readies for a 2nd rebound shot
- GK performs a proper **Low-ball Save** from Server 3
- If GK gives up a rebound-on Server 3's shot, GK **Recovers** quickly for any possible rebound

Set Up 2

- Use of regular size goal & the 18yd box
- Place ^1 2yds from the left post on a 45-degree angle from the post
- Server 1 sets up with balls at the feet 6yds from the left post down the end line
- Server 2 sets up about 3yds outside the left post & about 4 – 5yds up from the end line
- Server 3 sets up with balls at feet 6 – 8yds directly out from ^1
- GK starts in **Close Range Set Position** straddling ^1 & facing Server 2

Activity 2 (10-15mins)

- GK starts in **Close Range Set Position** straddling over ^1 & facing Server 2
- Server 1 starts the activity by saying "Go!"
- GK then quickly moves to the left post & gets into the **Cut Back Positioning**
- Server 1 strikes a low shot directly at the GK
- GK makes an appropriate **Low-ball Save**
- GK then **Bowls** the ball out to Server 2 using proper communication ("Yes & Server 2's name!")
    - o **Ball should be bowled out to Server 2 relatively slowly because the GK needs to chase the distribution out to Server 2**
- GK chases after the ball
- Server 2 hits the ball at the GK on the 1st touch
- GK must get out & make a **K-save** dropping the left knee down
- GK immediately **Recovers** to feet & back pedals behind ^1 & gets into **Close Range Set Position**
- Server 3 strikes a low hard ball to either side of the GK (close to the GK)
- GK makes appropriate **Low-ball Save**
- If GK gives up a rebound-on Server 3's shot, rebound is live for any Server
- GK returns to ^1 & straddles it facing Server 2 & readies for the next repetition
- Repeat 6X then GK's rotate

Coaching Points

- GK begins by straddling ^1 & facing Server 2 in proper **Close Range Set Position**
- All of GK's **Foot-work** is quick & clean
- GK sets up in proper **Cut Back Stance** at the left post
- Server 1 serves quality balls
- GK uses proper technique on the low ball save
- GK's **Distribution** to Server 2 is accurate, properly weighted, & done with proper communication ("Yes & Server 2's name!")
- GK quickly follows **Distribution** to Server 2
- GK performs a proper **K-save** with the left knee going down
- GK should not take big steps towards the ball but short, quick ones
- GK quickly **Recovers** to feet & readies for a 2nd rebound shot
- GK performs a proper **Low-ball Save** from Server 3
- If GK gives up a rebound on Server 3's shot, GK **Recovers** quickly for any possible rebound

U16 – U18 Training Session #7
1v1 Decision Making

Techniques used in this Session

- 2 Touch Passing
- 1 Touch Passing
- Volley
- Hands Low Catch
- Chest Down/Basket Catch
- Diamond/Contour Catch
- Controlled Collapsing to the Right/Left
- Bowling
- K-Save Stance
- Modern Set Position
- Close Range Set Position
- Containment Stance - 40/60 1v1 Situation

Key for Training Session

- ^ = cone (^1 – cone 1)
- X = Times (2X – 2 times)

Stage 1

Dynamic Warm-Up

Set up

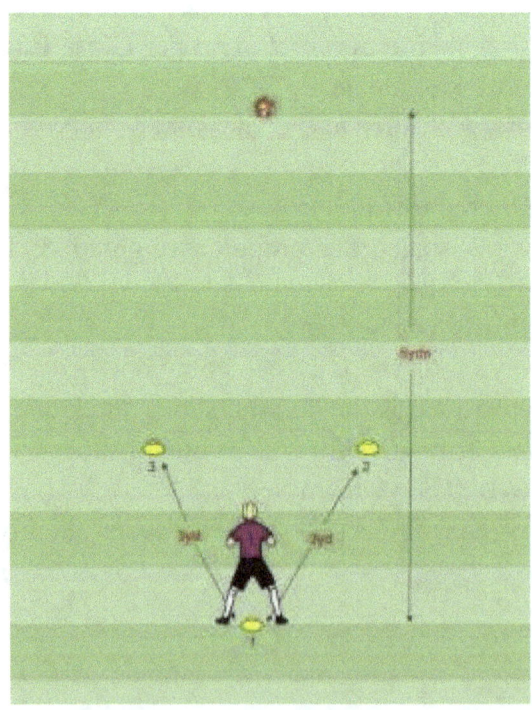

- Place 3 ^'s in a V shape, as shown above

- ^2 & ^3 each are at a 45-degree angle from ^1 & placed 3yds away
- Place a ball on the ground 6yds in front of ^1
- ^1 is the starting ^
- All of the dynamic movements performed between ^1 to ^2 & ^1 to ^3
- Movement back from ^2 to ^1 & ^3 to ^1 is a quick back pedal on both sides
- After back pedaling to ^1, GK then runs to the ball, scoops it up while calling "KEEPER!"
- GK puts ball back down & jogs back to start (^1)
- All movements done 1X or 2X each (depending on amount of time available for the whole session)

Activity 1 (5-8mins)

- Movements from ^1 to ^2 & ^1 to ^3
  - o Jog to ^; quick back pedal back to ^1
  - o High knees to ^; quick back pedal back to ^1
  - o Butt kicks to ^; quick back pedal back to ^1
  - o Skipping & forward arm circles to ^; quick back pedal back to ^1
  - o Skipping & arm circles backwards to ^; quick back pedal back to ^1
  - o Skipping & swinging arms across the chest to ^; quick back pedal back to ^1
  - o Open the gate to ^; quick back pedal back to ^1
  - o Close the gate to ^; quick back pedal back to ^1
  - o Lunges (lunging forward with one foot at a time – alternate feet) to ^; quick back pedal back to ^1
  - o Straight leg sweeps (bend forward & sweep the ground with both hands, take 3 small steps & do it again, etc.) to ^; quick back pedal back to ^1
  - o Twist body with elbows touching opposite knee to ^; quick back pedal back to ^1
  - o Side shuffle to ^2 facing inward; quick back pedal back to ^1
  - o Side shuffle to ^3 facing inward; quick back pedal back to ^1
  - o Carioca to ^2 facing inward; quick back pedal back to ^1
  - o Carioca to ^3 facing inward; quick back pedal back to ^1
  - o Quick feet forward to ^2; quick back pedal to ^1; quick feet forward to ^3; quick back pedal to ^1; sprint to ball
- Water break with additional static stretching

Coaching Points

- Reinforce proper execution of various movements
- Players shouldn't rush through these activities
- Movements should be executed deliberately, stressing the quality of each movement

Stage 2

K-Save Warm-Up & Stretch

Set Up

- Server has a ball in hand (substitute a heavy ball if available)
- GK starts on knees facing Server & 1yd away

Starting Position on Knees for the Activity

Photos Courtesy of Matt Broomall & Modern Goalkeeper Training Systems, LLC

Activity 1 (2mins)

- Server tosses ball towards the right ear of the GK
- GK raises right hand & catches the ball with 1 hand only
- At the same time, GK raises & opens right leg

- o GK plants right foot on the ground with the toes pointing laterally away from body (instep of right foot will be open towards the Server) forming a right angle with the right knee & the right hip
  - o Left knee remains facing forward & on the ground
  - o Hold stretch for 2secs
- GK tosses the ball back to Server & puts right knee back to the ground
- Server then tosses ball towards the left ear of the GK
- GK raises left hand & catches the ball with 1 hand only
- At the same time, GK raises & opens left leg
  - o GK plants left foot on the ground with the toes pointing laterally away from body (instep of left foot will be open towards the S) forming a right angle with the left knee & the left hip
  - o Right knee remains facing forward & on the ground
  - o Hold stretch for 2secs
- GK tosses the ball back to Server & puts left knee back to the ground
- Repeat 10X to both sides

Coaching Points

- Leg that raises opens to a full 90-degrees in order to get a full stretch in the groin area
- Toes on the foot of opened leg points laterally, not straight ahead
- Shoulders stay square to the Server on the catch – do not tilt on an angle towards the opened leg
- GK makes a clean 1 hand catch looking at the ball after it is in the hand
- The stretching activity is not hurried
- Slow movements required to get the full stretch & the feel of the save technique

Activity 2 (2mins)

- Repeat Activity 1 except
  - o Server tosses ball to left ear as right leg raises & opens
  - o Server tosses ball to right ear as left leg raises & opens
- Repeat 10X both sides

Coaching Points

- Leg that raises & opens stretches to a 90-degree angle of the opposite leg to get the full stretch in the groin area
- Toes on the foot of opened leg points laterally, not straight ahead
- Shoulders stay square to the Server on the catch – do not tilt on an angle towards the opened leg
- GK makes a clean 1 hand catch looking at the ball after it is in the hand
- The stretching activity is not hurried
- Slow movements required to get the full stretch & the feel of the save technique

Activity 3 (2mins)

- Repeat Activity 1 except
  - o As right leg raises & opens, Server tosses ball low & left of GK's left leg
  - o GK makes 1 hand catch with left hand & tosses ball back to Server after a 2sec hold
  - o As left leg raises & opens, Server tosses ball low & right of GK's right leg
  - o GK makes 1 hand catch with right hand & tosses ball back to Server after a 2sec hold

Coaching Points

- Leg that raises & opens stretches to a 90-degree angle of the opposite leg to get the full stretch in the groin area
- Toes on the foot of opened leg points laterally, not straight ahead
- Shoulders stay square to the Server on the catch – do not tilt on an angle towards the opened leg
- GK makes a clean 1 hand catch looking into the ball after it is in the hand
- The stretching activity is not hurried; slow movements required to get the full stretch & the feel of the save technique

Stage 3

K-Save/Recovery/Low Ball 2nd Shot

Set Up 1

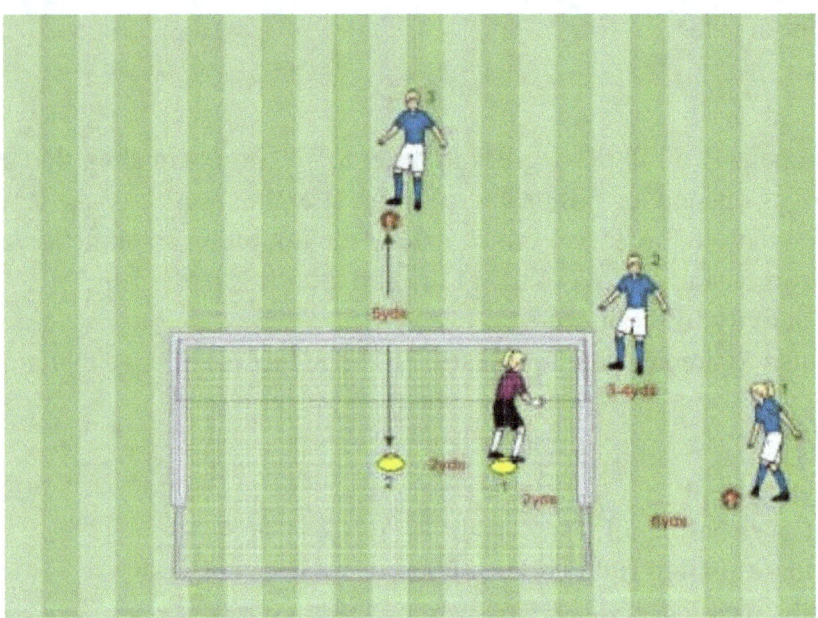

- Use of regular size goal & the 18yd box
- Place ^1 2yds from the right post on a 45-degree angle from the post
- Place ^2 2yds to the left of ^1
- Server 1 sets up with balls at the feet 6yds from the right post down the end line
- Server 2 sets up just outside the right post & about 3 – 4yds up from the end line
- Server 3 sets up with balls at feet 5yds directly out from ^2
- GK starts in **Close Range Set Position** straddling ^1 & facing Server 2

Close Range Stance/Blocking Stance

Photos Courtesy of Matt Broomall & Modern Goalkeeper Training Systems, LLC

Inside of the Foot Pass (IOF)

Bowling

Photos Courtesy of Matt Broomall

Hands Low Catch

Controlled Collapse Left

K-Save Technique Right

K-Save Technique Left

Photos Courtesy of Matt Broomall & Modern Goalkeeper Training Systems, LLC

Activity 1 (5 – 8mins)

- Server 1 starts the activity by saying "Go!"
- GK quickly moves to the right post & asks for the ball to be played to the feet using proper communication ("Yes & Server 1's name!")
- Server 1 passes the ball on the ground to GK
- GK uses **2 Touches** to receive & then pass the ball back to Server 1, using proper communication on passing the ball back to Server 1 ("Yes & Server 1's name!")
- GK then sets at the post
- Server 1 hits a 2ⁿᵈ ball on the ground to the GK who makes a **Hands Low Catch**
- GK then **Bowls** the ball out to Server 2 using proper communication ("Yes & Server 2's name!")
  - o **Ball should be bowled out to Server 2 relatively slowly because the GK needs to chase the distribution out to Server 2**
- GK chases after the ball
- Server 2 hits the ball at the GK on the 1ˢᵗ touch
- GK must get out & make a **K-Save** dropping the right knee down
- GK quickly **Recovers** & sets at ^1 in the **Close Range Set Position** but facing Server 3
- Server 3 strikes a low hard ball to ^2
- GK makes a **Controlled Collapsing Save to the Left**
- If there is a rebound, GK **Recovers** & readies to make an additional save
- Repeat 4X – 5X
- GK's rotate & repeat whole activity

Coaching Points

- GK begins by straddling ^1 & facing Server 2 in proper **Close Range Set Position**
- All of GK's **Foot-work** is quick & clean
- Server 1 serves quality balls
- GK uses proper technique on the low ball save

- GK's **Distribution** to Server 2 is accurate, properly weighted & done with proper communication ("Yes & Server 2's name!")
- GK quickly follows **Distribution** to Server 2
- GK performs a proper **K-Save** with the right knee going down
- GK should not take big steps towards the ball but short, quick ones
- GK quickly **Recovers** to feet & readies for a 2nd rebound shot
- GK performs a proper low ball save from Server 3
- If GK gives up a rebound on Server 3's shot, GK **Recovers** quickly for any possible rebound

Set Up 2

- **(Same Set Up as in Set Up 1 but on the opposite side of the goal)**

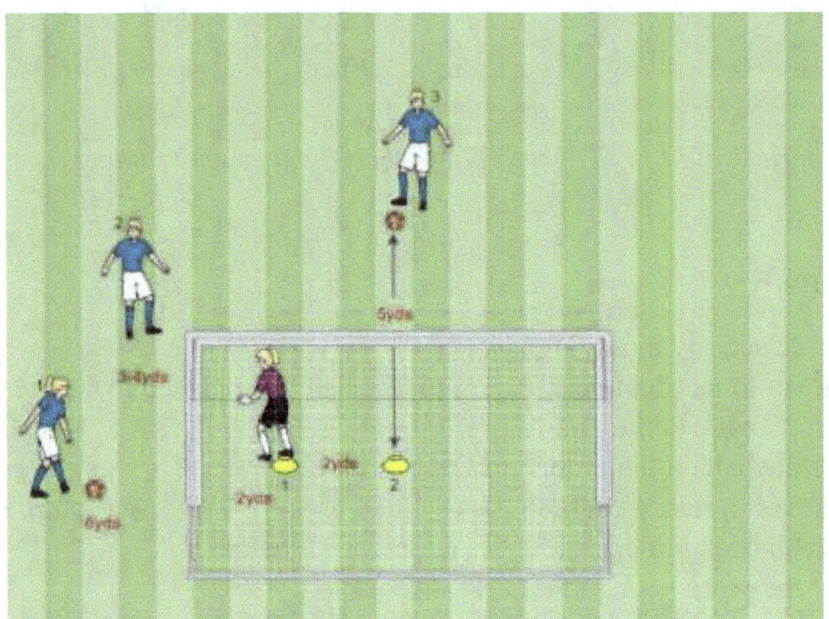

- Use of regular size goal & the 18yd box
- Place ^1 2yds from the left post on a 45-degree angle from the post
- Place ^2 2yds to the right of ^1
- Server 1 sets up with balls at the feet 6yds from the left post down the end line
- Server 2 sets up just outside the left post & about 3 – 4yds up from the end line
- Server 3 sets up with balls at feet 5yds directly out from ^2
- GK starts in **Close Range Set Position** straddling ^1 & facing Server 2

Chest Down/Basket Catch

Photos Courtesy Erin Guthrie Corsi

Controlled Collapse Right

Photos Courtesy of Matt Broomall & Modern Goalkeeper Training Systems, LLC

Activity 1 (5 – 8mins)

- Server 1 starts the activity by saying "Go!"
- GK quickly moves to the left post and asks for the ball to be played to the feet using proper communication ("Yes & Server 1's name!")
- Server 1 passes the ball on the ground to GK

- GK uses **1 Touch** to pass the ball back to Server 1, using proper communication on passing the ball back to Server 1 ("Yes & Server 1's name!")
- GK then sets at the post
- Server 1 hits a 2nd ball on the ground to the GK who makes a **Chest Down/Basket Catch**
- GK then **Bowls** the ball out to Server 2 using proper communication ("Yes & Server 2's name!")
  - **Ball should be bowled out to Server 2 relatively slowly because the GK needs to chase the distribution out to Server 2**
- GK chases after the ball
- Server 2 hits the ball at the GK on the 1st touch
- GK must get out & make a **K-Save** dropping the left knee down
- GK quickly **Recovers** & sets at ^1 in the **Close Range Set Position** but facing Server 3
- Server 3 strikes a low hard ball to ^2
- GK makes a **Controlled Collapsing Save to the Right**
- If there is a rebound, GK **Recovers** & readies to make an additional save
- Repeat 4X – 5X
- GK's rotate & repeat whole activity

Coaching Points

- GK begins by straddling ^1 & facing Server 2 in proper **Close Range Set Position**
- All of GK's **Foot-work** is quick & clean
- Server 1 serves quality balls
- GK uses proper technique on the low ball save
- GK's **Distribution** to Server 2 is accurate, properly weighted & done with proper communication ("Yes & Server 2's name!")
- GK quickly follows **Distribution** to Server 2
- GK performs a proper **K-Save** with the left knee going down
- GK should not take big steps towards the ball but short, quick ones
- GK quickly **Recovers** to feet & readies for a 2nd rebound shot
- GK performs a proper low ball save from Server 3
- If GK gives up a rebound on Server 3's shot, GK **Recovers** quickly for any possible rebound

Stage 4

K-Save/Recovery/Containment Stance

Set Up 1

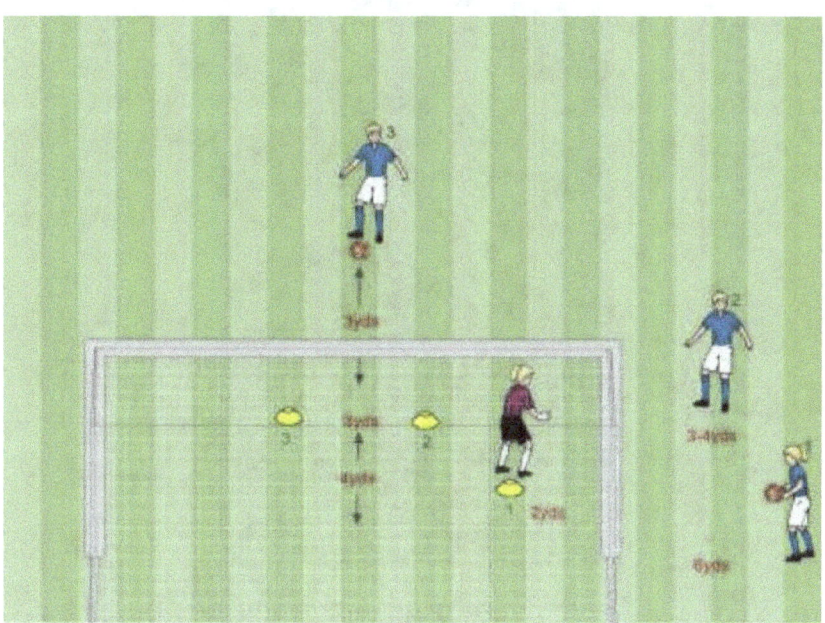

- Use of regular size goal & the 18yd box
- Place ^1 2yds from the right post on a 45-degree angle from the post
- Place ^2 & ^3 centrally in front of the goal about 4yds from the goal line & 3yds apart from each other
- Server 1 sets up with ball in the hands 6yds from the right post down the end line
- Server 2 sets up just outside the right post & about 3 – 4yds up from the end line
- Server 3 sets up with balls at feet 3yds directly out from ^2 & ^3
- GK starts in **Close Range Set Position** straddling ^1 & facing Server 2

Diamond/Contour Catch

Photo Courtesy of Matt Broomall

Containment Stance - 40/60 1v1 Situation

Photo Courtesy of Erin Guthrie Corsi

Activity 1 (5 – 8mins)

- Server 1 starts the activity by saying "Go!"
- GK quickly moves to the right post & gets set into the **Close Range Set Position**
- Server 1 **Volleys** the ball to the chest/face of the GK
- GK catches the ball using **Diamond/Contour Catch**
- GK then **Bowls** the ball back to Server 1, using proper communication ("Yes & Server 1's name!")
- GK then resets at the post
- Server 1 hits a 2nd ball on the ground to the GK who makes a **Hands Low Catch**

- GK then **Bowls** the ball out to Server 2 using proper communication ("Yes & Server 2's name!")
  - o **Ball should be bowled out to Server 2 relatively slowly because the GK needs to chase the distribution out to Server 2**
- GK chases after the ball
- Server 2 hits the ball at the GK on the 1st touch
- GK must get out & make a **K-Save** dropping the right knee down
- GK quickly **Recovers** & sets between ^2 & ^3 in the **Containment Stance** but facing Server 3
- Server 3 dribbles at game speed towards the GK & tries to get by the GK by dribbling or toe poking the ball through the 2^'s
- GK tries to keep the ball from going through the 2^'s
- If there is a rebound, GK **Recovers** & readies to make an additional save
- Repeat 4X – 5X
- GK's rotate & repeat whole activity

Coaching Points

- GK begins by straddling ^1 & facing Server 2 in proper **Close Range Set Position**
- All of GK's **Foot-work** is quick & clean
- Server 1 serves quality balls
- GK uses proper technique on the ball hit to chest & on low ball
- GK's **Distribution** to Server 1 & Server 2 is done with proper communication ("Yes & Server 1's/Server 2's name!")
- GK quickly follows **Distribution** to Server 2
- GK performs a proper **K-Save** with the right knee going down
- GK should not take big steps towards the ball but short, quick ones
- GK quickly **Recovers** to feet
- GK's **Containment Stance** is correct & GK waits for Server 3 to make the 1st move
- If GK gives up a rebound on Server 3's shot, GK **Recovers** quickly for any possible rebound

Set Up 2

- **(Same Set Up as in Set Up 1 but on the opposite side of the goal)**

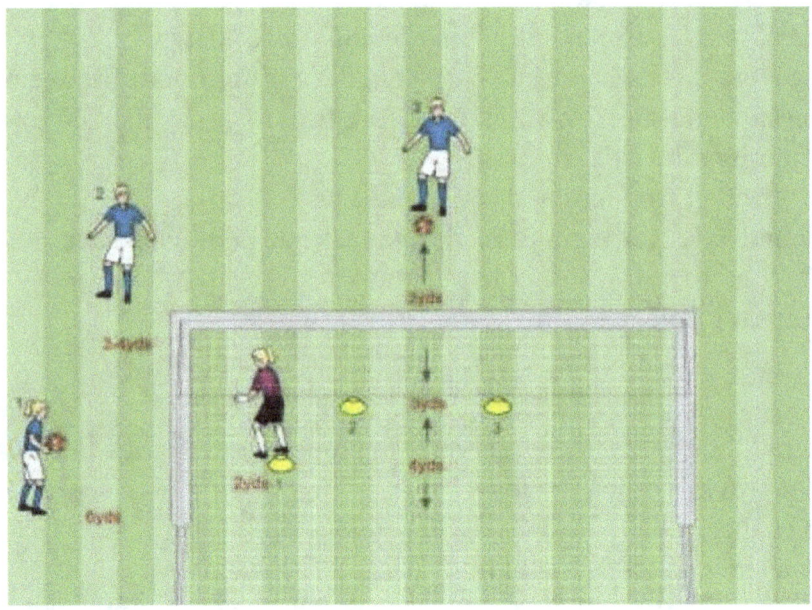

- Use of regular size goal & the 18yd box
- Place ^1 2yds from the left post on a 45-degree angle from the post
- Place ^2 & ^3 centrally in front of the goal about 4yds from the goal line & 3yds apart from each other
- Server 1 sets up with balls at the feet 6yds from the left post down the end line
- Server 2 sets up just outside the left post & about 3 – 4yds up from the end line
- Server 3 sets up with balls at feet 3yds directly out from ^2 & ^3
- GK starts in **Close Range Set Position** straddling ^1 & facing Server 2

Activity 2 (5 – 8mins)

- Server 1 starts the activity by saying "Go!"
- GK quickly moves to the left post & gets set into the **Close Range Set Position**
- Server 1 **Volleys** the ball to the chest/face of the GK
- GK catches the ball using **Diamond/Contour Catch**; GK then **Bowls** the ball back to Server 1, using proper communication ("Yes & Server 1's name!")
- GK then resets at the post
- Server 1 hits a 2nd ball on the ground to the GK who makes a **Hands Low Catch**
- GK then **Bowls** the ball out to Server 2 using proper communication ("Yes & Server 2's name!")
  - o **Ball should be bowled out to Server 2 relatively slowly because the GK needs to chase the distribution out to Server 2**
- GK chases after the ball
- Server 2 hits the ball at the GK on the 1st touch
- GK must get out & make a **K-Save** dropping the left knee down
- GK quickly **Recovers** & sets between ^2 & ^3 in the **Containment Stance** but facing Server 3
- Server 3 dribbles at game speed towards the GK & tries to get by the GK by dribbling or toe poking the ball through the 2^'s

- GK tries to keep the ball from going through the 2^'s
- If there is a rebound, GK **Recovers** & readies to make an additional save
- Repeat 4X – 5X
- GK's rotate & repeat whole activity

Coaching Points

- GK begins by straddling ^1 & facing Server 2 in proper **Close Range Set Position**
- All of GK's **Foot-work** is quick & clean
- Server 1 serves quality balls
- GK uses proper technique on the ball hit to chest & on low ball
- GK's **Distribution** to Server 1 & Server 2 is done with proper communication ("Yes & Server 1/Server 2's name!")
- GK quickly follows **Distribution** to Server 2
- GK performs a proper **K-Save** with the left knee going down
- GK should not take big steps towards the ball but short, quick ones
- GK quickly **Recovers** to feet
- GK's **Containment Stance** is correct & GK waits for Server 3 to make the 1st move
- If GK gives up a rebound on S3's shot, GK **Recovers** quickly for any possible rebound

Stage 5

Decision Making in 1v1 Situation

Set Up

- Use of full goal, 18yd box & space up to 30yds from the goal line
- Set up 2 dummies/flags 3yds apart and at the top of the "D" (arc)

- Server 1 starts with balls at feet about 2yds away from the "D" (arc) and in the middle of the dummies/flags/cones
- Server 2 & Server 3 set up on either side of the dummies/flags
- GK starts in goal approximately 2 – 3yds off the goal line (at the appropriate distance for a shot from 25 – 30yds from goal)

Modern Set Position

Photos Courtesy of Matt Broomall & Modern Goalkeeper Training Systems, LLC

Activity 1 (15 – 30mins)

- GK starts in **Modern Set Position** 2 – 3yds off the goal line
- Server 1 calls out "Server 2 or Server 3!" to indicate who goes for the ball
- Server 1 then passes the ball through the 2 dummies/flags (at varying distances) & the called Server attacks the ball
- The called Server must strike the ball 1st time on goal
- GK makes a decision on whether to go for the ball or hold ground for the shot
    o The decision is based on the distance/speed of the passed ball
- After the play is dead, GK resets & Server 1 once again calls out the name of a Server & repeats the activity
- GK repeats 6X – 8X & then GK's rotate

Variations

- Servers going after the ball can strike the ball on 1st or 2nd touch
- Servers can take as many touches as they like
- Change the angle of the set up so that the ball is coming from an angle, not straight on to the goal

Coaching Points

- GK must read the speed/angle of the ball coming into the 18yd box & set at proper distance from the ball at the shot
- GK's decisions
    - Can the GK get to the ball 1st
        - Clean save or deflected save
        - GK goes to the ball with the hands
        - GK yells "Keeper!" when going into the confrontation
        - If the ball is live after the save, GK **Recovers** & readies for an additional shot attempt
    - Can the GK get to the ball for a **50/50** confrontation
        - GK goes in with hands 1st & attempts to get a piece of the ball
        - If the ball is live after the save, GK **Recovers** & readies for an additional shot attempt
    - Does the attacker get to the ball 1st
        - What is the distance to the attacker?
            - 12 – 15yds, GK readies in the **Modern Set Position**
            - 4 – 8yds, GK readies in the **Close Range Set Position**
            - 2 – 3yds, GK gets into the **Containment Stance**
            - 1 – 2yds, GK goes in with the **K-Save**
- GK readies for possible rebound on all situations
- On any clean save made by the GK, the GK **Distributes** the ball back to Server 1 using proper communication ("Yes & Server 1's name!")

U16 – U18 Training Session #8
K-save/Close Range Shots/50-50 Balls

Techniques used in this Session

- **1 Touch Passing**
- **2 Touch Passing**
- **K-save Stance**
- **Close Range Set Position**
- **Cut Back Positioning**
- **50/50 Saves – Cobra Hand Positioning**
- **Controlled Collapse Catch Left & Right**
- **Recovery**

Key for Training Session

- ^ = cone (^1 – cone 1)
- X = Times (2X – 2 times)

Stage 1

Dynamic Warm-up

Set up

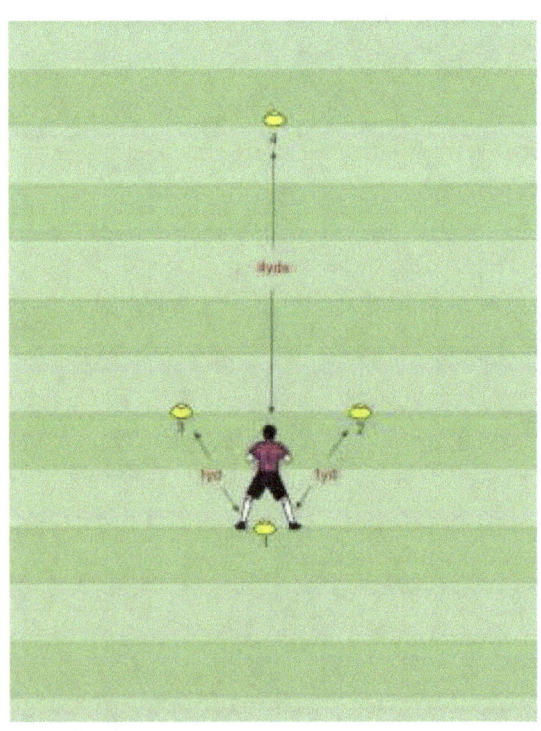

- Place 3 ^'s in a V shape, 1yd apart
- Place a 4th ^ 4yds away from ^2 & ^3
- ^1 is the starting ^; ^4 is the ending ^
- All starting **Foot-work** will be **fast feet (quick feet)** forward to ^3 & back to start; then fast feet forward to ^2 & back to start

- All of the dynamic movements will then be performed between ^1 & ^4
- Keepers will jog back to start (^1)
- All movements will be done 1X or 2X each (depending on amount of time available for the whole session)

Activity (5 – 8mins)

- Dynamic movements between ^1 & ^4 are (order can be varied or modified)
  - Jog up & jog back
  - High knees up & jog back
  - Butt kicks up & jog back
  - Skipping & performing forward arm circles up & jog back
  - Skipping & performing arm circles backwards & jog back
  - Skipping & swing arms across the chest & jog back
  - Open the gate & jog back
  - Close the gate & jog back
  - Inside up & jog back ("Inside" is performed in the following way)
    - With the body upright, dangle both arms down in front of the body towards feet
    - Pull one foot up & in so that hand touches the arch of the inside of that foot then the opposite foot up; done quickly
  - Outside up & jog back ("Outside" is performed in the following way)
    - Dangle arms straight down at the sides
    - Pull one foot up & slightly backwards so that hand touches the outside of the foot & then do the same with the opposite foot; done quickly
  - Facing sideways at ^1, get into set position; quick shuffle to ^4 & jog back; do the same in the opposite direction
  - Same as above except dynamic movement is carioca; do it facing both ways
  - Lunges up & jog back
  - Straight leg sweeps & jog back
  - GK's sprint to ^2 and circle around it with quick foot work in a counter-clockwise fashion; then back pedals with speed back to ^1
    - Repeat to ^3 (with speed) but in a clockwise fashion; finish by sprinting to ^4
- Take 2 minutes for a water break and static stretching on their own

Coaching Points

- Reinforce proper execution of various movements
- Players shouldn't rush through these activities
- Movements should be executed deliberately, stressing the quality of each movement

Stage 2

K-save Rhythm Work Utilizing 1 & 2 Touch Passing

Set Up 1

- Place 2 ^'s side by side 2yds apart
- Server 1 sets up on one side of the ^'s with a ball at feet 3yds from the ^'s
- Server 2 sets up on the opposite side of the ^'s with a ball at feet 2yds from the ^'s
- GK starts in the middle of the ^'s facing Server 1

Inside of the Foot Pass (IOF)

Photo Courtesy of Matt Broomall

K-Save Technique Right   **K-Save Technique Left**

Photos Courtesy of Matt Broomall & Modern Goalkeeper Training Systems, LLC

Activity 1 (3 – 5 mins)

- GK starts the activity by asking for the ball to be passed to the feet from Server 1, using proper communication ("Yes & Server 1's name!")
- Server 1 passes the ball to the GK
- GK uses **2 Touch Passing** to receive & pass the ball directly back to Server 1
  - GK uses any combination of the feet for the **2 Touches**
- As soon as the GK passes the ball back to Server 1, the GK quickly snaps around & faces Server 2
- Server 2 then makes a diagonal touch to the left or the right, follows the touch & strikes the ball into the GK
- GK quickly steps & executes a **K-save**
  - GK going to the right
    - Drops the left knee down
    - Right arm angled upward/left arm angled downward
    - Chest squared towards Server 2
  - GK going to the left
    - Drops the right knee down
    - Left arm angled upward/right arm angled downward
    - Chest squared towards Server 2
- After the **K-save**, the GK quickly **Recovers** to the feet anticipating a rebound
- GK goes back & resets between the ^'s facing Server 1
- Repeat the activity for 45 – 60secs
- Rotate the GK's & repeat the activity

Coaching Points

- GK uses proper communication when asking for the ball to be played to the feet
- Server 1 provides adequate services
- GK uses combination of both feet for the **2 Touch Passing**

- Server 2 serves a proper diagonal ball for the **K-save**
- GK uses proper technique for the **K-save** when going to the right & to the left
- GK **Recovers** quickly to the feet after the **K-save** anticipating a rebound shot

Set Up 2 (Same as Set Up 1)

Activity 2 (3 – 5mins)

- GK starts the activity by calling for the ball to be passed to the feet from Server 1, using proper communication ("Yes & Server 1's name!")
- Server 1 passes the ball to the GK
- GK uses **1 Touch Passing** to receive & pass the ball directly back to Server 1
  - o GK uses both left & right feet for the **1 Touch**
- As soon as the GK passes the ball back to Server 1, the GK quickly snaps around & faces Server 2
- Server 2 then makes a diagonal touch to the left or the right, follows the touch & strikes the ball into the GK
- GK quickly steps & executes a **K-save**
  - o GK going to the right
    - Drops the left knee down
    - Right arm angled upward/left arm angled downward
    - Chest squared towards Server 2
  - o GK going to the left
    - Drops the right knee down
    - Left arm angled upward/right arm angled downward
    - Chest squared towards Server 2
- After the **K-save**, the GK quickly **Recovers** to the feet anticipating a rebound
- GK goes back & resets between the ^'s facing Server 1
- Repeat the activity for 45 – 60secs
- Rotate the GK's & repeat the activity

Coaching Points

- GK uses proper communication when asking for the ball to be played to the feet
- Server 1 provides adequate services
- GK uses both feet for the **1 Touch Passing**
- Server 2 serves a proper diagonal ball for the **K-save**
- GK uses proper technique for the **K-save** when going to the right & to the left
- GK **Recovers** quickly to the feet after the **K-save** anticipating a rebound shot

Stage 3

Combination of K-save, Close Range Shot & 50/50 1v1 save

Set Up 1

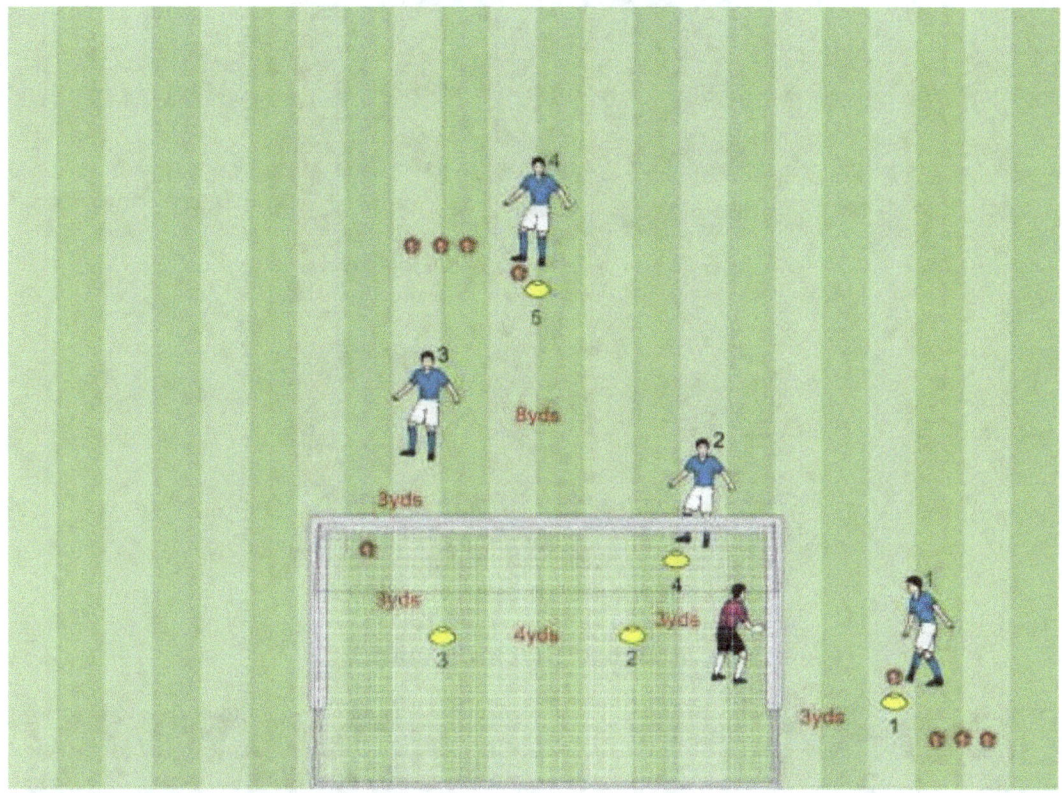

- Use of regular goal & the 18yd box
- Place ^1 along the end line 3yds outside the right post
- Place ^2 & ^3 4yds apart in the middle of the goal
- Place ^4 3yds off the goal line & at a 45-degree angle from the right post
- Place ^5 8 – 10yds off the goal line & in the middle of ^2 & ^3
- Place a ball 3yds off the goal line & just inside of the left post
- Server 1 sets up with balls at feet at ^1
- Server 2 sets up at ^4
- Server 3 sets up 3yds away from the ball & on a slight angle to the inside of the ball
- Server 4 sets up at ^5 with balls at the feet
- GK starts in **Cut Back Position** at the right post

Cut Back Positioning

Close Range Stance/Blocking Stance

Photos Courtesy of Matt Broomall & Modern Goalkeeper Training Systems, LLC

50/50 Cobra Technique

Photo Courtesy of Erin Guthrie Corsi

Activity 1 (18 – 20mins)

- GK starts at right post in the **Cut Back Position**
- Server 1 strikes a low ball at a controlled pace to Server 2
- As ball rolls out to Server 2, GK quickly moves with the ball towards Server 2
- Server 2 strikes the ball 1st time
- GK makes a **K-save** dropping right knee down
- GK then **Recovers** & quickly back pedals to the goal line between ^2 & ^3 & sets into **Close Range Set Position**
- Server 4 strikes a low hard ball anywhere between ^2 & ^3
- GK makes a save
- GK then quickly **Recovers** & sets into **Close Range Set Position** at ^3 facing Server 3
- Server 3 runs to the ball & strikes a low ball at the GK
  - GK reacts to Server 3's movement & quickly moves to the ball & makes a **50/50 Save** leading with the hands to the ball & collapsing on the left side
- After the play is dead, the GK goes back to the right post & resets
- Repeat whole activity
- GK repeats 5X – 6X
- GK's rotate & repeat whole activity

Coaching Points

- GK uses proper **Set Positions** throughout the activity
- Services are appropriate for the activity
- Observe & correct the execution of GK's **Set Positions** & saves
- The GK drops the correct knee down on the **K-save**
- On the **50/50 Save**, GK goes to the ball with the hands 1st
- GK's **Recoveries** are quick

Set Up 2

Same Set Up as in Set Up 1 but on the opposite side of the goal

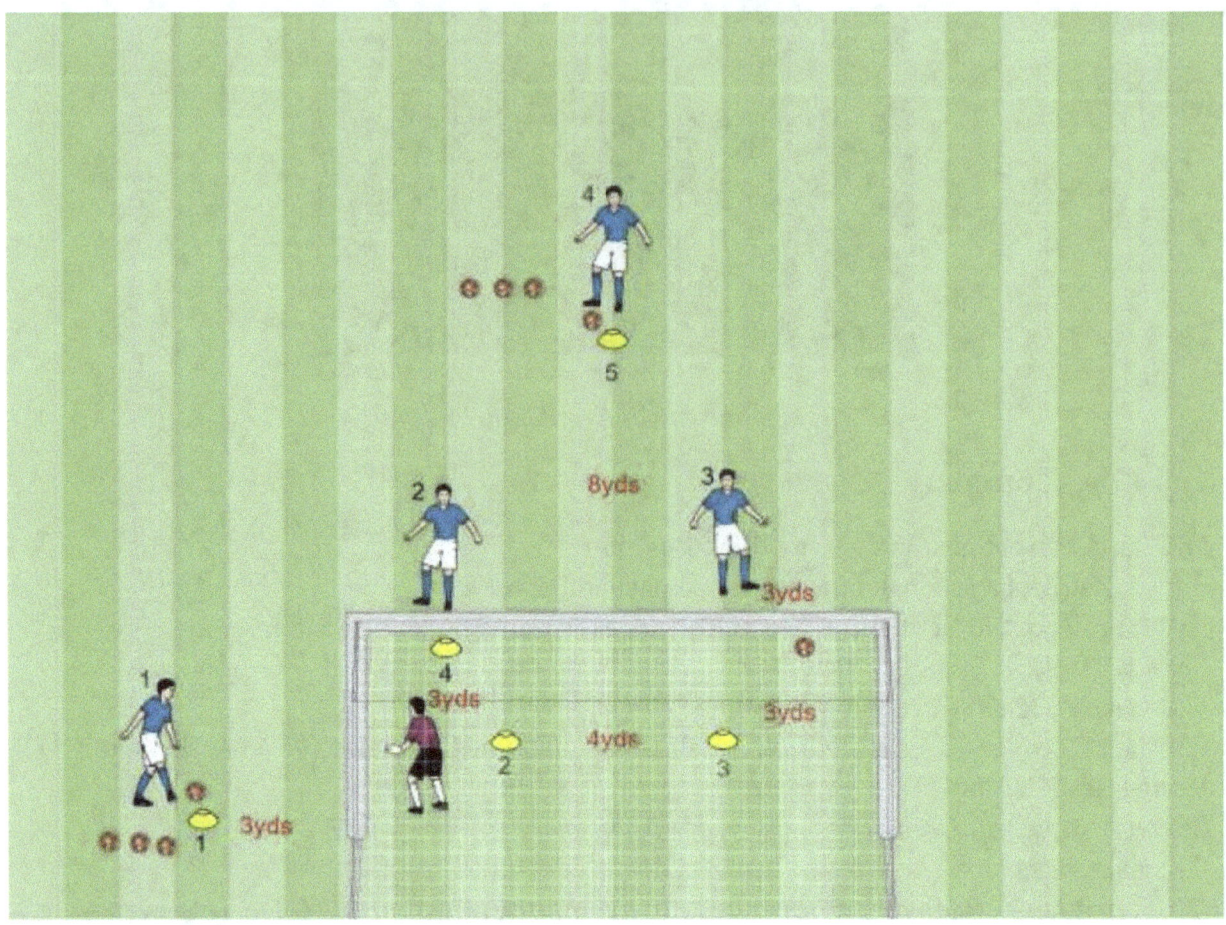

- Use of regular goal & the 18yd box
- Place ^1 along the end line 3yds outside the left post
- Place ^2 & ^3 4yds apart in the middle of the goal
- Place ^4 3yds off the goal line & at a 45-degree angle from the left post
- Place ^5 8 – 10yds off the goal line & in the middle of ^2 & ^3
- Place a ball 3yds off the goal line & just inside of the right post
- Server 1 sets up with balls at feet at ^1
- Server 2 sets up at ^4
- Server 3 sets up 3yds away from the ball & on a slight angle to the inside of the ball
- Server 4 sets up at ^5 with balls at the feet
- GK starts in **Cut Back Position** at the left post

Activity 2 (18 – 20mins)

- GK starts at left post in the **Cut Back Position**
- Server 1 strikes a low ball at a controlled pace to Server 2
- As ball rolls out to Server 2, GK quickly moves with the ball towards Server 2
- Server 2 strikes the ball 1ˢᵗ time
- GK makes a **K-save** dropping left knee down
- GK then **Recovers** & quickly back pedals to the goal line between ^2 & ^3 & sets into **Close Range Set Position**

- Server 4 strikes a low hard ball anywhere between ^2 & ^3
- GK makes a save
- GK then quickly **Recovers** & sets into **Close Range Set Position** at ^2 facing Server 3
- Server 3 runs to the ball & strikes a low ball at the GK
    o GK reacts to Server 3's movement & quickly moves to the ball & makes a **50/50 Save** leading with the hands to the ball & collapsing on the right side
- After the play is dead, the GK goes back to the left post & resets
- Repeat whole activity
- GK repeats 5X – 6X
- GK's rotate & repeat whole activity

Coaching Points

- GK uses proper **Set Positions** throughout the activity
- Services are appropriate for the activity
- Observe & correct the execution of GK's **Set Positions** & saves
- The GK drops the correct knee down on the **K-save**
- On the **50/50 Save**, GK goes to the ball with the hands 1st
- GK's **Recoveries** are quick

U16 – U18 Training Session #9
Long Range Distribution

Techniques used in this session

- **Modern Set Position**
- **Driven Balls**
- **Volleys**
- **Diamond/Contour Catch**
- **Chest Down/Basket Catch**
- **Front Smother**
- **High Ball Catching Technique**
- **Recovery**
- **Overhand (Windmill) Throw**
- **Laced Ball on the Ground**

The key for Training Session

- ^ = cone (^1 – cone 1)
- X = Times (2X – 2 times)

Stage 1

Dynamic Warm-Up

Set Up 1

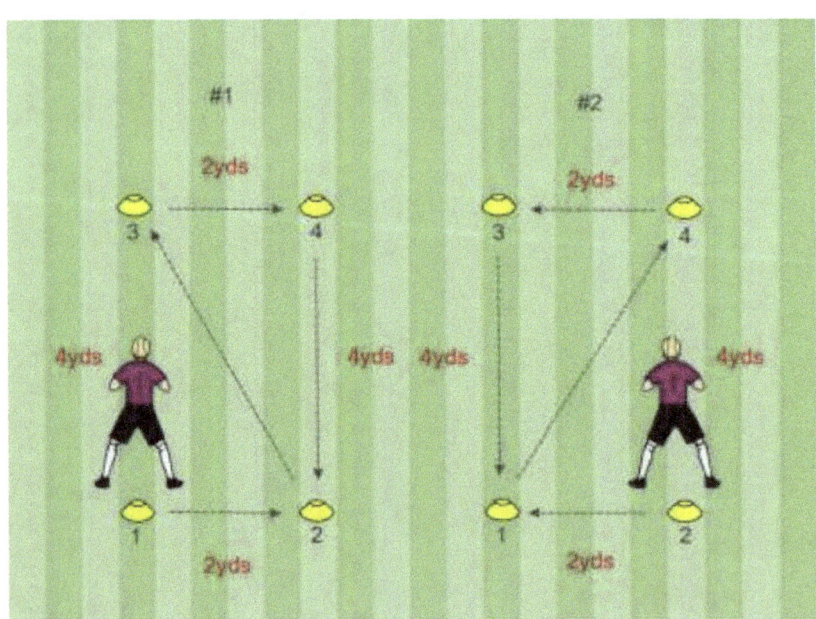

- Place ^1, ^2, ^3 & ^4 in a rectangle
- ^1/^2 & ^3/^4 are placed 2yds apart
- ^1/^3 & ^2/^4 are placed 4yds apart
- GK starts behind ^1

Activity 1 (5 – 8mins)

- GK starts in **Modern Set Position** directly behind ^1 facing forward (towards ^3)
- GK quickly shuffles to the right to ^2
- GK then performs a dynamic motion diagonally across to ^3
- GK then shuffles to the right to ^4
- GK backpedals to ^2
- GK stays at ^2 & reverses the process
- GK quickly shuffles to the left to ^1
- GK then performs the same dynamic motion diagonally across to ^4
- GK then shuffles to the left to ^3
- GK backpedals to ^1
- GK stays at ^1 & repeats the process but doing a different dynamic motion
- Dynamic motions
    - Jog
    - High knees
    - Butt kicks
    - Skipping & arm circles forwards
    - Skipping & arm circles backwards
    - Skipping & swinging arms across chest
    - Open the gate
    - Close the gate
    - Lunges (lunging forward with one foot at a time – alternate feet)
    - Straight leg sweeps (bend forward & sweep the ground with both hands, take 3 small steps & do it again, etc.)
    - Twist body with elbows touching opposite knee
    - Side shuffle to ^ facing inward
    - Side shuffle to ^ facing outward
    - Carioca to ^ facing inward
    - Carioca to ^ facing outward
    - Sprint to ^
- Water break with additional static stretching

Coaching Points

- Reinforce proper execution of various movements
- Players shouldn't rush through these activities
- Movements should be executed deliberately, stressing the quality of each movement

Stage 2

Rhythm Work – Overhand Throws/Driven Balls

Set Up 1

- Use of regular goal, the 18yd box & ½ field
- Server 1 sets up at the top of the arc (D) with balls at feet
- Server 2 sets up at the right corner of the 18yd box
- Server 3 sets up at the left corner of the 18yd box
- GK starts in **Modern Set Position** 2 – 3 yds off the goal line

Modern Set Position

Diamond/Contour Catch

Driven Balls

Laced Ball on the Ground

Photos Courtesy of Matt Broomall & Modern Goalkeeper Training Systems, LLC

Chest Down Front　　　　　　　　**Chest Down Side**

Photos Courtesy of Erin Guthrie Corsi

Overhand (Windmill) Throw

Photos Courtesy of Matt Broomall & Modern Goalkeeper Training Systems, LLC

Front Smother Catch

Photos Courtesy Erin Guthrie Corsi

Activity 1 (12 – 15min)

- GK starts in **Modern Set Position** 2 – 3yds off the goal line facing Server 1
- Server 1 strikes a **Driven Ball** to the GK who makes a save using the **Diamond/Contour Catch**
- GK **Overhand Throws** the ball out to Server 2
- GK runs outside of the frame of the goal on Server 2's side & asks for the ball to be played back to the feet using proper communication ("Yes & Server 2's name!")
- Server 2 strikes a low ball on the ground to the GK
- GK uses a touch with the feet to clean the ball up in the direction of Server 3
- GK strikes a **Driven Ball** to Server 3's hands using proper communication ("Yes & Server 3's name!")
- GK runs across the goal mouth & outside the frame of the goal on Server 3's side
- GK asks for another back pass this time from Server 3 using proper communication ("Yes & Server 3's name!")
- GK uses a touch with the feet to clean the ball up in the direction of Server 1
- GK then **Laces the Ball** on the ground to Server 1 using proper communication ("Yes & Server 1's name!")
- GK returns to original **Set Position** in the goal
- 2nd round is the same activity beginning with Server 1 hitting a **Laced Ball** on the ground to the GK
- GK makes a **Chest Down/Basket Catch** or a **Front Smother**
- GK **Recovers** & makes an **Overhand Throw** now to Server 3
- From there, the activity is the same as before but just to the opposite side
    - o GK receives back pass from Server 3

- o GK strikes **Driven Ball** to hands of Server 2
- o GK receives back pass from Server 2
- o GK **Laces the Ball** on the ground to Server 1
- o GK returns to goal
- o GK uses proper communication on all back passes & **Distributions**
- GK repeats 6X – 8X on both sides
- GK's rotate & repeat activity

Coaching Points

- GK begins in proper **Modern Set Position** & 2 – 3yds off the goal line
- All services are executed properly and accurately
- GK uses proper communication when receiving the ball & when **Distributing** the ball ("Yes & Server's name!")
- GK's 1st touch on back passes is under control & pushed in the direction of the intended receiver
- GK uses proper technique on **Diamond/Contour Catch, Chest Down Catch & Front Smother**
- GK uses correct technique on the **Overhand Throw**
    - o **Overhand Throw** should be thrown into the ground, not at S's chests
    - o Makes it easier for teammates to clean up & move up field or pass back, especially if there is some pressure on the outlet receiver
- Proper technique & accuracy are stressed in **Driven & Laced Balls**
- **Driven Balls** should be struck to the hands of Servers
- **This activity is performed at game speed & with game intention**

Stage 3

Long Distribution Activity

Set Up 1 (Not to Scale)

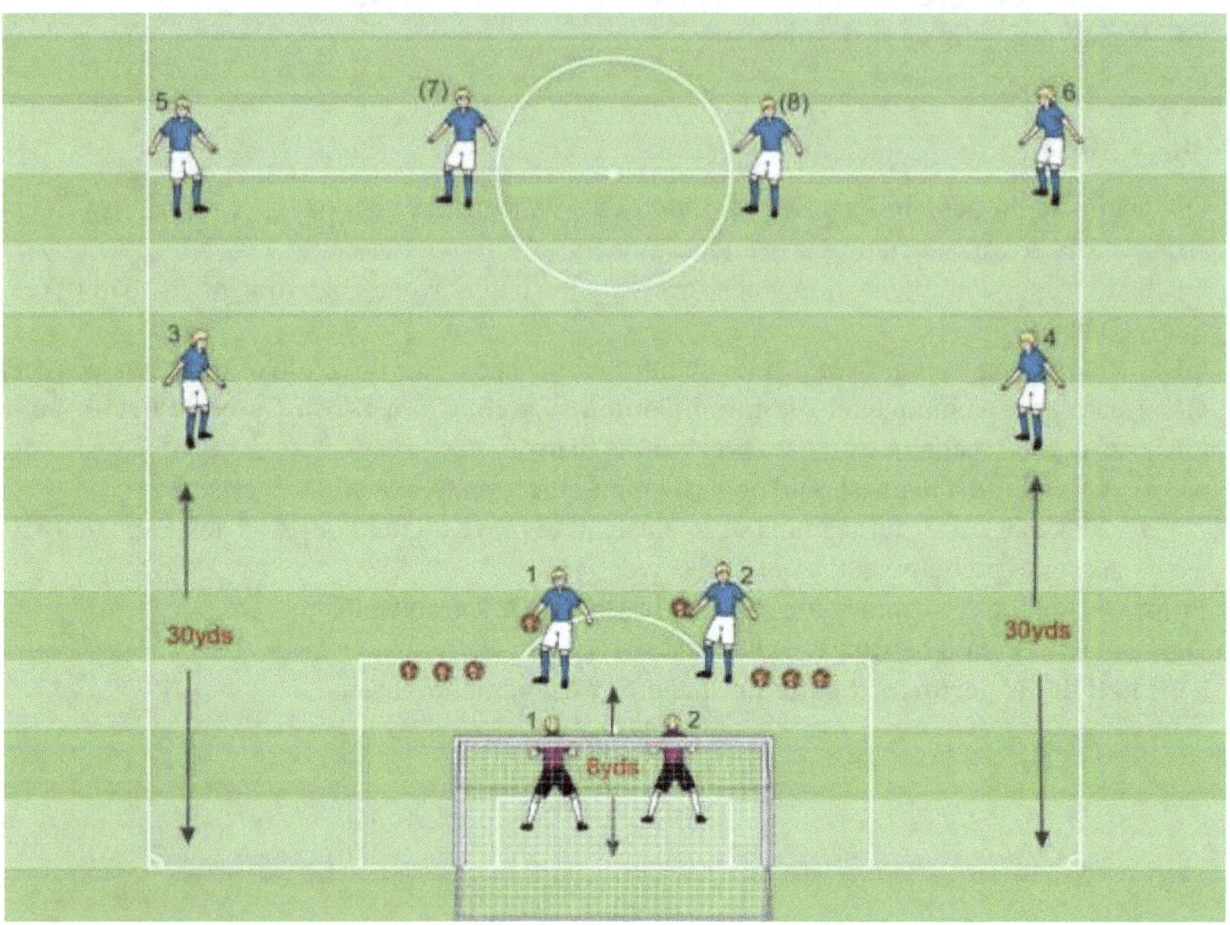

- Use of regular size goal, the 18yd box & ½ field
- Use of field players is helpful, otherwise have additional GK's to handle
- Server 1 & Server 2 set up 8yds from goal with ball in hands
- Server 3 sets up near left side line 30yds from goal
- Server 4 sets up near the right-side line 30yds from goal
- Server 5 sets up near the left side line 45 – 50yds from goal
- Server 6 sets up near the right-side line 45 – 50yds from goal
- (Server 7) & (Server 8) can be additional field players for added distribution options
- GK1 sets up in left half of the goal in line with Server 1
- GK2 sets up in the right half of the goal in line with Server 2
- GK1 & GK2 work simultaneously

High Ball Catching Technique (Diamond/Contour Catch)

Right Knee up Front   **Left Knee Up Front**

Photos Courtesy of Erin Guthrie Corsi

Activity 1 (15 – 20mins)

- GK1 & GK2 start in **Modern Set Position** 2yds off the goal line
- Server 1/Server 2 **Volley** a ball to GK1's/GK2's hands
- GK's make a **Diamond/Contour Catch**
- GK1 **Overhand Throws** to Server 3 using proper communication ("Yes & Server 3's name!")
- GK2 **Overhand Throws** to Server 4 using proper communication ("Yes & Server 4's name!")
- Server 3 & Server 4 keep the balls
- GK1/GK2 reset
- Server 1/Server 2 take a 2nd ball in hands & toss high balls to GK1/GK2
    - Server 1 tosses to GK1's left
    - Server 2 tosses to GK2's right
    - GK1 catches the ball using **High Ball Catching Technique (Diamond/Contour Catching Technique)** driving the left knee upwards & yelling "Keeper!"
    - GK2 catches the ball using **High Ball Catching Technique (Diamond/Contour Catching Technique)** driving the right knee upwards & yelling "Keeper!"
- GK1 drops the ball to the ground using a two-hand back spin to stop the ball's movement quickly
- GK1 strikes a **Driven Ball** to Server 5 using proper communication ("Yes & Server 5's name!")
- At the same time, GK2 drops the ball to the ground using a two-hand back spin to stop the ball's movement quickly
- GK2 strikes a **Driven Ball** to Server 6 using proper communication ("Yes & Server 6's name!")

- Server 5 & Server 6 collect the balls & then strike the balls back to Server 1 & Server 2 respectively on the ground using **Laced Ball Technique** & using proper communication ("Yes & Server's name!")
- GK1 then quickly moves to the left outside of the frame of the goal, asks for the ball to be played back by Server 3, using proper communication ("Yes & Server 3's name!")
- GK1 collects the ball & **Drives** another ball out to Server 5 using proper communication ("Yes & Server 5's name!")
- At the same time, GK2 then quickly moves to the right outside of the frame of the goal, asks for the ball to be played back by Server 2, using proper communication ("Yes & Server 2's name!")
- GK2 collects the ball & **Drives** another ball out to Server 6 using proper communication ("Yes & Server 6's name!")
- Server 5 & Server 6 collect the balls & then strike the balls on the ground back to Server 1 & Server 2 respectively using **Laced Ball Technique** & using proper communication ("Yes & Server's name!")
- This whole process counts as 1 repetition
- GK's repeat 4X – 5X to each side
- Rotate any GK's in & repeat activity

Coaching Points

- **This activity is performed at game speed & with game intention**
- All catching techniques used by the GK's is proper
- GK's use proper communication on all **Distributions** & receiving of back passes ("Yes & Server's names!")
- **Overhand Throws** are thrown into the ground so that the ball skips into the receiver's feet
- All **Driven Balls** should be attempted to the hands of the Servers receiving the ball
- **Laced Balls** are accurate & struck with pace along the ground
- GK's are in control of the pace of the activity
  - o If it's too slow – speed it up
  - o If it's too fast – slow it down
  - o Learn to control tempo
- GK's demand accuracy & proper pace on all services
- All participants have a role in the activity & all should perform with intent
- This activity has multiple moving parts
- It is good training for GK's to stay within each moment of completing each segment before going onto the next

Variation using additional servers (Server 7 & Server 8)

Set Up (Same as above but now utilizing additional Server 7 & Server 8)

Activity 1 (15 – 20mins)

- GK1 & GK2 start in **Modern Set Position** 2yds off the goal line
- Server 1/Server 2 **Volley** a ball to GK1's/GK2's hands
- GK's make a **Diamond/Contour Catch**
- GK1 **Overhand Throws** to Server 3 using proper communication ("Yes & Server 3's name!")
- GK2 **Overhand Throws** to Server 4 using proper communication ("Yes & Server 4's name!")
- Server 3 & Server 4 keep the balls

- GK1/GK2 reset
- Server 1/Server 2 take a 2nd ball in hands & toss high balls to GK1/GK2
  - Server 1 tosses to GK1's left
  - Server 2 tosses to GK2's right
  - GK1 catches the ball using **High Ball Catching Technique (Diamond/Contour Catching Technique)** driving the left knee upwards & yelling "Keeper!"
  - GK2 catches the ball using **High Ball Catching Technique (Diamond/Contour Catching Technique)** driving the right knee upwards & yelling "Keeper!"
- GK1 drops the ball to the ground using a two-hand back spin to stop the ball's movement quickly
- GK1 strikes a **Driven Ball** to Server 5 using proper communication ("Yes & Server 5's name!")
- At the same time, GK2 drops the ball to the ground using a two-hand back spin to stop the ball's movement quickly
- GK2 strikes a **Driven Ball** to Server 6 using proper communication ("Yes & Server 6's name!")
- Server 5 & Server 6 collect the balls & then strike the balls back to Server 1 & Server 2 respectively on the ground using **Laced Ball Technique** & using proper communication ("Yes & Server's name!")
- GK1 then quickly moves to the left outside of the frame of the goal, asks for the ball to be played back by Server 3, using proper communication ("Yes & Server 3's name!")
- Server 1 now calls out the name of either: "Server 5 or Server 7!"
- GK1 collects the ball & **Drives** another ball out to the Server whose name was called by Server 1 using proper communication ("Yes & Server 5's or Server 7's name!")
- At the same time, GK2 then quickly moves to the right outside of the frame of the goal, asks for the ball to be played back by Server 2, using proper communication ("Yes & Server 2's name!")
- Server 2 now calls out the name of either: "Server 6 or Server 8!"
- GK1 collects the ball & **Drives** another ball out to the S whose name was called by Server 2 using proper communication ("Yes & Server 6's or Server 8's name!")
- Server 5/Server 7 & Server 6/Server 8 collect the balls & then strike the balls back to Server 1 & Server 2 respectively on the ground using **Laced Ball Technique** & using proper communication ("Yes & Server's name!")
- This whole process counts as 1 repetition
- GK's repeat 4X – 5X to each side
- Rotate any GK's in & repeat activity

Coaching Points

- **This activity is performed at game speed & with game intention**
- GK's must now adjust to another option of **Distributing** the ball based on Server 1/Server 2 name calling
- All catching techniques used by the GK's is proper
- GK's use proper communication on all **Distributions** & receiving of back passes ("Yes & Server's names!")
- **Overhand Throws** are thrown into the ground so that the ball skips into the receiver's feet
- All **Driven Balls** should be attempted to the hands of the Servers receiving the ball
- **Laced Balls** are accurate & struck with pace along the ground
- GK's are in control of the pace of the activity
  - If it's too slow – speed it up
  - If it's too fast – slow it down

- o Learn to control tempo
- GK's demand accuracy & proper pace on all services
- All participants have a role in the activity & all should perform with intent
- This activity has multiple moving parts
- It is good training for GK's to stay within each moment of completing each segment before going onto the next

U16 – U18 Training Session #10
Training with the Team

Introduction

- This session will offer a few different ideas on training the GK with the team
- These ideas could be used with just keepers in a camp environment, as well, where there are multiple players

Key

- ^'s = cones
- **GKC** = GK Coach

TRAINING FORMAT

Dynamic Warm-Up (8 – 10mins)

- All sessions should begin with a minimal 8 – 10mins of a **Dynamic Warm-Up**
- Any **Dynamic Warm-Up** used in Sessions 1 – 9 in this age group is fine
- **Coaching Points** are applied as with all **Dynamic Warm-Ups**

Rhythm Work (20 – 30mins)

- A minimum of 20 – 30mins of **Rhythm Work** with the GK's is essential prior to training with the team, to get them into a good form before joining the team
- **Rhythm Work** should consist of the following
  - **Foot-work** Patterns
  - **Foot Skills** (Touches)
  - All forms of **Handling**
  - The **Rhythm Work** should be in line with the team session if applicable, for example
    - Crossing/near post-far post patterns – GK's work on **High Balls**
    - **Distribution** – GK's work on **Driven Balls/Throws**
    - Shooting – GK's work on handling **Low/Mid & High Balls**
- The **Rhythm Work** can be drawn from the library of ideas from the previous age groups

Tactical Session with the Team (20 – 30mins)

11v11 Game (20 – 30mins)

GK Coach's Positioning

- For the tactical portions of the sessions, **GKC's** should position themselves behind the goal so that
  - They can observe what is happening on the field from the GK's position
  - The communication between the GK & **GKC** is easier

Training Session 1

Distribution: Directional Possession

Set Up

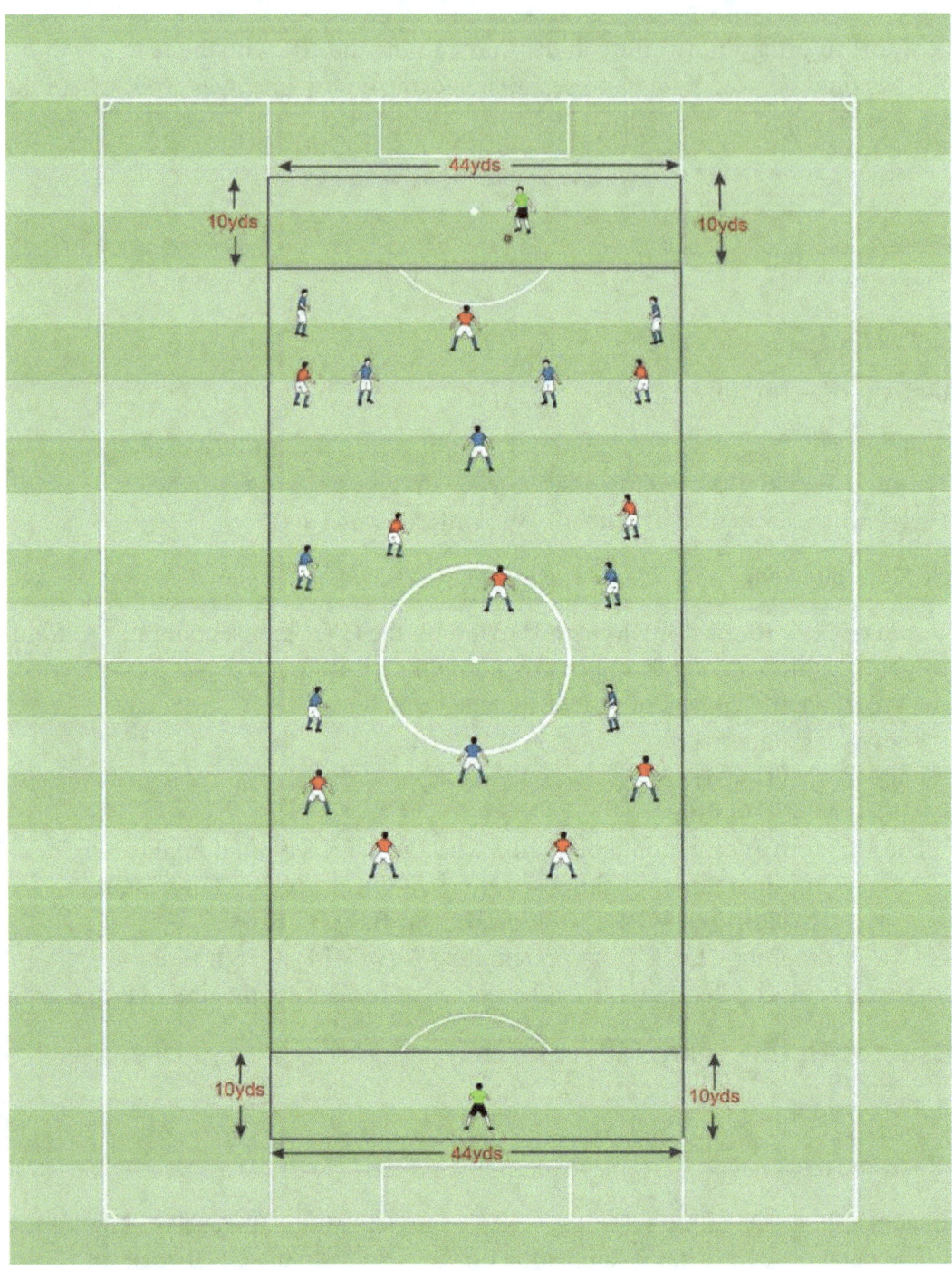

- Use of full field
- 10 v 10 field players + 2 GK's
- Field size (for 10 v10)
    - o Length of the field
        - ■ End lines run from the corners of the 18yd box on one end of the field to the corners of the 18yd box on the other end of the field

- o Width
    - 44yds wide (width of 18yd box)
  - o Mark off midfield line
  - o Mark off with ^'s a line 10yds back from each 18yd line
  - o This activity can be played with lesser #'s – field size would need to be adjusted
- Field players line in accordance with their position on the field
- GK's set up at each end behind opposite 18yd lines
- **Both GK's are always on the side of the group in possession,** so in other words
  - o If Team A has the ball, both GK's are with team A
  - o If Team B has the ball, then both GK's are with Team B
- One team of 10 wears pinnies

Activity 1 (20 – 30mins)

Rules of the game

- The purpose of the game is to
  - o Team A must start by getting the ball to one of the GK's at either end of the field (it doesn't matter which keeper is first to receive the ball because they are both on the side of the team with the ball)
  - o Then Team A must move the ball until it gets to the GK at the opposite end of the field
  - o Then Team A must return the ball to the GK who touched the ball first
  - o When Team A does this, then that Team A gets **1pt**
  - o Play continues until Team A loses the ball by interception or hits the ball out of bounds, Team B then starts play by getting the ball to one of the GK's at either end of the field & play repeats
- Example
  - o Team A gets possession
  - o Team A gets the ball to GK1
  - o GK1 **Distributes** the ball back to Team A
  - o Team A moves the ball down the field to GK2
  - o GK2 **Distributes** the ball back to Team A
  - o Team A gets the ball back to GK1 for a point
  - o Team A maintains possession of the ball until Team B intercepts or gains possession by Team A hitting the ball out of bounds
  - o Once Team B gets the ball, their play begins by getting the ball to one of the GK's at either end of the field & the scoring process is repeated
  - o **It doesn't matter which GK gets the ball first, the ball just has to work its way to the opposite GK and back to the original GK for the point**
- GK's can only use their feet
- GK's cannot cross over the 18yd line onto the field
- Players cannot cross the 18yd line into the GK's area
- GK's can run anywhere side-side behind the 18yd line but can only go to a depth of 10yds back from the 18yd line
- Any ball going beyond 10yds deep is considered out of bounds & the other team gets possession
- The initial ball back to one of the GK's can be a ball of any length (short pass or long pass) and the ball from the GK out to any player can be the same
- Both GK's are outlets for the team in possession of the ball
- The team in possession can pass the ball back to any GK at any time & in any direction to maintain possession of the ball
- Length of possession is not a factor

- Possession of the ball & movement of the ball between GK's is the purpose
- The ball passed to GK1 to start the scoring phase can be of any length (can be from the offensive or defensive half of the field)
- The ball passed to GK2 can be of any length (can be from the offensive or defensive half of the field)
- However, getting the ball back to GK1 to score a point **cannot** be a long pass from the defensive half of the field
- The ball must get into the offensive half of the field (the side in which the 1st GK touched the ball to start the play) & then to the original GK to get the point
    o This keeps the game from getting into just striking long balls
- The coach may use touch restrictions as they see fit

Coaching Points

- GK's must move side to side behind the 18yd line as the ball moves side to side on the field
    o This allows them to be an accessible & constant outlet to maintain possession for the team in possession
- GK's must communicate to the team in possession to let them know they are there as an outlet
- Field players always looking to both GK's as being outlets to maintain possession
- The possession game should involve short & long ball passing
    o Avoid getting into a one-dimensional type of passing game
- This activity, when practiced on a consistent manner, creates trust between field players & GK's
- Builds communication, team work & most importantly, gets the GK's involved in ball possession with the team

Training Session 2

5v5 + GK's Shooting Game

Set Up

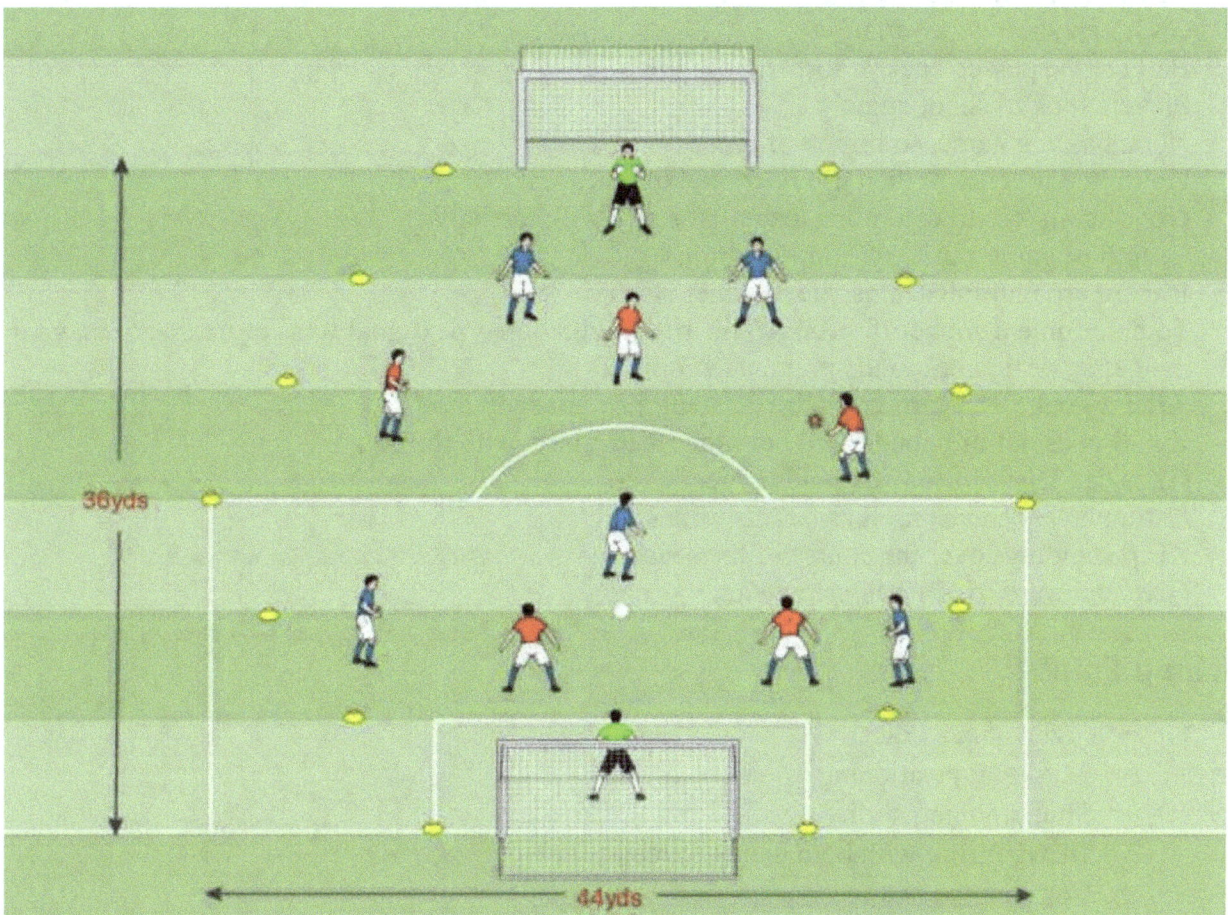

-   Use of regular size goals
-   Length of field = 36yds
-   Width of field = 44yds
-   Use of 18yd box
-   18yd line acts as midfield line
-   Shape of field is a diamond
-   Use ^'s to mark off side lines
-   Place starting ^'s 4yds from each post from both goals
-   Line rest of ^'s every 5yds out to corners of the 18yd box to form diamond-shape field
-   Supply plenty of balls at all 4 goalposts
-   5v5 field players
-   One GK in each goal
-   Each team of 5 players has
    -   3 players in their attacking 3rd
    -   2 players in their defensive 3rd
    -   It is always 3v2 in each team's attacking 3rd

Activity (15 – 20mins)

- This is a shooting game – players can shoot from anywhere on the field
- Players must stay in their half – cannot cross the line
- Any player can shoot
- GK's can shoot as a variation
- Ball can be passed back & forth across the line
- Players look to shoot quickly
- Not a passing game, so limit # of passes
- Unlimited touches & then use restricted touches
- Use of coin toss to determine team that starts with the ball
- Length of game can vary from 1 – 4mins
- If there are multiple teams, play winner stays on
- To determine a winner if there is a tie after regulation – next goal wins or next shot on goal wins the game, or tie goes to the previous winner
- After a goal, play starts from the GK who just got scored on
- If ball goes out of bounds – GK of other team starts with the ball
- GK's can **Distribute** with hands or feet
- Extra players can be used as targets, if desired
- Keep standings over the course of the season
- Give an award to championship team

Coaching Points

- Observe & evaluate GK's
  - o Angles & positioning
  - o Shot-stopping ability
  - o **Distribution** with both hands & feet
  - o Competitive nature
  - o Communication
- Maintain shooting integrity – this is not a passing game
- Shots can be taken from anywhere on the field
- All players look to shoot & to shoot quickly

Training Session 3

6v4 – 7v5 Buildup Activity & Defensive Organization

Set Up for 6v4

- Use of regular goal & half field
- Offense has 6 players (3 Forwards; 3 Midfielders)
- Defense has 4 players (set up in Flat Back 4)
- **6v4**
    - Offense has
        - 3 Midfielders
            - Right Midfielder
            - Center Midfielder (Attacking MF)
            - Left Midfielder
        - 3 Forwards
            - Outside Right Forward
            - Center Forward
            - Outside Left Forward

    - Defense has
        - 4 Backs
            - Outside Left Back
            - Left Center Back
            - Right Center Back
            - Outside Right Back
- Defense sets up at approximately the 30yd line
- Midfielders start at just past midfield line with balls at feet

- Forwards set up a few yards in front of the Defensive line
- GK starts about 10 – 12yds off goal line & in line with the ball being served

Activity (10 – 15mins)

- Right Midfielder starts the activity by raising the head, touching the ball forward & serving a long ball into the 18yd box
- As the Right Midfielder raises the head & touches the ball, GK orders the Backs to **"Drop!"**
- Backs quickly turn & drop towards the 18yd box
- GK makes a decision
    o Whether to catch or collect the ball with the feet/body by yelling: **"Keeper!"**
        ▪ GK either clears the ball on a 1X clearance back towards the Right Midfielder (if possible, otherwise just clears the ball back up field), or collects the ball & strikes a **Driven Ball** back out to the Right Midfielder
        ▪ Offense then attacks **6v4**
    o Or, directs the Backs to clear the ball by yelling: **"Away!"**
        ▪ Backs then clear the ball back to the Right Midfielder (if possible, otherwise just clear the ball back up field)
        ▪ Offense then attacks **6v4**
- Offense attacks in a game-like fashion according to the tactics developed by the head coach
- Defense defends in a game-like fashion according to the tactics developed by the head coach
- GK organizes the Defense with communication
- Play is dead once
    o Offense scores
    o GK collects the ball
    o Defense clears/breaks up the play
    o Ball goes out of bounds
- Once play is over, Offense & Defense set up once again to restart
- Play then restarts this time by the Central Midfielder raising the head, touching the ball forward & serving a long ball into the 18yd box
- After the play is over, the Left Midfielder starts the activity in the same manner

Coaching Points to the GK

- This is obviously a number's down situation for the GK & the Defense
    o Communication, concentration, defensive organization, movement, working as a unit are all high priorities
    o Defense must have an attitude of not allowing shots or goals
- **Long Service Considerations**
    o Reading a long ball, communicating to the Defense to **"Drop!"**, making sure that the Defense's recovery runs are proper & organized
    o GK communicates to the Defense early & loudly
    o Defense's recovery runs should
        ▪ Sideways running, not back pedaling or shuffling
        ▪ Funnel back & inwards to the 18yd box, not straight-line runs
        ▪ Body positioning should be towards the center of the field so Defense can easily see the ball & opposition
    o GK then yells out proper command **"Keeper!"** or **"Away!"** early and loudly

- o If ball is cleared, clearance should be high, far & wide or directly to a target up field if possible
- o As ball is cleared out or if the GK collects the ball & then **Distributes**, GK should yell
  - ▪ **"UP!"** to get the Defense up field & ready to defend the wave of attack & to push forward the offsides line
  - ▪ **"Organize!"** as a command for the Defense to get their shape & be ready for the attack

- **Organizing the Defense against the attack**
  - o Outside Backs are no deeper than the Center Backs
    - ▪ Keeps Offense on-sides
  - o No major gaps between the back 4
    - ▪ Rule of thumb
      - • Minimum distance between Backs – 10yds
      - • Maximum distance between Backs – 15yds
    - ▪ GK communicates these movements
      - • **"Stay Attached!"**
  - o Backs move side-to-side/up & back together as a unit
    - ▪ GK communicates these movements
      - • **"Slide left!"; Slide right!"**
      - • **"Push up!"; "Drop back! Get organized!"**
  - o Weakside Backs have their bodies open to the field & their heads on a swivel
    - ▪ GK communicates this
      - • **Right Back – "Open your body, turn your head!"**
  - o If a Center Back moves forward to stop penetration, rest of the Backs pinch together to cover the vacated space by the advancing Center Back
    - ▪ GK communicates this
      - • **"Pinch!"**
  - o Once the advancing ball is stopped & redirected by the Offense, Backs get reorganized
    - ▪ GK communicates this
      - • **"Organize!"**
  - o If GK collects the ball on a shot, through ball or cross, GK should start a counterattack by **Distributing** the ball to a target

- **GK's positioning**
  - o Once the ball is in the attacking 3rd, GK should be 2 – 3yds off the goal line
  - o As the ball moves from side-to-side, GK mirrors these movements but with lesser steps
    - ▪ GK must not move too much to one side or the other – this could cause GK to be out of position
  - o GK must protect the near post when the ball is on an angle
  - o If the ball breaks through the plane of the Backs, GK should be ready to charge the ball & attempt to possess or clear
    - ▪ GK must communicate this decision & movement ("Keeper!")
  - o If a crossing situation develops, GK should be positioned properly in the goal mouth
    - ▪ If ball is deep in the corner, rule of thumb
      - • 1 step back from the center of the goal line
      - • 1 step off the goal line
      - • Body turned on a 45-degree angle to the field

- If cross is coming in from farther up field
    - GK lines up closer to the front half of the goal being prepared for either a cross or possible shot
- On all crosses, GK must communicate intentions early & loudly ("Keeper!" or "Away!")

Set Up for 7v5

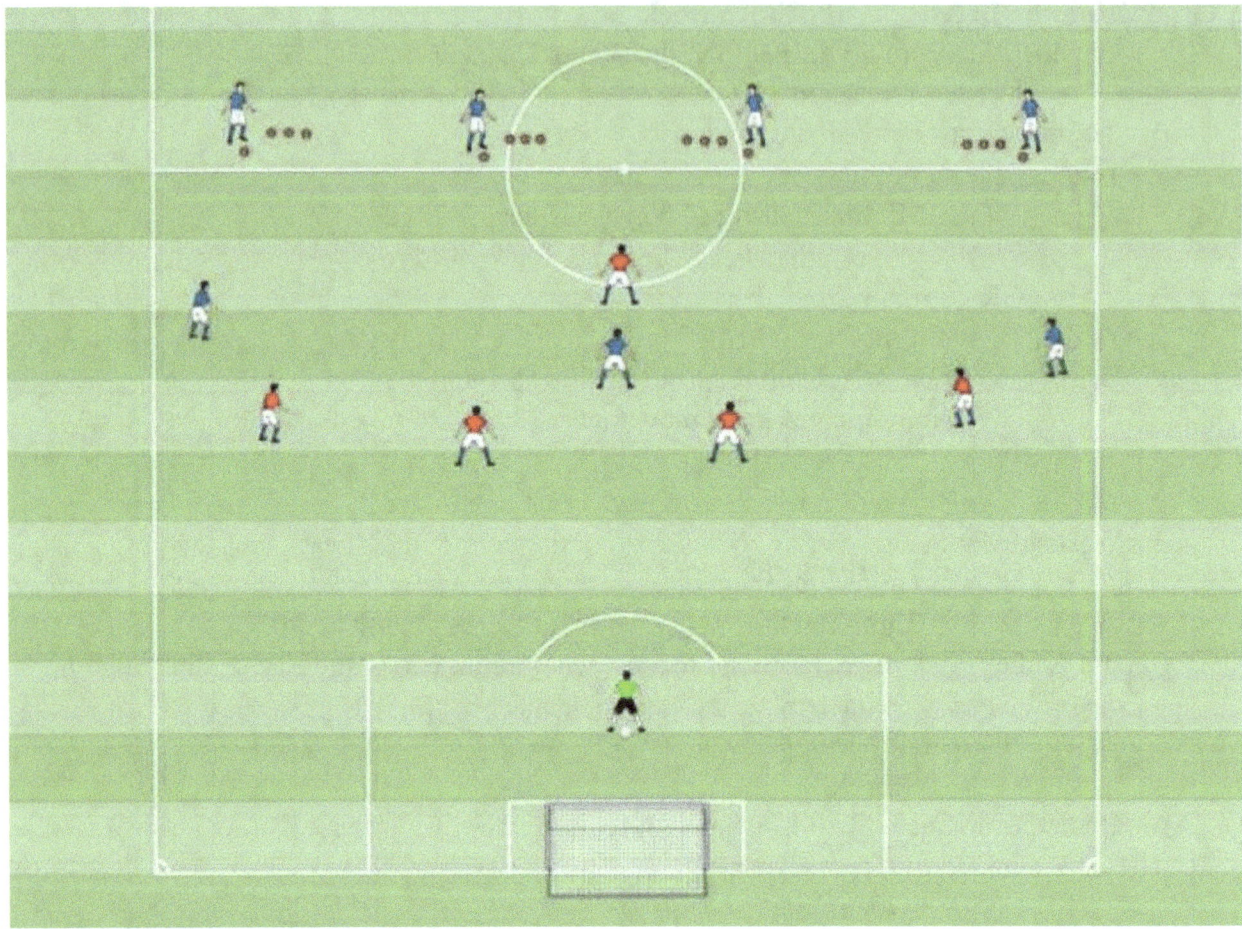

- Use of regular goal & half field
- Offense has 7 players (3 Forwards; 4 Midfielders, or 3 Midfielders & 1 Outside Back)
- Defense has 5 players (set up in Flat Back 4; Defensive Midfielder in front of 2 Center Backs)
- 7v5
    - Offense has
        - 4 Midfielders
            - RMF – Right Midfielder
            - Center Midfielder (Attacking MF)
            - Left Midfielder
            - Possible Outside Back moving forward into the attack
        - 3 forwards
            - Outside Right Forward
            - Center Forward
            - Outside Left Forward
    - Defense has

- 4 Backs
  - Outside Left Back
  - Left Center Back
  - Right Center Back
  - Outside Right Back
- 1 Midfielder
  - Defensive Midfielder
- Back 4 sets up at approximately the 30yd line
- Defensive Midfielder sets up about 10yds – 15yds in front of the back 4
- Midfielders start at just past midfield line with balls at feet
- Forwards set up a few yards in front of the Back 4 line
- GK starts about 10 – 12yds off goal line & in line with the ball being served

Activity (1 – 12mins)

- **Defensive Midfielder**
  - Sets up in front of the 2 Center Backs
  - Responsibility is to predominately protect the space in front of the 2 Center Backs
  - Be mindful of the Attacking Center Midfielder, but also be aware of any other player advancing into the space in front of the 2 Center Backs (in case the Center Midfielder is pull out of that space)
- Right Midfielder starts the activity by raising the head, touching the ball forward & serving a long ball into the 18yd box
- As the Right Midfielder raises the head & touches the ball, GK orders the Back's to **"Drop!"**
- Backs & Defensive Midfielder quickly turn & drop towards the 18yd box
- GK makes a decision
  - Whether to catch or collect the ball with the feet/body by yelling: **"Keeper!"**
    - GK either clears the ball on a 1X clearance back towards the Right Midfielder (if possible, otherwise just clears the ball back up field), or collects the ball & strikes a **Driven Ball** back out to the Right Midfielder
    - Offense then attacks **7v5**
  - Or, directs the Backs to clear the ball by yelling: **"Away!"**
    - Backs then clear the ball back to the Right Midfielder (if possible, otherwise just clear the ball back up field)
    - Offense then attacks **7v5**
- Offense attacks in a game-like fashion according to the tactics developed by the head coach
- Defense defends in a game-like fashion according to the tactics developed by the head coach
- GK organizes the Defense with communication
- Play is dead once
  - Offense scores
  - GK collects the ball
  - Defense clears/breaks up the play
  - Ball goes out of bounds
- Once play is over, Offense & Defense set up once again to restart
- Play then restarts this time by the Center Midfielder raising the head, touching the ball forward & serving a long ball into the 18yd box
- After the play is over, the Left Midfielder starts the activity in the same manner

Coaching Points to the GK

- This is obviously a number's down situation for the GK & the Defense
  - Communication, concentration, defensive organization, movement, working as a unit are all high priorities
  - Defense must have an attitude of not allowing shots or goals
- **Long Service Considerations**
  - Reading a long ball, communicating to the Defense to **"Drop!"**, making sure that the Defense's recovery runs are proper & organized
  - GK communicates to the Defense early & loudly
  - Defense's recovery runs should
    - Sideways running, not back pedaling or shuffling
    - Funnel back & inwards to the 18yd box, not straight-line runs
    - Body positioning should be towards the center of the field so Defense can easily see the ball & opposition
  - GK then yells out proper command **"Keeper!"** or **"Away!"** early and loudly
  - If ball is cleared, clearance should be high, far & wide or directly to a target up field if possible
  - As ball is cleared out or if the GK collects the ball & then **Distributes**, GK should yell
    - **"Up!"** to get the Defense up field & ready to defend the wave of attack & to push forward the offsides line
    - **"Organize!"** as a command for the Defense to get their shape & be ready for the attack
- **Organizing the Defense against the attack**
  - Outside Backs are no deeper than the Center Backs
    - Keeps Offense on-sides
  - No major gaps between the Back 4
    - Rule of thumb
      - Minimum distance between Backs – 10yds
      - Maximum distance between Backs – 15yds
    - GK communicates these movements
      - **"Stay Attached!"**
  - Backs move side-to-side/up & back together as a unit
    - GK communicates these movements
      - **"Slide left!"; "Slide right!"**
      - **"Push up!"; "Drop back! Get organized!"**
  - Weakside Backs have their bodies open to the field & their heads on a swivel
    - GK communicates this
      - Right Back – **"Open your body, turn your head!"**
  - If a Center Back moves forward to stop penetration, rest of the Backs pinch together to cover the vacated space by the advancing Center Back
    - GK communicates this
      - **"Pinch!"**
  - Once the advancing ball is stopped & redirected by the Offense, Backs get reorganized
    - GK communicates this
      - **"Organize!"**

- o If GK collects the ball on a shot, through ball or cross, GK should start a counterattack by **Distributing** the ball to a target
- o GK must read & organize the positioning & movement of the Defensive Midfielder with communication
    - ▪ Defensive Midfielder does not back track in to the back line unless attacker being defended by Defensive Midfielder penetrates to the Back 4
    - ▪ Defensive Midfielder must realize who is a Forward & who is a Midfielder
        - • Defensive Midfielder may have to track a Forward dropping deep into the midfield but should not chase that Forward back into the back line – should release the Forward to the Backs
        - • Defensive Midfielder defends a space & anyone who enters it
            - o Should not chase players out of the Defensive Midfielder's zone
            - o Should pass these roving players off to other Defenders

- **GK's positioning**
    - o Once the ball is in the attacking 3rd, GK should be 2 – 3yds off the goal line
    - o As the ball moves from side-to-side, GK mirrors these movements but with lesser steps
        - ▪ GK must not move too much to one side or the other – this could cause GK to be out of position
    - o GK must protect the near post when the ball is on an angle
    - o If the ball breaks through the plane of the Backs, GK should be ready to charge the ball & attempt to possess or clear
        - ▪ GK must communicate this decision & movement ("Keeper!")
    - o If a crossing situation develops, GK should be positioned properly in the goal mouth
        - ▪ If ball is deep in the corner, rule of thumb
            - • 1 step back from the center of the goal line
            - • 1 step off the goal line
            - • Body turned on a 45-degree angle to the field
        - ▪ If cross is coming in from farther up field
            - • GK lines up closer to the front half of the goal being prepared for either a cross or possible shot
    - o On all crosses, GK must communicate intentions early & loudly ("Keeper!" or "Away!")

Player Evaluation/Assessment Process – Tryouts

It should be understood that the assessment and evaluation of players at tryouts is not always easy and can be quite stressful for all involved. There is quite a variance in the comfort levels of goalkeepers in tryouts; this should be taken into consideration when rating the players. Remember that although this is a position in which character, leadership, and communication must be displayed, many keepers are nervous when it comes to demonstrating their abilities in front of coaches for the first time. The atmosphere at tryouts should be positive, organized, and display professionalism to help create a comfort level for all players. Coaches need to make the process an enjoyable one.

Although technical evaluation can be done in a controlled environment, it is essential to see the players in game situations.

The players should be evaluated in the following

1) Appearance
2) Ability to listen and understand directives
3) Technical ability
4) Tactical sense
5) Communication skills
6) Leadership abilities

The evaluation process should allow ample time so that these qualities can be fully evaluated.

Evaluation Activities

Warm-Up
Dynamic warm-up
Get the heart rate up
Additional stretching

Technical Work
Foot work
Foot skills
Handling
Distribution

Games to Goal
Small-Sided Games (5v5 – 8v8)
Full-Sided Games (11v11)

Additional Considerations

1) In the beginning (after the warm-up), allow the keepers to do some touches with a partner on their own for a few minutes; observe initiative
2) Use full size goals; NOT poles or cones for makeshift goals
3) Encourage communication
4) Combine foot work, foot skills, and handling into Rhythm Work for efficiency of the technical work
5) Use the games to evaluate
   a. Positioning and angles
   b. Organization of the defense
   c. Distribution

6) Encourage the keepers to get out of their comfort zones
7) Let the keepers know it's okay to make mistakes

<u>Activities to Avoid</u> (those that don't transfer to the game)

1) Rapid fire activities

Goalkeeper Code of Conduct

As a Club Goalkeeper I will...

1. Train and play to the best of my ability
2. Display mutual respect for other players, coaches, and parents
3. Win and lose respectfully
4. Always display good sportsmanship
5. Respect officials and accept their decisions
6. Arrive prepared to all matches and training (i.e.: proper mental attitude and equipment; bringing a ball to training)
7. Respect coaches and trainers
8. Attend all training sessions. If I cannot, I will notify the coach/trainer in advance knowing that if I do not, I may not be playing in the next match
9. Be neat and professional in my appearance (i.e.: proper uniforms, boots polished for all matches)
10. Greet coaches with a hand shake and eye contact at the beginning of training/games/events, and do the same when leaving training/games/events
11. Maintaining eye contact when speaking to someone or being spoken to by someone
12. Not participate in any hazing or bullying
13. Keep training areas and game fields neat and clean
14. Use appropriate language at all times
15. Conduct myself properly at any function while representing the Club
16. Be responsible for my school work and work hard to do well in school
17. Refrain from using alcohol, tobacco products, and drugs (unless prescribe by a doctor)
18. Represent the Club both on the pitch and off
19. Give proper notice to the Club if I intend on leaving for a different club

Any actions in violation of the GK Code of Conduct may result in suspension from practice, games, and possible expulsion from Club events.

Player Signature _____

Parent Signature(s) _____

Coach's Signature _____ Date _____

Goalkeeper Coach Code of Conduct

As a coach, I understand that I have the responsibility to follow the Club Code of Conduct. I will...

1. Be a teacher and mentor to all players
2. Maintain a positive attitude
3. Maintain a professional training environment
4. Maintain a professional appearance – uniform clean, shirt tucked in, etc.
5. Come prepared to every training session
6. Keep training sessions organized
7. Maintain a library of training sessions
8. Follow all Club protocols
9. Display sportsmanship
10. Be punctual to all training sessions and matches
11. Always use appropriate language
12. Respect all players, coaches, parents, referees, managers, and club officials
13. Refrain from using drugs (unless prescribed), alcohol, or tobacco at any training session, match, or event
14. Learn and respect the laws of the game
15. Maintain open lines of communication with players, parents (when appropriate), other coaches, and club officials

Any actions in violation of the Coach Code of Conduct may result in suspension from practice, games, and possible expulsion/termination from the Club.

Coach's Signature _____ Date _____

Goalkeeper Parent Code of Conduct

As a parent of the Club Goalkeeper, I will…

1. Be encouraging and supportive with respect to my child's play on the field
2. Respect the officials and accept their decisions at all times
3. Refrain from speaking or showing disrespect to opposing players or goalkeepers
4. Discuss any issues concerning my child with the Goalkeeper Coach of the Club:
    a. At an appropriate time
    b. Not immediately prior to, during, or directly after any match
5. Make sure that my child arrives to all training sessions, matches, or other events at the appropriate times
6. Accept the responsibility for my child to attend all training sessions; if they cannot attend a session, I will notify the Goalkeeper Coach in advance
7. Make sure that my child is properly prepared for all training and matches (equipment, nutrition, and fluids)
8. Refrain from the use of tobacco or alcohol at any training session, match, or event
9. Refrain from shouting comments from the sidelines during any training session, match, or event (unless to show support for my child during a match)
10. Refrain from interfering with any training session
11. Refrain from engaging in any unsportsmanlike conduct with any official, coach, manager, trainer, player, or other parent
12. Maintain open lines of communication with the club Goalkeeper Coach in regard to my child's growth and development in the position, but not to the point of being overbearing
13. Give proper notice to the Club if my Goalkeeper intends on leaving for a different club

Any actions in violation of the Parent Code of Conduct may result in the suspension of my child from practice, games, and possible expulsion from Club events.

Parent Signature(s) _____

Coach's Signature _____ Date _____

Match Analysis

A **Match Analysis** can be an invaluable tool to help goalkeepers learn tactics and to understand the game. This analysis can be done by a coach observing a keeper's performance in a match or by a keeper watching the game either on a device or live.

Technical mastery is imperative; athletic development is one of the cornerstones of the position; mental development can make or break a keeper's success; tactical understanding of the game is the ultimate component that will help keepers reach their potential. This aspect cannot be ignored by the coach or the club.

GK coaches and their goalkeepers should have conversations about tactics pre-game, at the half and post-game.

Following are guidelines to help in a **Match Analysis** of a keeper. A **Match Analysis** should be performed on a regular basis.

Technical

- All aspects of the keeper's technical performance should be noted, including
  - Set position
  - Positioning
  - Shot stopping
  - Dealing with back passes and through balls
  - Distribution
  - Handling
  - Communication

Tactical

- Keepers need to fully understand the coach's tactics so that they can help implement them on the field
- This is a major responsibility of a goalkeeper
- If there are problems during the first half, there should be a quick discussion between the GK and the coach at the half to solve them
  - This helps to prevent reoccurrences during the second half

Additional Tactical Considerations

- **Watching Weak-Side Defense**
  - Many breakdowns in defense occur on the weak-side of the defensive unit
  - These include
    - **Poor body positioning of the Outside Back (OB)**
      - Weakside back ball watching and body not opened up to the field
      - Head needs to be on a swivel
    - **OB's deeper than the deepest Center Back (CB)**
      - OB's should hold their line with the deepest CB
        - If not, this keeps the whole line subject to allowing opponent to stay on sides
        - General rule for OB's

- ▪ stay attached to the CB and be no deeper than any CB
- **Organization of the Back Line**
    - o GK's need to be the organizer of the back line
        - ▪ Move the pieces
        - ▪ Read the game, make a decision, communicate, execute
    - o Watch for large gaps in the back line
        - ▪ Gaps cause attacking possibilities for the opponent
        - ▪ Back line should move left/right together and up/back together

- **Protecting the Hole**

    - o Protect the area in front of the CB's
    - o Generally, a defensive midfielder's (DMF) responsibility
    - o If DMF gets pulled out of position, another player needs to be pulled in to cover the space

- **Transition**

    - o When the ball gets turned over or when the ball is in between possession
        - ▪ immediate organization

- **Corner Kick Organization**

    - o Understand coach's defensive organizational plan
    - o Quick organization of the defense
    - o High concentration situation
    - o Hold defense accountable

- **Setting Walls**

    - o Organize quickly
        - ▪ Determine desired number in the wall
        - ▪ Always best to be able to see the ball
    - o Know whether the restart is a direct/indirect kick
        - ▪ don't get caught off guard
    - o High concentration situation

Additional considerations for keepers

- o There are levels of high concentration, low concentration, but never **no concentration**
- o GK's should always study and analyze the game in front of them
- o GK's need to learn to read the game
- o Anticipate what could break down (anticipate mistakes)
- o Be a leader

Additional considerations for coaches

- o Coach should chart how goals were scored
    - ▪ What broke down (defensive mistake or error on the part of the keeper) and discuss
- o Use of video for review
- o Be constructive during post-game sessions
    - ▪ Don't break keeper's confidence

Paul D. Blodgett, M.Ed

Guidelines for Goalkeeper Positioning on Crosses and Corner Kicks

Proper positioning in goal for a deeper angled cross or corner kick
- Rule of Thumb
    - o Middle of goal or one step back from the middle of the goal
    - o One step off the line
    - o Body angled on a 45-degree angle towards the ball

Proper positioning in goal for cross coming from a higher angle up field
- Rule of Thumb
    - o Favoring the near post (a shot can be taken)
    - o Body opened on a 45-degree angle towards the ball
    - o GK is ready for either a shot or a cross

Decision making on High Balls
- When the cross is struck, GK's need to hold their ground & read the flight of the ball before attacking it
- How to go for the ball depends upon its flight pattern
    - o Inswinger ball (ball curving inward to the goal)
    - o Outswinger ball (ball curving outward away from the goal)
    - o A floater ball with lots of back spin (ball will rise upwards more)
    - o Low hard driven ball with little spin (ball will come into the area low, hard and fast)

Effect of the wind on each of these kicks
- Is the ball coming towards the 6yd box or going outside of it? Stay or go?
- What is the quickness/speed of the GK?
- How tall is the GK?
- What is the GK's range?
- What is the pathway to the ball like? Crowded (punch or get set for a shot) or is there an open lane (go collect the ball)?

Basic Positioning for an Outswinger

Basic Stance for an Inswinger

Photos Courtesy of Matt Broomall and MGTS

Three Zone System Inside the 18 Yard Box

Success In Soccer Magazine (www.successinsoccer.com) was a periodical that was a collaboration between US Youth Soccer and the German Soccer Federation (I believe the periodical may now be defunct). In the May, 2011 Issue 3, there was an article by Gerd Bode (a German association coach) analyzing the goals that were scored in the 2010 Men's World Cup: "World Cup 2010: Giving away the goals". A quick synopsis of the article:

- 80% of the goals scored in the 2010 men's World Cup were scored inside the 18yd box during the run of play
- After analyzing the positioning and the efforts of the goalkeepers, it was determined that many mistakes were committed by these world class keepers, mostly due to improper positioning depending from where the shots were taken
- Gerd Bode's article: "shows that many keepers make fundamental mistakes even at the highest level." (Page #3)
- The article covers positioning and drills to practice that positioning in order to help keepers at younger and older levels understand where to position themselves on shots and plays developing in different areas of the 18yd box

The article breaks down the 18yd box into three different zones: Zone 1; Zone 2; and Zone 3 (see diagram and descriptions that follow). The article describes the positioning for the keeper in each of these three zones and offers drills to help them practice this positioning.

3 Zones Inside the 18yd Box

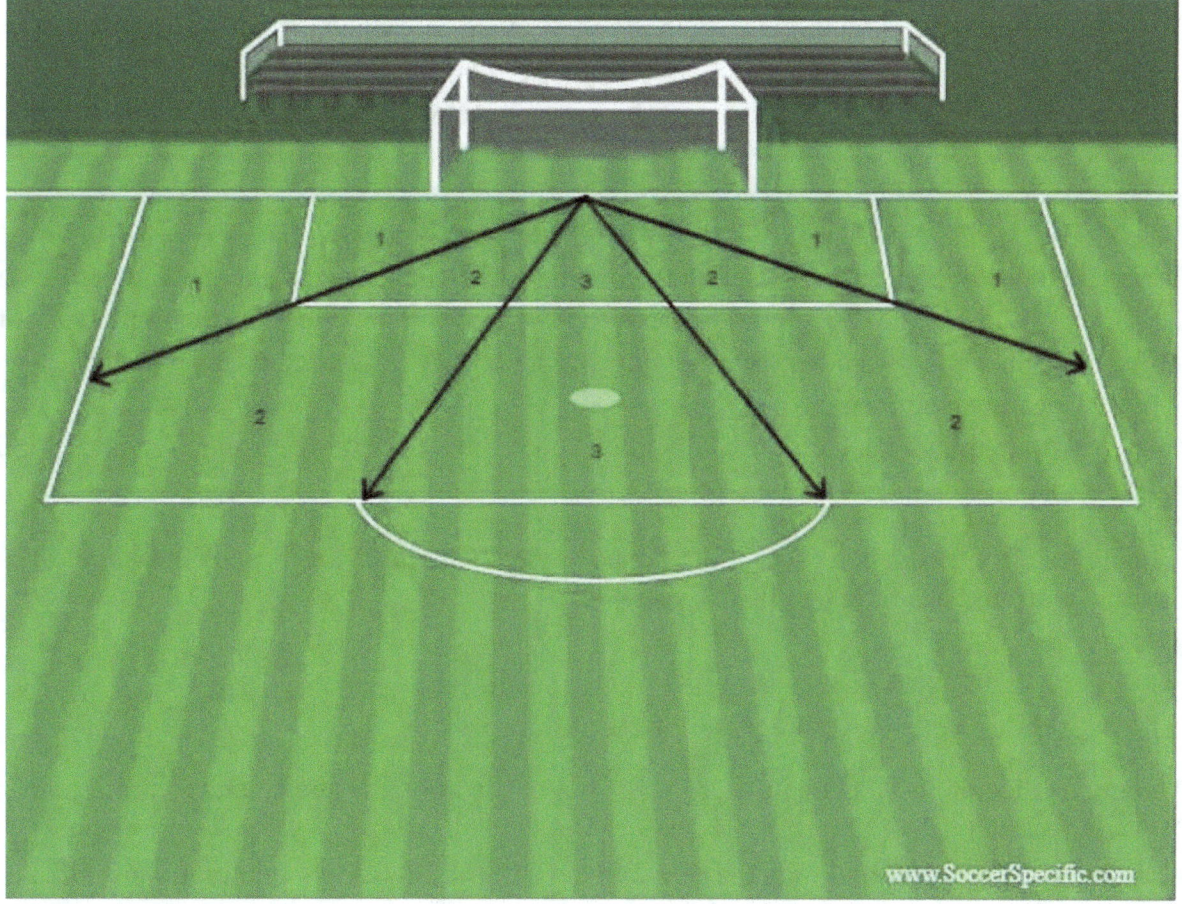

www.SoccerSpecific.com

<u>Zone 1</u>

Zone 1 is the area within the 18yd box that is described as follows:

- A triangle (slice of pie) in which one side begins at the midpoint of the goal line and extends outwards along the bi-line to the 18yd box line; the other demarcation begins at the midpoint of the goal line, once again, and extends outwards through the corner of the goal box (6yd box) to the 18yd box (see accompanied diagram)
- To demonstrate this Zone, cones or a rope may be used; this helps create an easy visual for the goalkeepers

The positioning of the keeper for shots within this Zone should be at the near post.

- 1st situation: Ball (attacker) is along the endline, outside of the 6yd box but within the 18yd box
    - o GK sets up at the near post but in a **Cut Back Stance**
- 2nd situation: Ball (attacker) is along the endline, at or inside the 6yd box
    - o GK squares up to the attacker with the ball at the post
    - o Keeper's heels are placed on the imaginary line from the post extended onto the field
    - o Keepers should not venture out to the ball beyond the near post on either shots or on an advancing attacker who is dribbling the ball directly towards the goal in this situation; rather they should maintain their position at the post; reasons:

- When the GK leaves the post in this situation, it is difficult to recover back into the goal on a rebound or on a cut back pass
- If the GK ventures away from the post, it forces the defense to cover the goal and to try and defend their attacker at the same time

Zone 2

Zone 2 is the area within the 18yd box that is described as follows:

- A triangle (slice of pie) that begins at the midpoint of the goal line and extends outwards through the corner of the goal box (6yd box) towards the 18yd box. The other demarcation begins at the midpoint of the goal line and extends outwards to where the D (arc) connects with the 18yd box line (see accompanied diagram)
- To demonstrate this Zone, cones or a rope may be used; this helps create an easy visual for the goalkeepers

The positioning of keepers for shots within this Zone should be about 2 – 3 steps off their line; the area that needs to be protected is a little less than 4yds wide.

Zone 3

Zone 3 is the area inside of the 18yd box described as follows:

- A triangle (slice of pie) that begin at the midpoint of the goal line and extends to both junctions of the D to the 18yd line
- A use of cones or string outlining the area may be helpful for keepers to initially visualize this Zone

This is the most difficult area for a keeper to cover since the greatest portion of the goal is exposed. The keeper should try and protect a goal of about 5yds across in this situation. Balls struck to the upper or lower corners, especially if they are hit with a bend/speed, are extremely difficult to stop. Keepers should always make the effort to make these saves, but if they work on covering a 5yd goal in this Zone, then they may achieve more success.

Initial positioning for the keeper is as follows:

- For balls being struck anywhere from about the 35yd line to 15 yards from goal, the keeper should start no higher than the 3yd line; any ball struck at goal from within these distances should be more easily handled when starting at this point; if keepers set up on the 6yd line or even farther, balls can fly over their heads
- For balls being struck from as close as 12yds, keepers should set up closer to the 6yd line and get into the **Close Range, Blocking Stance**
- If the keepers are able to do so, depending on the touch of the attacker, they should try and close down the attacker into a 1v1 scenario

Setting Up Walls

Below is a graphic that can be used as a standard reference for goalkeepers when determining how many defensive players should be put into the wall.

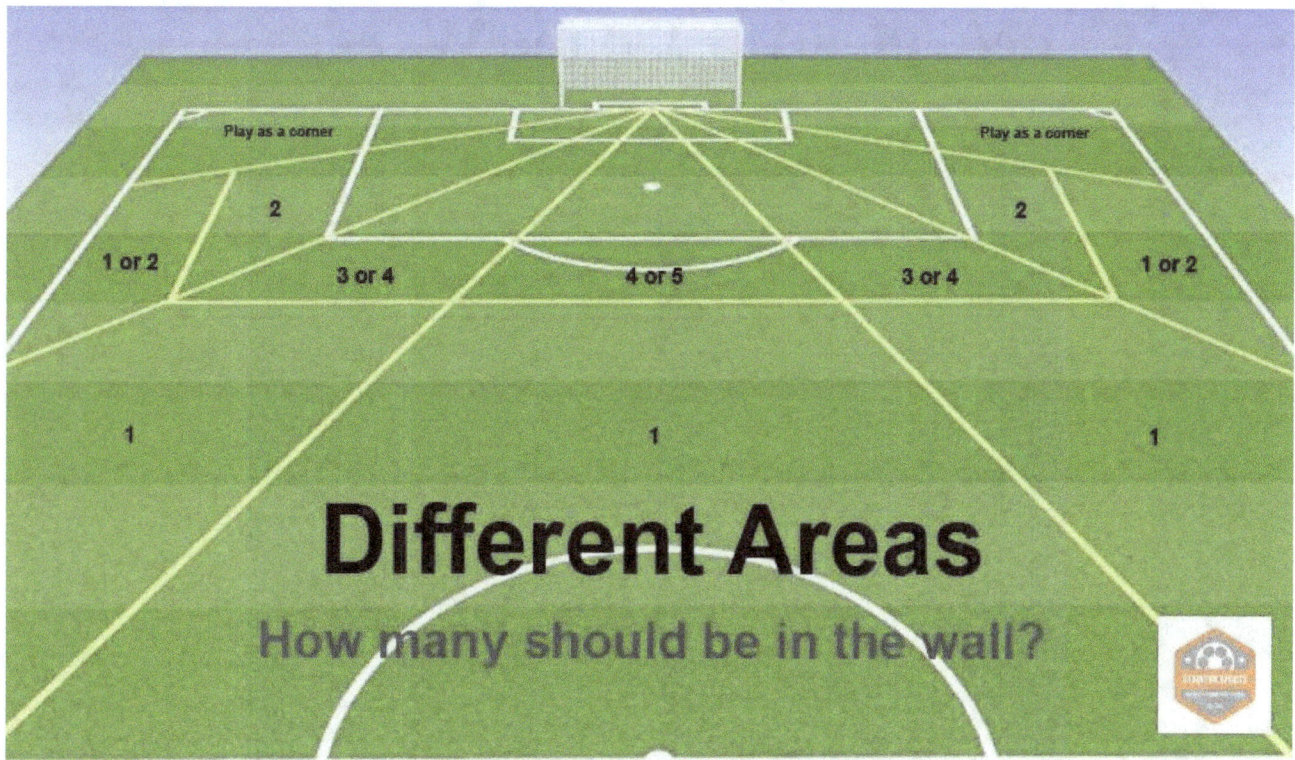

Courtesy of Rick Stainton; Stainton Sports; Head Women's Soccer Coach at UMBC

Organization:

- It is the goalkeeper's responsibility to set up the Wall
- This is a high concentration situation, therefore all must be completely focused
- Quickly determine how many players need to be in the Wall
- The defensive player protecting the post turns to face the GK, who sets up the Wall from the post
- The GK instructs the Wall to move in the direction that will properly cover the post (to the left or to the right)
- Line up the defensive player who is covering the post, so that the he/she straddles the "line" from the post to the ball (to help cover a bending ball around the post)
- The tallest defensive player in the Wall should be the one protecting the post
- As best as possible, the GK needs to see the ball

This situation MUST be practiced often, so that everyone involved understands what to do.

Goalkeeper Shooting Games (Alphabetically)

Beginner 1v1 Goalie Wars

Set up

- Create a 10yd X 5yd grid with a mid-line
  - o Cone 1 – cone 4 outline the field
  - o Cone 5 – cone 8 represent the midline
- Both GK1 & GK2 must stay within their own half
- 1v1 competition
- **GKC (GK Coach)** stands at midfield side-line with multiple balls to keep play moving along if balls are hit astray

Activity

- One GK starts with the ball in hands
- GK with the ball can move anywhere in their half
- GK's score a point if they can **Bowl** the ball across the opposing GK's end line
- Opposing GK tries to keep the ball from crossing their own end line
- The game continues back & forth
- GK retains possession on any ball that goes out of bounds on their side of the field

- **GKC** serves ball into GK's to keep play moving along
- Play two halves, each one minute in length
- After a short break, GK's change halves
- Start of 2nd half, other GK starts with the ball

Coaching Points

- Evaluate all previous techniques in a competitive environment

Beginner 1v1 Goalie Wars with Variations

Set up

- Create a 10yd X 5yd grid with a mid-line
  - o Cone 1 – cone 4 outline the field
  - o Cone 5 – cone 8 represent the midline
- Both GK1 & GK2 must stay within their own half
- 1v1 competition
- **GKC (GK Coach)** stands at midfield side-line with multiple balls to keep play moving along if balls are hit astray

Activity

- One GK starts with the ball in hands
- GK with the ball can move anywhere in their half
- GK's score a point if they can **Bowl** the ball across the opposing GK's end line
- Opposing GK tries to keep the ball from crossing their own end line
- The game continues back & forth
- GK retains possession on any ball that goes out of bounds on their side of the field
- **GKC** serves ball into GK's to keep play moving along
- Play two halves, each one minute in length
- After a short break, GK's change halves
- Start of 2nd half, other GK starts with the ball

Variation
- GK can **Bowl** or **Kick** the ball

Coaching Points

- Evaluate all previous techniques in a competitive environment

Beginner Goalie Wars with Small (Pug) Goals

Set up

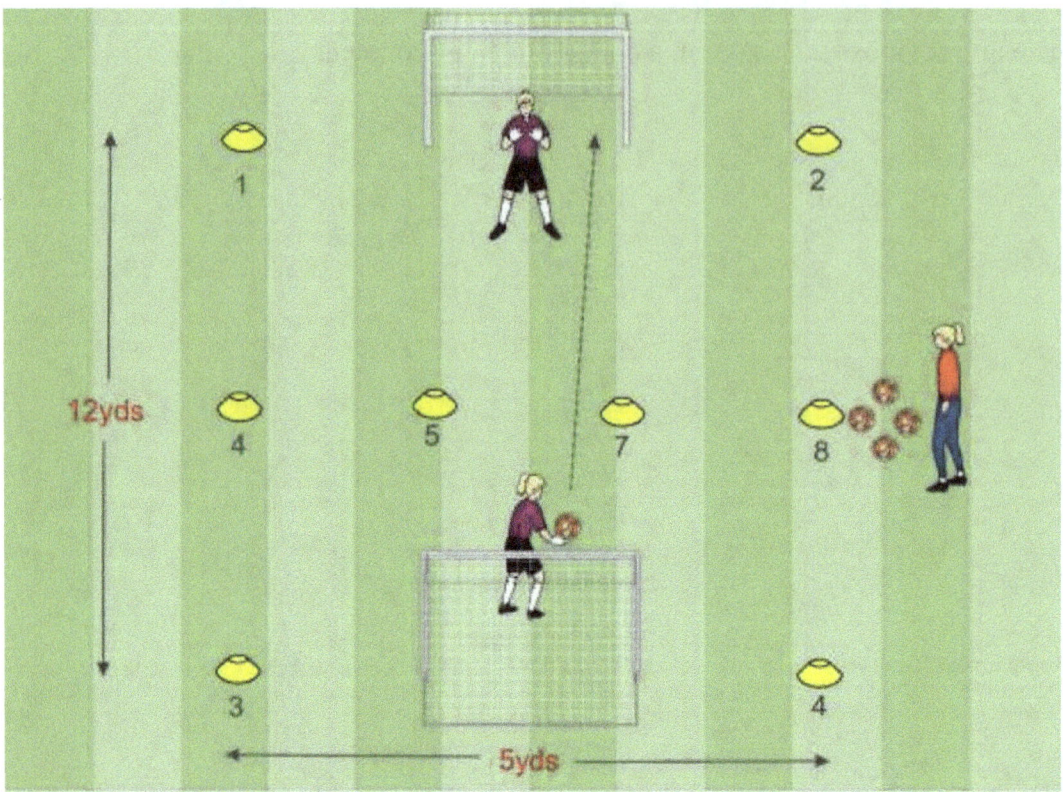

- Create a 12yd X 5yd grid with a midline
    - Cone 1 – Cone 4 outline the field
    - Cone 5 – Cone 8 represent the midline
- Put Pug Goals (or a suitable substitute) at the mid-point of each goal line
- GK's will stand within their own half
- 1v1 competition
- **GKC (GK Coach)** stands at midfield side-line with multiple balls to keep play moving along if balls are hit astray

Activity

- One GK starts with the ball in hands or at feet
- Starter can move anywhere in their half & will score a point if they can **Bowl OR Kick** the ball past the opposing GK, or into the Pug Goal
- Ball needs to be on the ground, not a mid or high ball
- Opposing GK tries to keep the ball from entering pug goal or crossing over their own end line
- Scoring
    - **1pt** for ball going over end line
    - **2pts** for ball going into pug goal
- GK's incorporate any learned **Chest Down/Basket Catch, Front Smother** or **Controlled Collapse**
- The game continues back & forth
- Play two halves, each one minute in length

- After a short break, GK's change halves

Coaching Points

- Evaluate all previous techniques in a competitive environment

Beginner's Hand Ball – Keep Away

Set up

- Divide GK's into two equal groups
- 1 ball (age appropriate size)
- Field size – no restrictions on size

Activity 1 (10 – 15mins)

- Team that wins coin toss starts with the ball
- Team with the ball rolls, tosses, or throws the ball to teammates
- Team tries to maintain possession (play keep-a-way)
- It doesn't matter if the ball touches the ground
- Possession goes to the team who picks up the ball

Coaching Points

- Decision making in a game situation
- Evaluate all previous techniques in a competitive environment
- Communication by GK's

Bull in the Channel with GK Start – Live Activity

Set-Up

Diagram 1

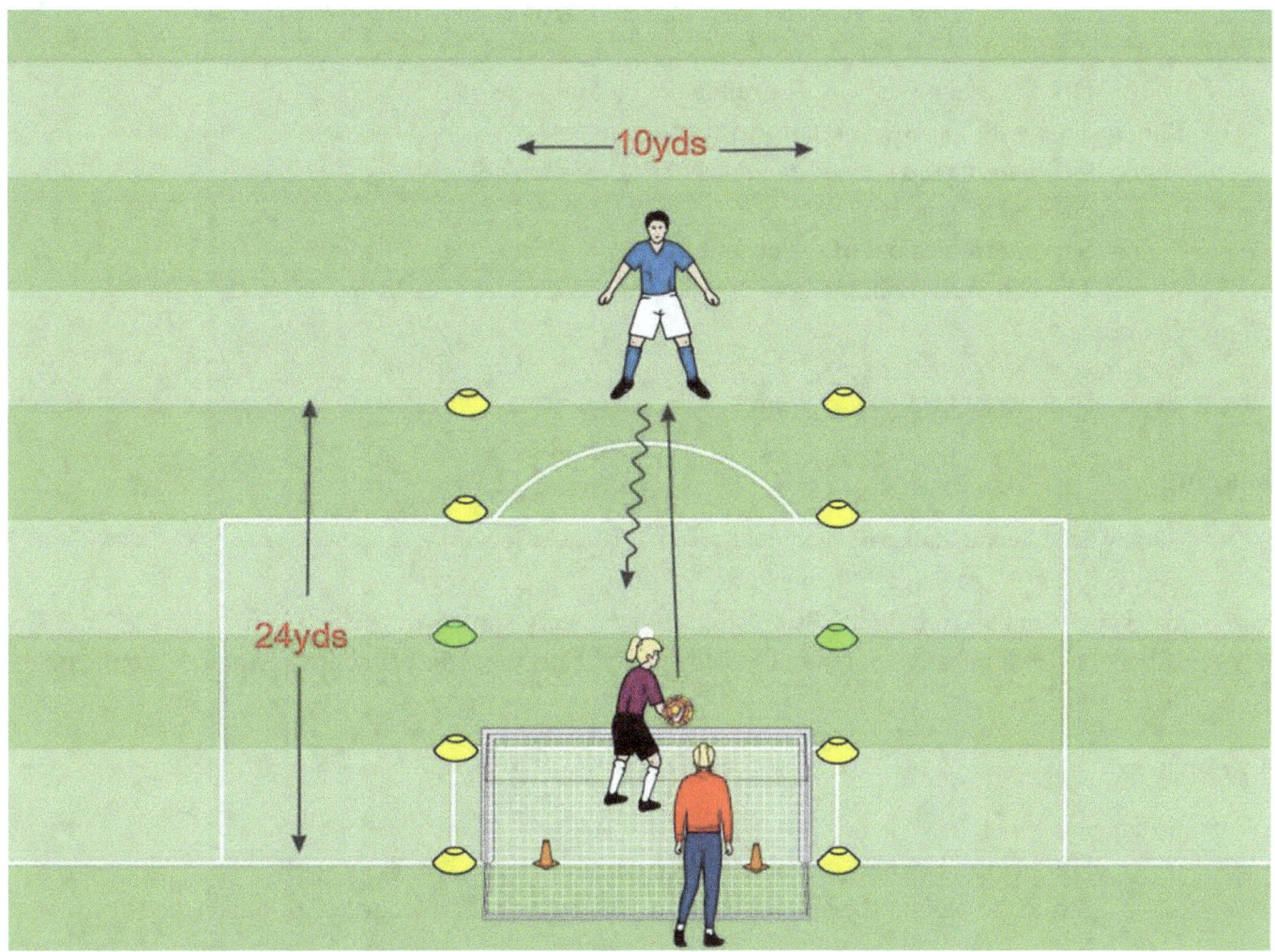

- Use of the 18yd box area with a goal
- Channel is set-up in front of the goal – 10yds wide X 24yds long
- Place cones to mark the channel (place cones every 6yds) starting at the goal line & extending to the top of the D (arc – 24yds from the goal line); green cones represent the 12yd line
- Place 2 midsized cones side by side on the goal line, inside the goal posts (each cone is placed on the goal line 2yds in from each post – making 2 small targets for Server to be used in a variation)
- Server starts at the top of the D
- GK starts 2 – 3 yds off the line with the ball
- **GKC (GK Coach)** sets up behind the goal

Activity 1 (10 – 15mins)

- GK starts with the ball
- GK **Distributes** the ball (either with feet or hands) out to Server using proper communication ("Yes & Server's name!")

196

- Server must stay at cone 1 until the ball gets there
- As ball is **Distributed** out, GK follows the **Distribution** to close down the distance to Server
- Server collects the ball & attacks the goal by dribbling the ball
- GK confronts Server & attempts to
    o Steal the ball
    o Force Server to dribble or, strike the ball out of bounds (out of the channel)
- Server attempts to
    o Dribble around the GK & dribble the ball into the goal
- Play restarts with the GK **Distributing** the ball if
    o GK disrupts the play & ball goes out of the channel
    o GK collects the ball
    o Server dribbles out of the channel
    o The ball ends up in the goal
- GK repeats 6X
- GK's switch & repeat activity
- Keep score if you desire a competition

Scoring

- Server dribbles the ball past the penalty spot: **1pt for Server**
- Server dribbles the ball all the way into the goal: **1pt for Server**
- GK keeps the ball from being dribbled past the penalty spot: **1pt for GK**
- If ball gets past penalty spot but GK recovers & keeps the ball from being dribbled into the goal: **1pt for GK**

Variations

- Server can either
    o Dribble the ball past the penalty spot
    o Strike the ball on the ground into 1 of the 2 targets at the corners of the goal: **1pt for Server**
    o Take a shot directly after collecting the **Distribution** from GK (2 touches)
    o Live play – Server can attack/shoot at anytime

Coaching Points

- Decision making & proper execution of techniques on the part of the GK in live situations
    o Distance/close range shooting
    o 60:40 situation
    o 50:50 situation
    o 40:60 situation

Paul D. Blodgett, M.Ed

Bull in the Channel Variation – Live Activity

Set-Up

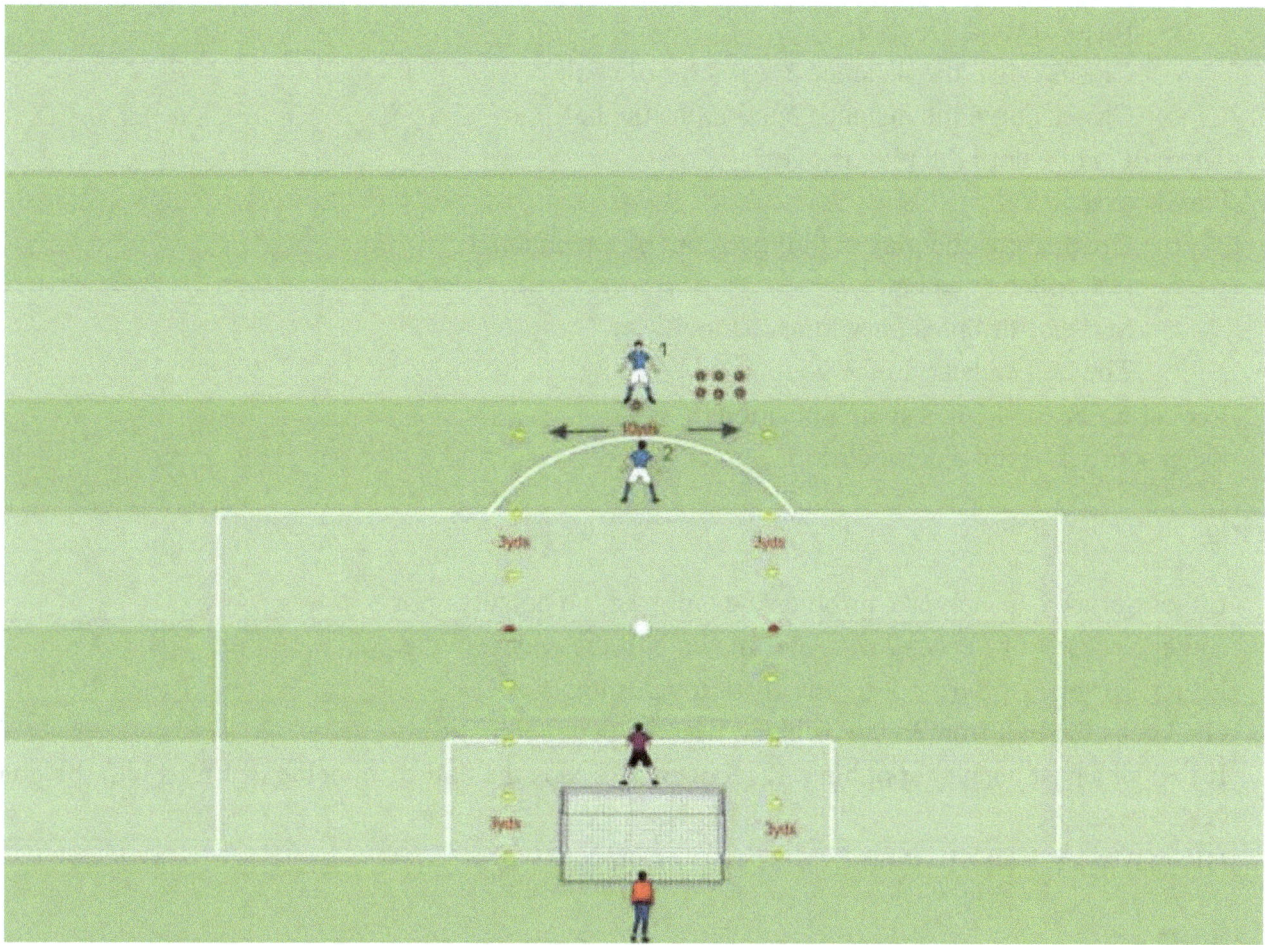

- Use of the 18yd box area with a regular size goal
- Channel is set-up in front of the goal – 10 yds wide X 24yds long
- Place cones to mark the channel (place cones every 3yds); start at goal line & extend to the top of the D (arc – 24yds from the goal line)
- Cones at the top of the D (arc) are the starting cones for Server 1
- Server 1 starts at the top of the D with a ball at feet
- Server 2 starts 1yd in front of Server 1, facing the goal with feet spread apart
- GK starts 2 – 3 yds off the line
- **GKC (GK Coach)** sets up behind the goal

Activity 1 (10 – 15mins)

- Server 1 starts with the ball
- Server 1 has 2 options to start the activity
  - Pass the ball through the legs of Server 2 at varying distances
    - Server 2 chases the ball then either
      - Strikes it on target with the 1ˢᵗ touch
      - Tries to dribble around the GK & dribble into the goal

- o Server 1 touches the ball around Server 2 then either
    - Strikes it on target with the 1st touch
    - Tries to dribble around the GK & dribble into the goal
- GK makes a decision
    - o Readies for a 1X shot
    - o Closes down the distance & goes for the ball
    - o Closes down the distance & contains the ball
- The ball is live until the play is over
- Play is over if
    - o GK disrupts the play & ball goes out of the channel
    - o GK collects the ball
    - o Server 1 dribbles out of the channel
    - o The ball ends up in the goal
- Repeat 6X & then GK's switch positions
- Keep score if desire a competition

Scoring

- Either Server 1 or Server 2 dribbles the ball past the penalty spot: **Server +1pt**
- Either Server 1 or Server 2 **dribbles** the ball all the way into the goal: **Server +1pt**
- Either Server 1 or Server 2 scores on 1st touch shot: **Server +1pt**
- GK keeps the ball from being dribbled past the penalty spot: **GK +1pt**
- If ball gets past penalty spot but GK recovers & keeps the ball from being dribbled into the goal: **GK +1pt**
- GK makes save on any shot: **GK +1pt**

Variations

- Servers can only dribble the ball into the goal
- Servers must shoot on 1st touch
- Servers can shoot on the 2nd touch
- Live play – Servers can attack/shoot at any time
- Add players to both attack & defense

Coaching Points

- Decision making & proper execution of techniques on the part of the GK in live situations
    - o 60:40 situation (**Controlled Collapsing Save**)
    - o 50:50 situation (**Controlled Collapsing Save/Cobra Technique**)
    - o 40:60 situation (**Containment Stance**)
- GK is patient & waits for attacking player to make the 1st move
- GK reads the length of the attacker's touches when making decision to go for the ball
- GK is ready for a shot at any time
- If there's a loose ball after a save, GK has the mentality of getting up & either resetting or pursuing

Crossing/Shooting Games

1. 3 Zone Crossing/Goalie War Game

Set Up

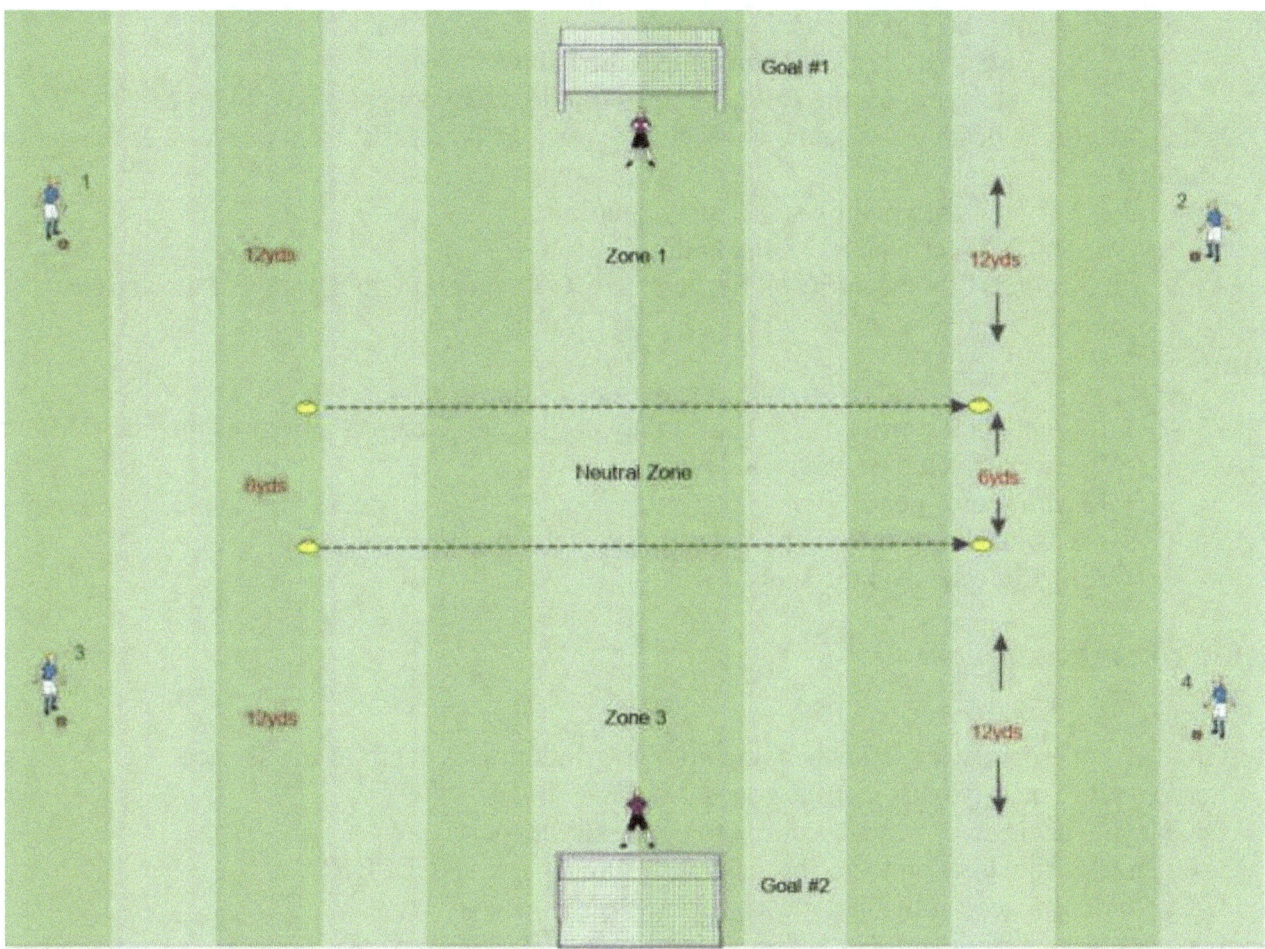

- Place Goal 1 & Goal 2 facing opposite of one another 30yds apart
- With cones, mark off 3 zones
  - Zone 1 is 12yds out from Goal 1
  - Neutral zone is marked off 6yds from Zone 1
  - Zone 3 is 12yds from Goal 2
- GK1 & GK2 set up in each goal
- Place Server 1, Server 2, Server 3 & Server 4 in each corner with balls

Variation

- Adjust positioning of Servers due to the number of Servers available

Activity

- GK's set up & get ready for a cross (**Driven Ball**) from Server 1
- Server 1 can serve the ball into any of the 3 zones

- o If ball is served into Zone 1
  - GK1 collects the ball yelling "**Keeper!**"
  - GK2 must yell "**AWAY!**"
  - GK1 then gets to throw or kick the ball at GK2 to try & score
- o If the ball is served into Zone 2
  - GK2 collects the ball yelling "**Keeper!**"
  - GK1 must yell "**AWAY!**"
  - GK2 then gets to throw or kick the ball at GK1 to try & score
- o If the ball is served into the Neutral Zone
  - Either GK1 or GK2 can collect the ball
  - Whoever gets the ball can then shoot to the opponent's goal to score
- When the play is dead, GK's set up to receive a cross (**Driven Ball**) from Server 2 & the game continues
- Server 3 & Server 4 then hit crosses, & play continues
- Servers can score directly on a crossed ball
- After 2 or 3 rounds of services by all Servers, new GK's get into goal & repeat the activity

Scoring

- GK's collect the cross: **+1pt** (but if they don't yell "**Keeper!**", point is disqualified)
- Server scores on the cross, GK loses Pt: **-1pt**
- GK who scores goal: **+1pt**
- If GK who shoots misses the target completely, that GK gets: **-1pt**
- GK makes a save on the shot: **+1pt**

Coaching Points

- GK's set up properly in goal depending upon the direction & depth of the service
- Servers serve quality balls into the zones
- GK's make decision on whether or not to go for the cross
- If GK makes the decision to go for the ball, GK must yell "**KEEPER!**"
- GK who doesn't go for the ball must yell "**AWAY!**"
- GK uses proper **High Ball Collecting Technique**
- GK gets into good **Set Position** for the shot
- GK's use good technique whether **Distributing** the ball or making a save
- **Distribution** is on point & proper communication is used

2. Crossing/Shooting Game

Set Up

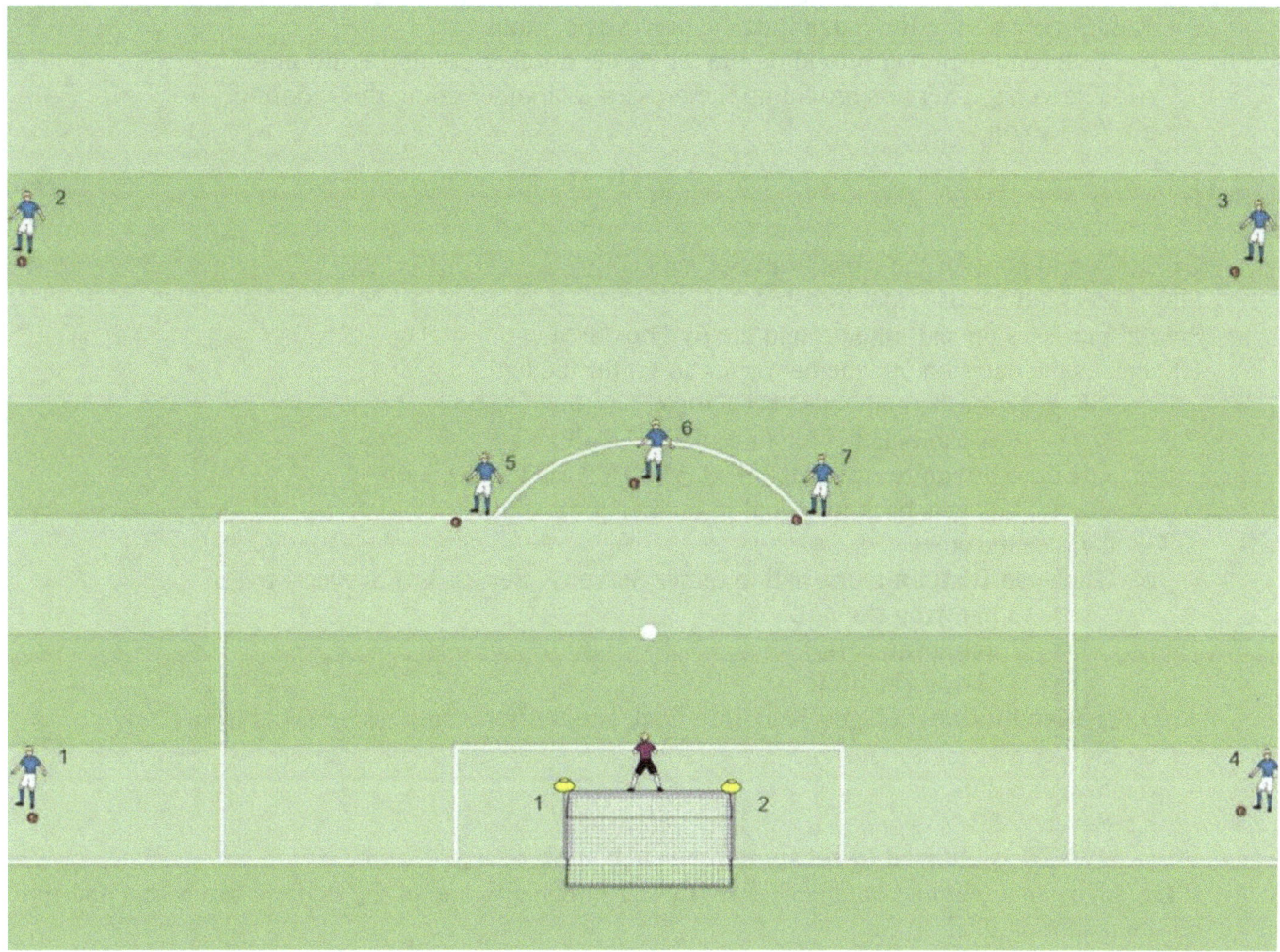

- Use of regular size goal & the defensive third of the field
- Place cone 1 at post & 3yds off goal line
- Place cone 2 at other post & 3yds off goal line
- Server 1 placed deep into the corner left of the goal with balls
- Server 2 is placed 25 – 30yds up the field on the same side as Server1 & near the touch line with balls
- Server 3 is placed on the opposite side of the field from Server 2, 25 – 30yds up the field & near the touch line with balls
- Server 4 is placed deep in the corner right of the goal with balls
- Server 5 is placed at the junction of the D (the arc) & the 18yd line with balls
- Server 6 is placed in the center of the D just outside of the 18yd line with balls
- Server 7 is placed opposite of Server 5 at the junction of the D & the 18yd line with balls
- GK sets up in the center of the goal

Variation

- Artificial dummies or additional players can be added into the 6yd box area for obstruction to the GK
- If GK & Server #'s are limited, adjust the serving positions to
    o 2 servers: 1 Server providing the crosses & another doing the shooting
    o 3 servers: 2 Servers providing the crosses & another doing the shooting
    o And so on…

Activity

- GK sets up in goal for the cross from Server 1
- Play starts with a cross from Server 1
- Server 1 crosses the ball into/around the 6yd box area
- GK makes the decision on whether or not to go for the ball
    o GK goes for the ball yells "**KEEPER!**" on the decision
        ▪ GK can either catch or punch the ball away
    o GK does not go for the ball yells "**AWAY!**" on the decision
        ▪ GK gets back into goal & readies for a shot
- If GK handles the cross
    o Then can **Distribute** the ball to either Server 2, Server 3 or Server 4 by
        ▪ **Throwing the ball**
        ▪ **Lacing the ball**
        ▪ **Driving the ball**
- After the **Distribution**, GK gets back into goal, gets set for 3 successive shots from
    o Server 5 1st
    o Server 6 2nd
    o Server 7 3rd
    o *****GK is allowed to get set before each shot*****
- If GK gives up a rebound on the 3rd shot (ONLY), then any one of the Servers can take a one-time rebound shot on goal
- If GK cannot handle the cross and yells "**AWAY!**", or if the GK **Punches** the ball away
    o GK gets back into goal, gets set for 3 successive shots from
        ▪ Server 5 1st
        ▪ Server 6 2nd
        ▪ Server 7 3rd
    o *****GK is allowed to get set before each shot*****
- If GK gives up a rebound on the 3rd shot (ONLY), then any one of the Servers can take a one-time rebound shot on goal
- Activity is repeated starting with crosses from Server 2, then Server 3 & Server 4 (all Servers take their turn on serving in a cross, regardless of which Server starts, so there are always 4 successive crosses)
- After 1 round, the next GK steps into goal & repeats whole activity

Scoring

- GK collects the cross: +1pt (Pt does not count if GK forgets to yell "**KEEPER!**")
- GK **Punches** the ball away: +1pt (Pt does not count if GK forgets to yell "**KEEPER!**")
- GK makes save but is not clean: +1pt
- GK makes a clean save (sticks the ball): +2pts
- GK hits target on **Distribution**: +1pt

- If Server 1 can drive the ball between the post & cone 1 (& it stays lower than crossbar height) before GK gets to the ball, GK loses Pt: **-1pt**
- If Server 4 can drive the ball between the post & cone 2 (& it stays lower than crossbar height) before GK gets to the ball, GK loses Pt: **-1pt**
- Server 5, Server 6 or Server 7 scores a goal (or whoever scores any rebound shot), GK loses Pt: **-1pt**
- GK who earns most points is exempt from an additional activity (i.e. sit-ups, push-up, etc.)

Coaching Points

- GK's set up properly in goal depending upon the direction & depth of the service
- Servers serve good balls into the zones
- GK's make decision on whether or not to go for the cross
- If GK makes the decision to go for the ball, GK must yell "**KEEPER!**"
- GK doesn't go for the ball, must yell "**AWAY!**"
- GK uses proper **High Ball Collecting Technique**
- GK gets into good **Set Position** for the shot
- GK's use good technique whether **Distributing** the ball or making a save
- **Distribution** is on point and proper communication is used

3. 3 Goal Crossing/Shooting Game

Set Up

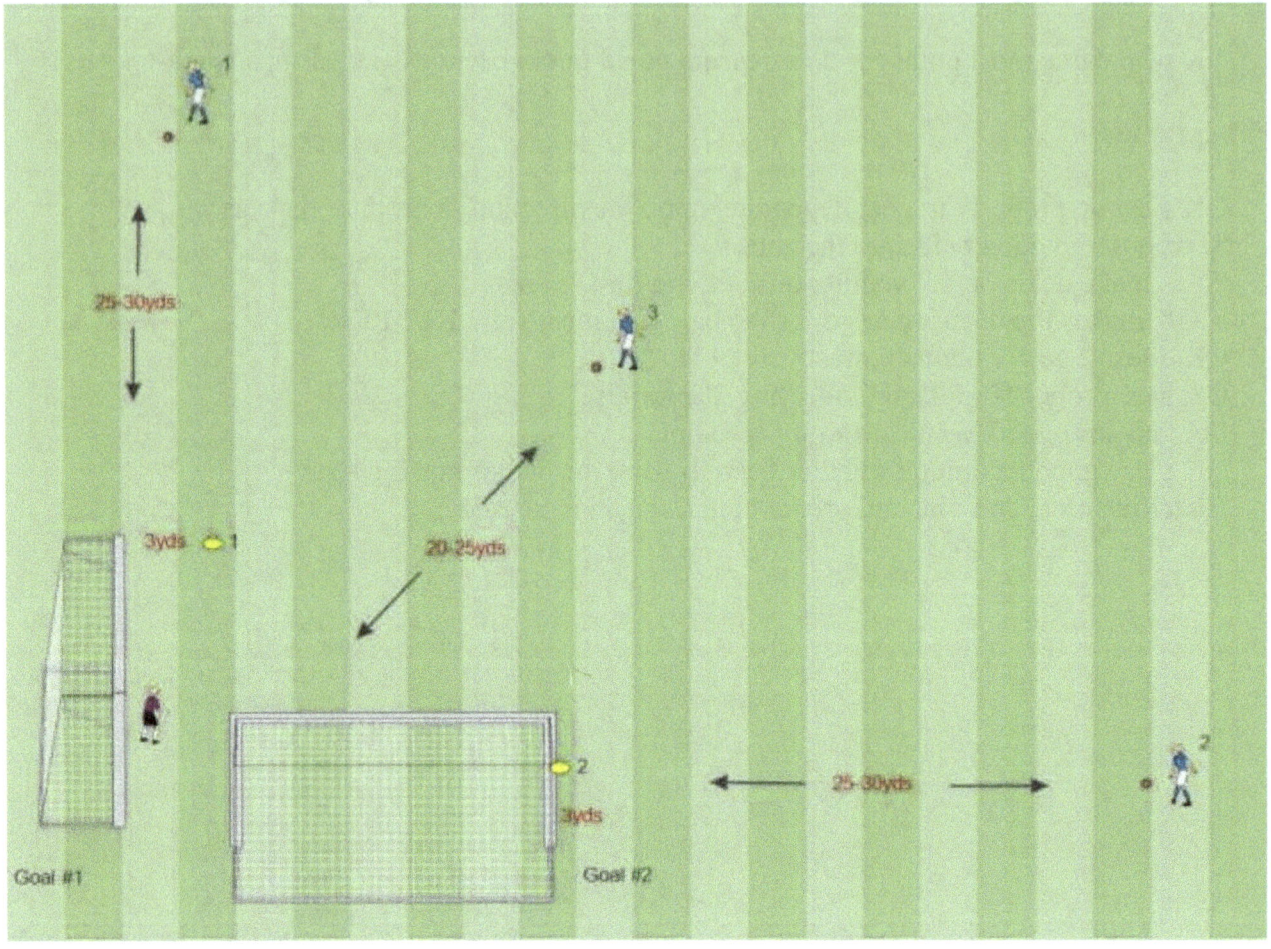

- Set up 2 full sized goals at a right angle to each other (post to post)
- Place cone 1 3yds in from the near post (towards Server 1)
- Place cone 2, 3yds in from the near post (towards Server 2)
- The 2 big goals are G1 & G2
- The cones & the post make up G3 depending upon which Server is serving the ball into the area
    - When Server 1 is serving
        - G1 is the nearer big goal
        - G2 is the farther big goal
        - G3 is the distance between the post & cone 1
    - When Server 2 is serving
        - G1 is the nearer big goal
        - G2 is the farther big goal
        - G3 is the distance between the post & cone 2
- Server 1 sets up with balls 15 – 20yds from the post of G1
- Server 2 sets up with balls 12 – 15yds from the post of G2
- Server 3 sets up with balls 15 – 20yds out from the junction of the two far posts of G1 & G2

Activity (10 – 15mins)

- GK sets up for a cross from Server 1
- Server 1 crosses the ball towards either G1, G2 or G3
    - Server 1 can **Drive**, **Punt** or **Throw** the ball in
- GK attempts to **Collect or Punch** away the crossed ball by making a decision to go or to stay
    - If GK goes, yells "KEEPER!" & **Catches** or **Punches** the ball
    - If GK stays, yells "AWAY!" & gets back into **Modern Set Position** for a shot
- If the GK collects the ball
    - GK **Distributes** the ball back to Server 1 by **Overhand Throwing, Lacing or Driving** the ball using proper communication ("Yes & Server 1's name!")
    - GK then looks out to Server 3 who points to either G1 or G2
    - GK must hurry into the **Modern Set Position** into that particular goal for a shot from Server 3
    - GK attempts to stop the shot
- If GK yells "AWAY!":
    - GK then looks out to Server 3 who points to either G1 or G2
    - GK must hurry into the **Modern Set Position** into that particular goal for a shot from Server 3
    - GK attempts to stop the shot
    - If GK makes a clean save, GK **Distributes** the ball back to Server 3 using proper communication ("Yes & Server 3's name!")
- GK then sets up for a cross from Server 2
- Server 2 crosses the ball towards either G1, G2 or G3
- GK attempts to **Collect or Punch** away the crossed ball by making a decision to go or to stay
    - If GK goes, yells "KEEPER!" & **Catches or Punches** the ball
    - If GK stays, yells "AWAY!" & gets back into **Modern Set Position** for a shot
- If the GK collects the ball
    - GK **Distributes** the ball back to Server 2 by **Overhand Throwing, Lacing or Driving** the ball using proper communication (Yes & Server 2's name!")
    - GK then looks out to Server 3 who points to either G1 or G2
    - GK must hurry into the **Modern Set Position** into that particular goal for a shot from Server 3
    - GK attempts to stop the shot
- If GK yells "AWAY!"
    - GK then looks out to Server 3 who points to either G1 or G2
    - GK must hurry into the **Modern Set Position** into that particular goal for a shot from Server 3
    - GK attempts to stop the shot
    - If GK makes a clean save, GK **Distributes** the ball back to Server 3 using proper communication ("Yes & Server 3's name!")
- GK then resets for a cross from Server 1 & the activity is repeated to both sides
- Repeat 3X – 4X to each side & rotate GK's

Variations

- Rebound on shots can be live
- Can have additional shooter alongside Server 3

Scoring Variations

- GK collects the cross: **+1pt for GK** (Point does not count if GK forgets to yell "KEEPER!")
- GK punches the ball away: **+1pt for GK** (Point does not count if GK forgets to yell "KEEPER!")
- Server 1 or Server 2 drive ball directly into either G1 or G2: **-1pt for GK**
- GK keeps the ball from going through G3: **+1pt for GK**
- GK can't keep ball from going through G3: **-1pt for GK**
- GK makes save but is not clean: **+1pt for GK**
- GK makes a clean save (sticks the ball): **+2pts for GK**
- GK hits target on **Distribution**: **+1pt for GK**
- Server 3 scores a goal: **-1pt for GK**

Coaching Points

- GK's set up properly in goal depending upon the direction & depth of the service
- Server's serve good balls into the zones
- GK's make decision on whether or not to go for the cross
- GK's use proper **High Ball Catching Technique**
- GK's yell "Keeper!" when they make the decision to go for the ball
- GK's yell "Away!" when they make the decision not to go for the ball
- Correct leg goes up on the catch
- GK makes good decision on whether to **Catch or Punch** the ball
- GK gets into good **Modern Set Position** for the shot
- **Distribution** is on point & proper communication is used

4. Crossing/Shooting Activity

Set Up

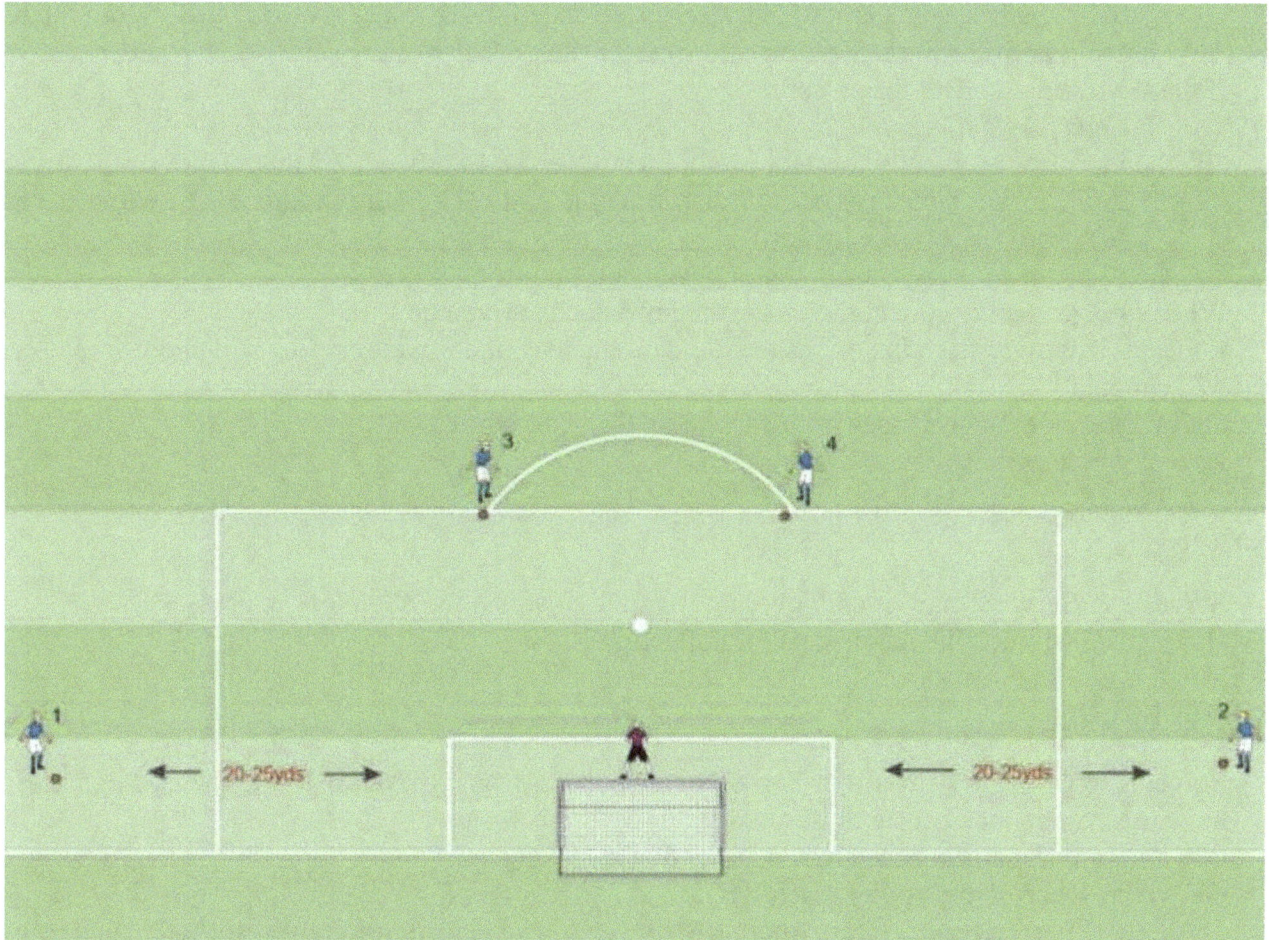

- Use of regular size goal
- Use of 18yd box area
- Server 1 & Server 2 set up 20 – 25yds from the post along the end line with balls
- Server 3 & Server 4 set up at the junction of the "D" & the 18yd line with balls
- GK sets up in goal

Activity

- Server 1 will be 1st to serve a cross
- GK sets up in goal to receive a cross from Server 1
- Guideline for GK's positioning on the cross:
    o Start at middle of the goal
    o Take 1 step backwards
    o Take 1 step off the line
    o Adjust body so that it is on a 45-degree angle facing the field
- Server 1 serve a cross into the 6yd box; GK goes for the ball
- **If the GK can collect the cross:**
    o Yells "Keeper!" early and collects the ball
    o Jumps up bringing the right knee upwards

- o Distributes the ball back to Server 1 with a throw or kick & uses proper communication ("Yes & Server 1's name!")
- GK then turns for a touch/shot from S4 & then a 2nd touch/shot from Server 3 **(touch/shot means S touches the ball 1st & then shoots, so is hitting a rolling ball; not a still ball)**
  - o If GK makes a clean save, will distribute the ball back to the shooter by **Bowling** the ball & using proper communication
- If the GK cannot collect the cross:
  - o Yells "Away!" early
- GK then turns & gets ready for a touch/shot from Server 4 & then a 2nd touch/shot from Server 3
  - o If GK makes a clean save, will distribute the ball back to the shooter by **Bowling** the ball & using proper communication
- GK then sets up for a cross from the opposite end line from Server 2
- When GK goes up to collect the cross, the left knee is driven up
- Repeat the activity from the opposite side with the exception that Server 3 will shoot 1st & Server 4 will shoot 2nd
- GK will receive 3 – 4 crosses from each side, then GK's rotate
- Repeat whole activity

Variations

- Server 1 & Server 2 can set up higher up the field to adjust the angle of the crosses
- Have the GK punch the ball instead of collecting it

Coaching Points

- Server's serve quality crosses; if Server's cannot hit a proper driven ball into the 6yd box area, have them volley the ball in or throw it in
- GK's set up properly for the crossing situation
- GK yells "Keeper" or "Away" early!
  - o **Yelling "Keep!" is improper; the power of the command comes in the 2nd syllable**
- GK executes high ball catch with proper technique:
  - o Feet are chopping while ball is in the air to prepare for take off
  - o GK drives correct knee upwards:
    - ▪ Right knee goes up on crosses from the left
    - ▪ Left knee goes up on crosses from the right
  - o GK catches the ball on the way up, not on the way down
  - o GK catches the ball in front of the face, not above or behind the head
  - o GK lands on both feet
- All **Distributions** are executed properly using proper communication
- GK quickly prepares for shots
- GK makes attempt to make the save

Distribution: Directional Possession

Set Up

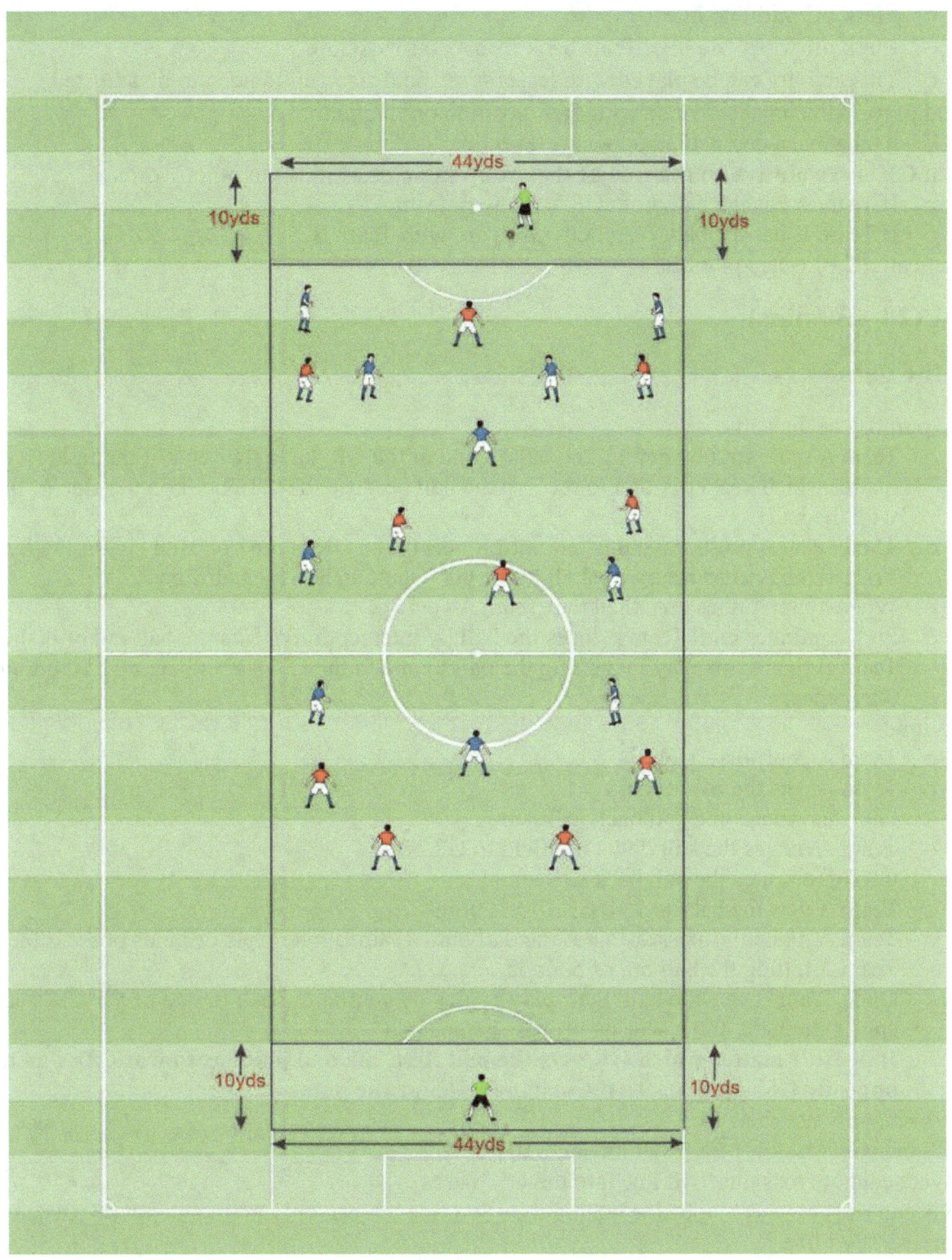

- Use of full field
- 10 v 10 field players + 2 GK's
- Field size (for 10 v10)
  - ○ Length of the field

- End lines run from the corners of the 18yd box on one end of the field to the corners of the 18yd box on the other end of the field
- o Width
  - 44yds wide (width of 18yd box)
- o Mark off midfield line
- o Mark off with ^'s a line 10yds back from each 18yd line
- o This activity can be played with lesser #'s – field size would need to be adjusted
- Field players line in accordance with their position on the field
- GK's set up at each end behind opposite 18yd lines
- **Both GK's are always on the side of the group in possession**, so in other words
  - o If Team A has the ball, both GK's are with team A
  - o If Team B has the ball, then both GK's are with Team B
- One team of 10 wears pinnies

Activity 1 (20 – 30mins)

Rules of the game

- The purpose of the game is to
  - o Team A must start by getting the ball to one of the GK's at either end of the field (it doesn't matter which keeper is first to receive the ball because they are both on the side of the team with the ball)
  - o Then Team A must move the ball until it gets to the GK at the opposite end of the field
  - o Then Team A must return the ball to the GK who touched the ball first
  - o When Team A does this, then that Team A gets **1pt**
  - o Play continues until Team A loses the ball by interception or hits the ball out of bounds, Team B then starts play by getting the ball to one of the GK's at either end of the field & play repeats
- Example
  - o Team A gets possession
  - o Team A gets the ball to GK1
  - o GK1 distributes the ball back to Team A
  - o Team A moves the ball down the field to GK2
  - o GK2 distributes the ball back to Team A
  - o Team A gets the ball back to GK1 for a point
  - o Team A maintains possession of the ball until Team B intercepts or gains possession by Team A hitting the ball out of bounds
  - o Once Team B gets the ball, their play begins by getting the ball to one of the GK's at either end of the field & the scoring process is repeated
  - o **It doesn't matter which GK gets the ball first, the ball just has to work its way to the opposite GK and back to the original GK for the point**
- GK's can only use their feet
- GK's cannot cross over the 18yd line onto the field
- Players cannot cross the 18yd line into the GK's area
- GK's can run anywhere side-side behind the 18yd line but can only go to a depth of 10yds back from the 18yd line
- Any ball going beyond 10yds deep is considered out of bounds & the other team gets possession
- The initial ball back to one of the GK's can be a ball of any length (short pass or long pass) and the ball from the GK out to any player can be the same
- Both GK's are outlets for the team in possession of the ball

- The team in possession can pass the ball back to any GK at any time & in any direction to maintain possession of the ball
- Length of possession is not a factor
- Possession of the ball & movement of the ball between GK's is the purpose
- The ball passed to GK1 to start the scoring phase can be of any length (can be from the offensive or defensive half of the field)
- The ball passed to GK2 can be of any length (can be from the offensive or defensive half of the field)
- However, getting the ball back to GK1 to score a point **cannot** be a long pass from the defensive half of the field
- The ball must get into the offensive half of the field (the side in which the 1st GK touched the ball to start the play) & then to the original GK to get the point
  - This keeps the game from getting into just striking long balls
- The coach may use touch restrictions as they see fit

Coaching Points

- GK's must move side to side behind the 18yd line as the ball moves side to side on the field
  - This allows them to be an accessible & constant outlet to maintain possession for the team in possession
- GK's must communicate to the team in possession to let them know they are there as an outlet
- Field players always looking to both GK's as being outlets to maintain possession
- The possession game should involve short & long ball passing
  - Avoid getting into a one-dimensional type of passing game
- This activity, when practiced on a consistent manner, creates trust between field players & GK's
- Builds communication, team work & most importantly, gets the GK's involved in ball possession with the team

5v5 + GK's Shooting Game

Set Up

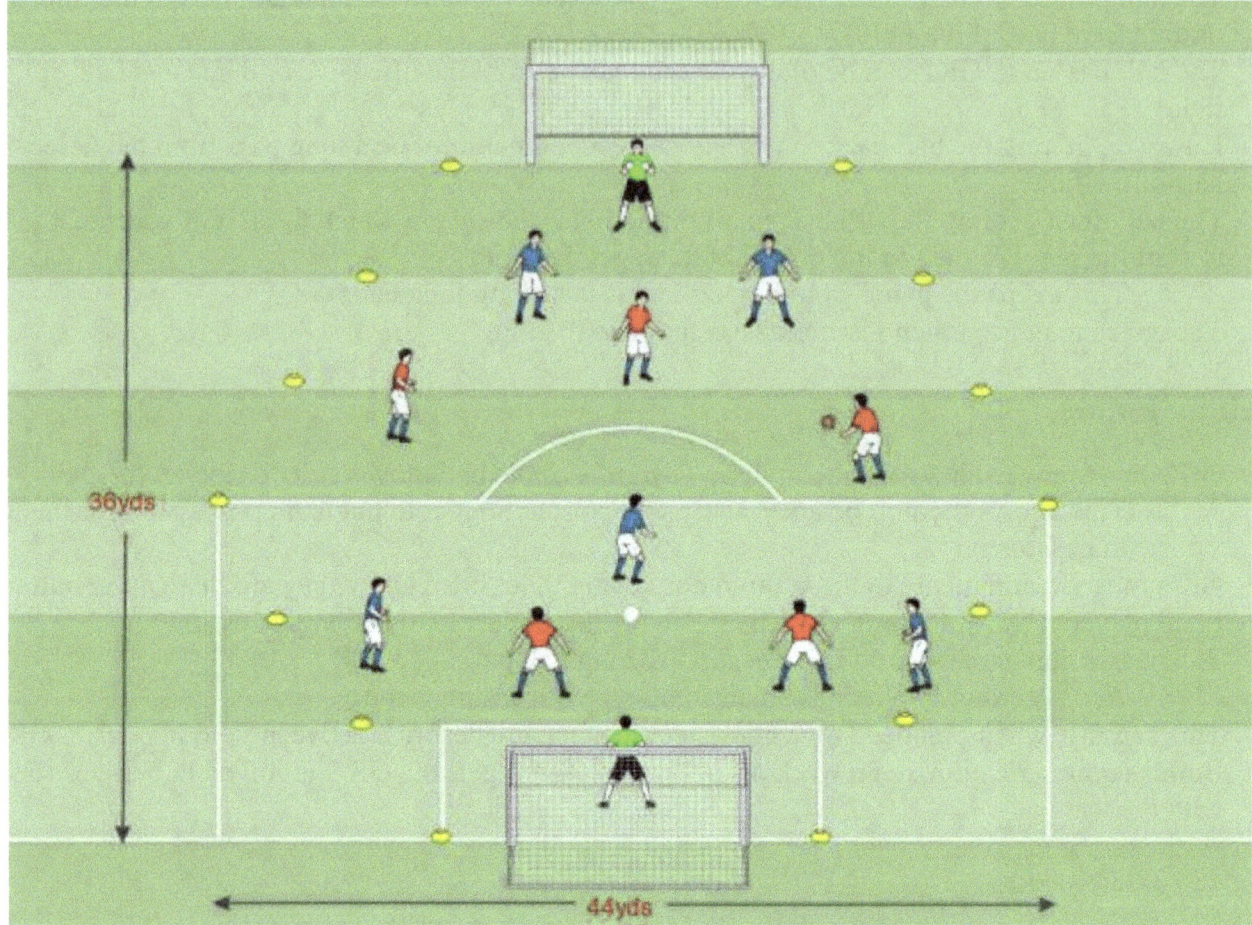

- Use of regular size goals
- Length of field = 36yds
- Width of field = 44yds
- Use of 18yd box
- 18yd line acts as midfield line
- Shape of field is a diamond
- Use cones to mark off the side-lines
- Place starting cones 4yds from each post
- Line rest of cones every 5yds out to corners of the 18yd box to form diamond-shape field
- Supply plenty of balls at all 4 goalposts
- 5v5 field players
- One GK in each goal
- Each team of 5 players has
    - 3 players in their attacking 3rd
    - 2 players in their defensive 3rd
    - It is always 3v2 in each team's attacking 3rd
    - There is no neutral area
- Additional players can be placed around the field to keep ball in play

Activity (15 – 20mins)

- This is a shooting game – players can shoot from anywhere on the field
- Players must stay in their half – cannot cross the line
- Any player can shoot
- GK's can shoot as a variation
- Ball can be passed back & forth across the line
- Players look to shoot quickly
- Not a passing game, so limit # of passes
- Unlimited touches & then use restricted touches
- Use of coin toss to determine team that starts with the ball
- Length of game can vary from 1 – 4mins
- If there are multiple teams, play winner stays on
- To determine a winner if there is a tie after regulation
  - Next goal wins or next shot on goal wins the game
  - Tie goes to the previous winner
- After a goal, play starts from the GK who just got scored on
- If ball goes out of bounds, GK of other team starts with the ball
- GK's can distribute with hands or feet
- Extra players can be used as targets, if desired
- Keep standings over the course of the season
- Give an award to championship team

Coaching Points

- Observe and evaluate GK's
  - Angles & positioning
  - Shot-stopping ability
  - Distribution with both hands & feet
  - Competitive nature
  - Communication
  - Dealing with man down situations in the GK's half of the field
- Maintain shooting integrity – this is not a passing game
- Shots can be taken from anywhere on the field
- All players look to shoot & to shoot quickly

Four Corner Shooting Game

Set Up

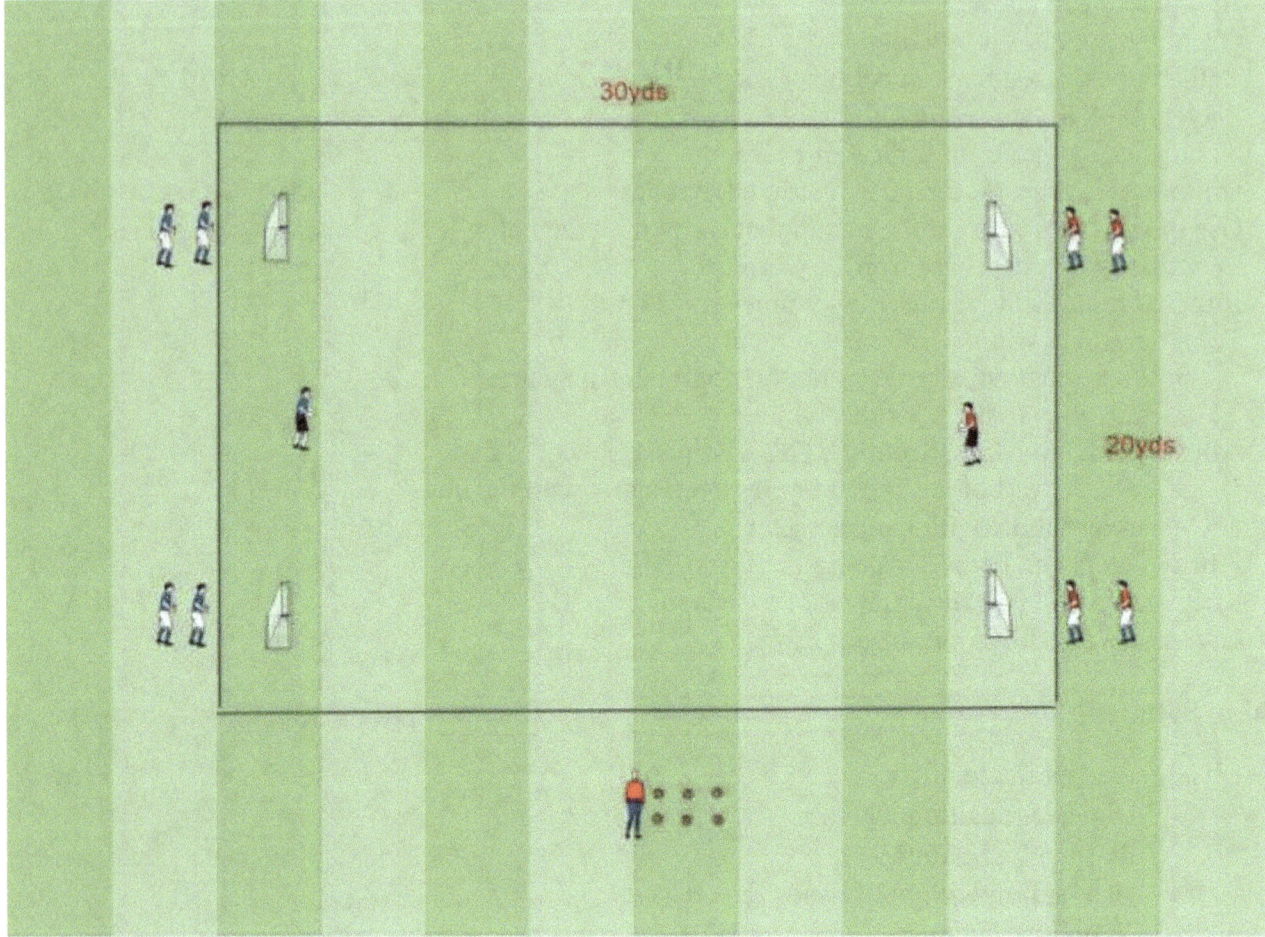

- Make a grid 20yds X 30yds
- Goals are placed at each corner of the grid
    - Use cones for goals
    - Goals 4yds wide
- **GKC (GK Coach)** positioned at mid-line with all of the balls
- 2 teams wearing different colored pinnies
- Each team is told which goals are theirs to defend
- Each team splits into halves
- Players on one team line up in a straight line behind a specific goal on their half of the grid
- Opposing team players line up at opposite sides of the grid
- 1 GK for each team starts on their end-line within the grid

Activity

- **GKC** serves a ball onto the field of play
- 1st player in each of the 4 lines run onto the field & 3v3 game begins
    - 2 field players + 1 GK/team
- Play continues until a goal is scored into one of the four goals or the ball goes out of bounds
- When this happens

- Those players retreat to the back of their respective lines
- GK's stay on
- Play restarts with the coach serving another ball into play

Coaching Points

- Decision making in a game situation
- Passing & receiving
- GK's
  - Protecting a goal
  - **Set Position**
  - **Foot-work**
  - Body behind the ball
  - **Handling Techniques**
  - **Distribution**
  - **Communication**

Live 1v1 Situation #1

Set Up

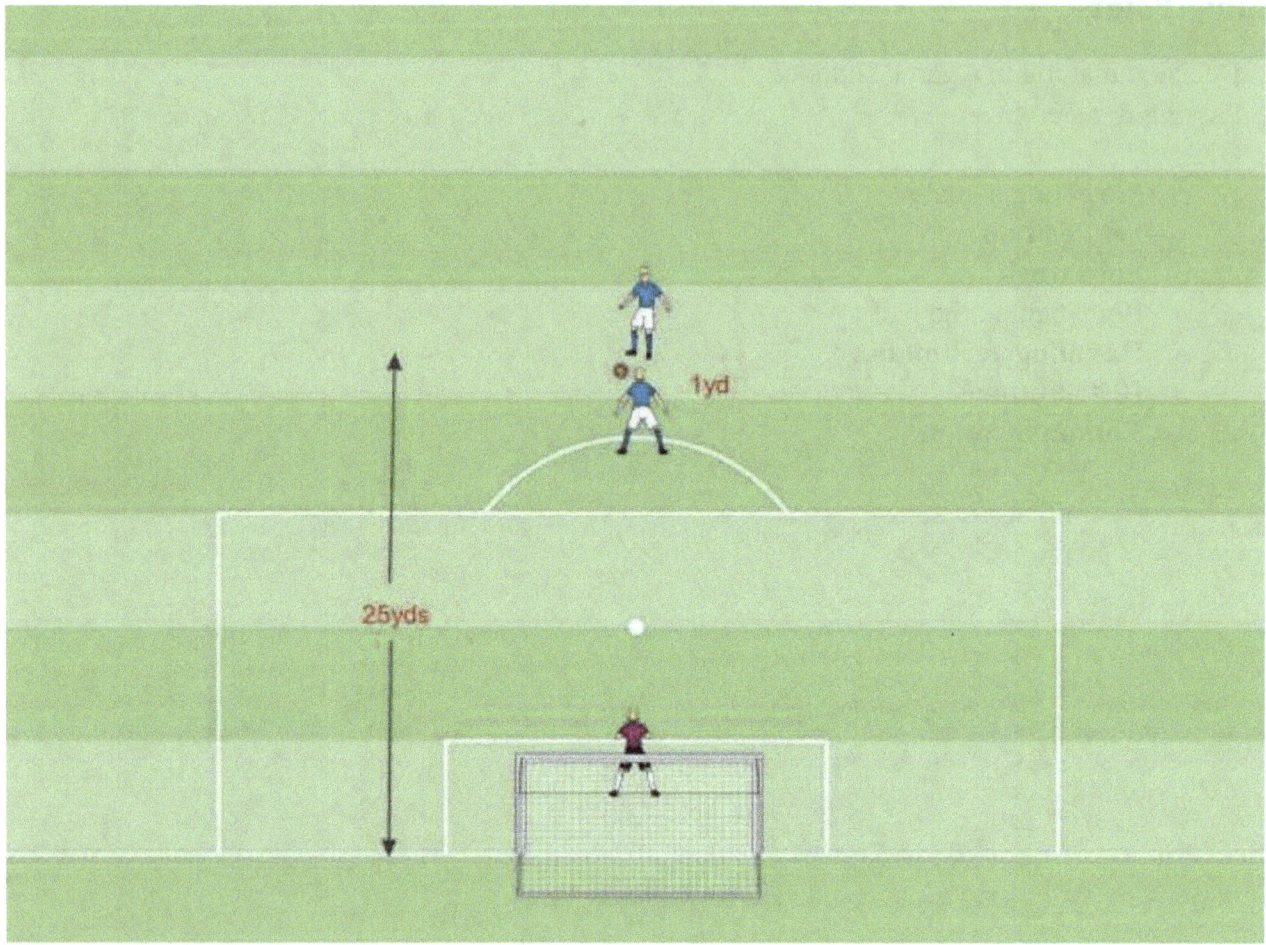

- GK sets up in goal, 2 – 3yds off line
- Server 1 starts with ball at feet, facing the goal & 25yds from goal
- Server 2 sets up 1yd from Server 1
- Server 2's back is to Server 1 & legs are straddled open

Activity 1 (10 – 15mins)

- GK starts 2 – 3yds off line in **Modern Set Position**
- Server 1 starts the activity by striking the ball between Server 2's open legs
- Server 2 chases after ball & makes the decision to
  - o Take on & try to dribble around the GK
  - o Take a 1 time shot on goal
- GK must
  - o Read speed/path of the ball
  - o Make a decision on whether to go for the ball or get set for the 1X shot
- Rebounds are live
- Repeat 6X for each GK
- Repeat whole activity several times for each GK

Variations

-   Server 1 & Server 2 start by facing each other
-   Add a defender(s) to chase Server 2

Coaching Points

-   Server 1 provides good services
-   Server 2 either dribbles or takes a shot on 1st touch
-   GK starts 2 – 3yds off line
-   GK makes a decision
-   GK executes proper technique, whether getting set for the shot or taking off & confronting attacker by going in with a **Low-ball Collapsing Save**

Live 1v1 Situation #2

Set Up

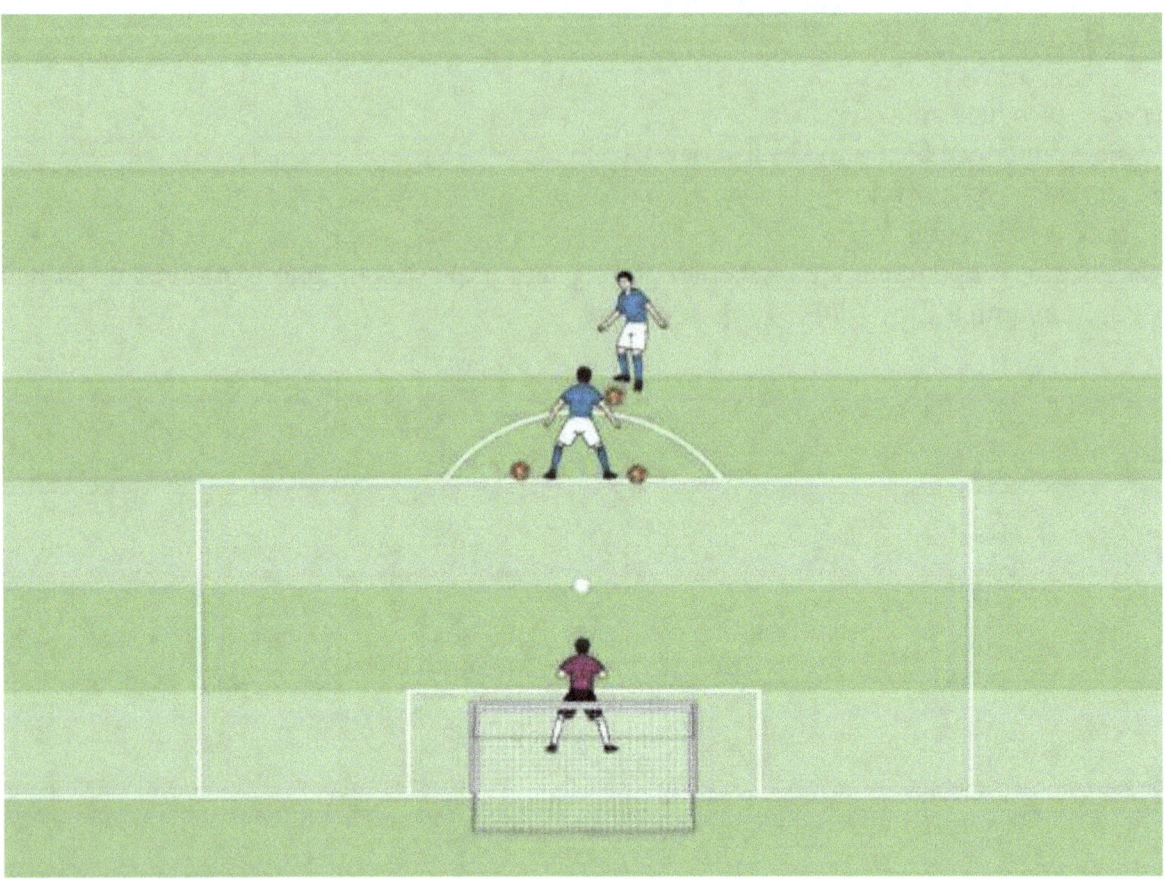

- Use of 18yd box & goal
- GK sets up in goal, 2 – 3yds off line
- Server 1 starts with ball at feet, facing the goal & at the top of the D (arc)
- Server 2 sets up 1yd from Server 1
- Server 2's back is to the goal (facing Server 1) & legs are straddled open
- A ball is placed either side of Server 2
- Starting distances for Server 1 & Server 2 may be closer to the goal depending upon kicking ability of Server 1

Activity 1 (10 – 15min)

- Play starts with Server 1
- Server 1 has the option of
  - Passing the ball through Server 2's legs at varying distances
    - Server 2 then turns & runs onto the rolling ball creating a 1v1 situation with the GK
  - Shooting either ball at the side of Server 2
  - If Server 1 shoots one of the balls at the side of Server 2, after the shot is saved by the GK or goes wide, Server 1 must then hit a 2nd ball through the legs of Server 2 at varying distances
    - Server 2 then turns & runs onto the rolling ball creating a 1v1 situation with the GK

- In either case, each play must end with a ball struck through Server 2's legs creating 1v1 situations with the GK
- Depending upon how far Server 1 hits the through ball, live situations will occur creating
  - **60:40 situations**
  - **50:50 situations**
  - **40:60 situation**
- Once the 1v1 situation plays out, everyone resets & Server 1 starts again with either option
- Repeat 6X, then switch roles of all players
- Keep repeating whole activity until session is over

Variation

- Can create a competition with scoring if desired

Coaching Points

- Decision making & proper execution of techniques on the part of the GK in live situations
  - **60:40 situation**
  - **50:50 situation**
  - **40:60 situation**
- Good services supplied by the attacking players

Liverpool Pass Back Shooting Game

Set Up

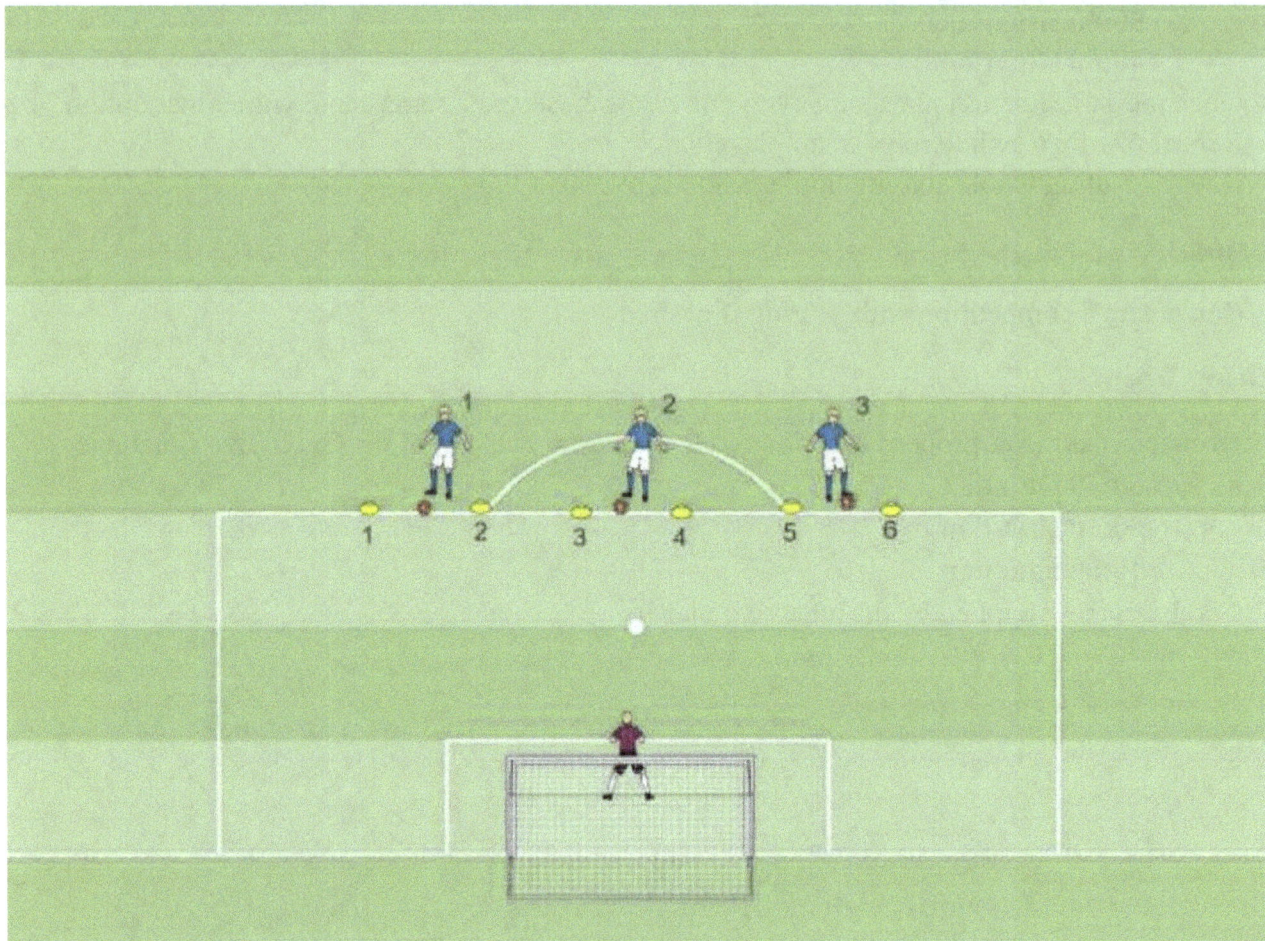

- Use of Goal & 18yd box
- All cones placed along the 18yd box

  o Cone 2 placed at the junction of the D (arc) & the 18yd line
  o Cone 1 placed along side of ^2, 4 yds from ^2 (going away from the D)
  o Cone 3 & cone 4 (^4) placed along side of each other in the middle of the D, 4yds apart
  o Cone 5 (^5) placed at the junction of the D & the 18yd line
  o Cone 6 (^6) placed along side of cone 2 (^2), 4 yds from cone 2 (^2) (going away from the D)

- These cones act as the pass back targets & the shooting area for each Server
- Server 1 sets up between cone 1 & cone 2 with balls
- Server 2 sets up between cone 3 & cone 4 with balls
- Server 3 sets up between cone 5 & cone 6 with balls
- GK starts in the middle of the goal

Activity 1 (10 – 15mins)

- GK starts in **Modern Set Position** 2 yards off the goal line & in the middle of the goal
- GK sprints right to the outside of the frame of the goal & asks for the ball from Server 3 using proper communication ("Yes! & Server 3's name")

- o   Server 3 plays a back pass on the ground to the GK
- o   GK controls the back pass, returns the ball directly back to Server 3 with a **1 or 2 Touch Pass** once again using proper communication with Server 3 ("Yes & Server 3's name!")
- GK then sprints back into goal & gets into position for a shot from Server 1
- After making the save (or if a goal is scored or if the ball is struck wide by Server), GK gets set again for a 2nd shot from Server 2 & this repeats for a 3rd shot from Server 3
- **All shots by Server's must be a touch/shot – not a still ball shot**
- Rebounds are alive ONLY on the 3rd shot
- If a rebound is given – Server 1, Server 2 & Server 3 can all go after the rebound
- Rebound is a 1X shot
- After the play is dead, GK resets in the middle of the goal & begins the sequence again by sprinting out to the left of the goal for a pass back from Server 1
- The activity repeats with a back pass, return pass to Server 1 & 3 successive shots, this time with
  - o   Server 3 shooting 1st; Server 2 shooting 2nd & Server 1 shooting 3rd
- The activity is repeated for 3X each side

Scoring

- GK passes the ball directly back between the 2 target cones where the Servers are located with a 1 or 2 touch pass: **GK +1pt**
- GK makes the save: **GK +1pt**
- GK sticks the ball cleanly (cannot use the body & cannot bobble the ball): **GK +2 pts**
- Any Server scores a goal: **Server +1pt**
- Any Server scores on the rebound: **Server +1pt**
- Any Server misses the target: **Server -1pt** (Servers can go in the hole on scoring)
- Point possibilities stay alive if rebound is given up on 3rd shot until ball is either in the net or out of bounds
- Game is over after competing GK's have completed the same # of back passes & shots

Variations

- Vary the type of service on the back pass (ground ball, mid ball or high ball)
- Points can be adjusted as to how the GK handles & delivers the back pass
- GK receives the ball from Server 3, cleans it up & passes across to the Server 1
  - o   Server 1 then takes 1st shot; Server 2 takes 2nd shot & Server 3 takes 3rd shot
- The **GKC (GK Coach)** may use only 2 Server's is #'s dictate

Coaching Points

- GK's follow the rules of the game
- **GKC** reinforces all points covered in the session in regard to
  - o   Handling techniques
  - o   Kicking techniques
  - o   Communication

Liverpool Pass Back Shooting with Clearance

Set Up

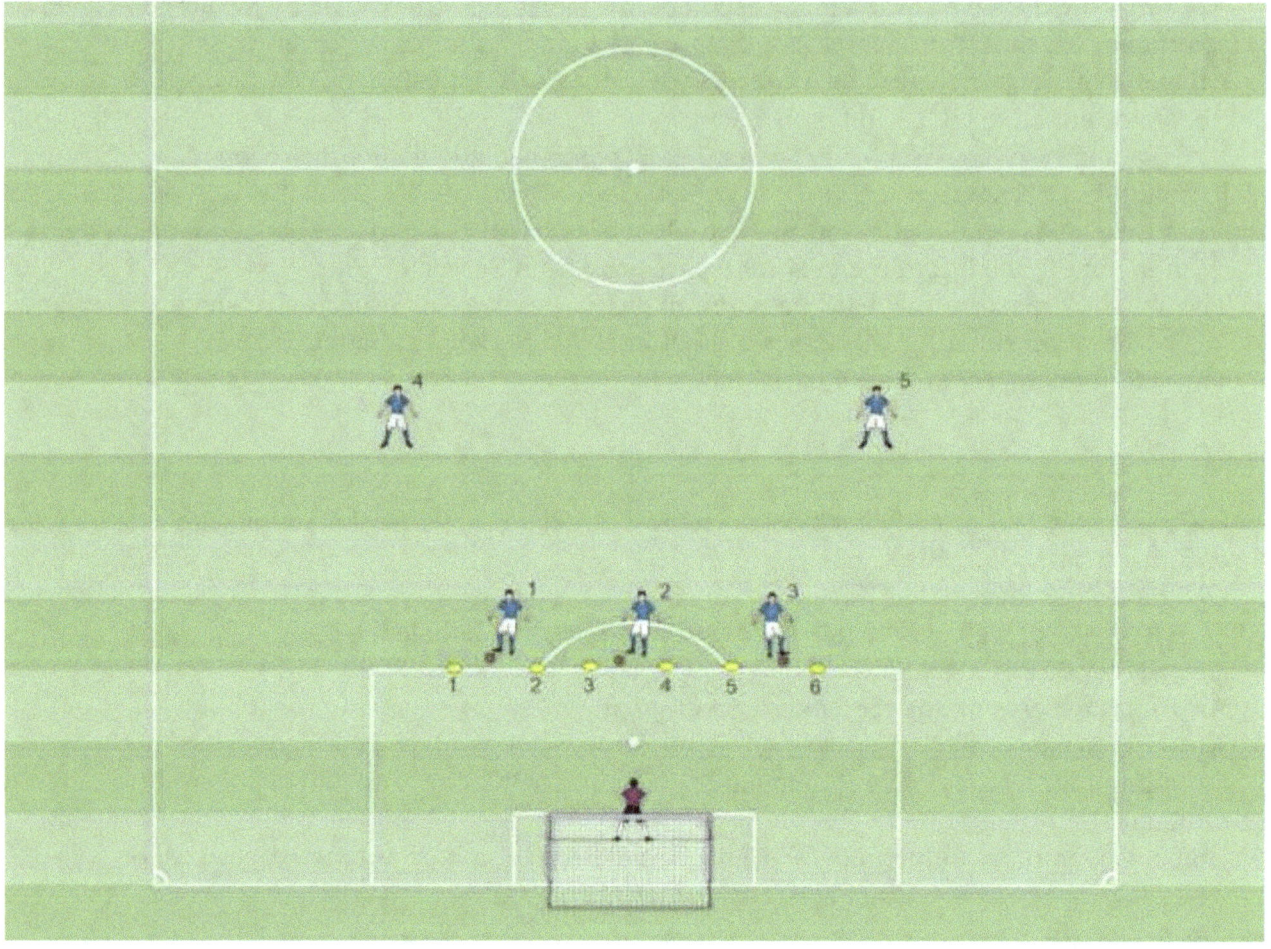

- Use of regular size goal & ½ of field
- All cones placed along the 18yd box
    - Cone 2 placed at the junction of the D (arc) & the 18yd line
    - Cone 1 placed along-side of cone 2, 4 yards from cone 2 (going away from the D)
    - Cone 3 & cone 4 placed along-side of each other in the middle of the D, 4yds apart
    - Cone 5 placed at the junction of the D & the 18yd line
    - Cone 6 placed along-side of cone 5, 4 yards from cone 5 (going away from the D)
- These cones act as the pass back targets & the shooting area for each Server
- Server 1 sets up between cone 1 & cone 2 with balls at feet
- Server 2 sets up between cone 3 & cone 4 with balls at feet
- Server 3 sets up between cone 5 & cone 6 with balls at feet
- Server 4 & Server 5 set up in different spots on the field 35 – 40yds from goal with balls at feet
- GK starts in the middle of the goal, 2 yds off the goal line & in **Modern Set Position**

Activity 1 (10 – 15mins)

- GK starts in **Modern Set Position** 2yds off the goal line & in the middle of the goal
- GK quickly runs to the right outside & of the frame of the goal & asks for the ball from Server 3 using proper communication ("Yes & Server 3's name!")
- Server 3 plays a back pass on the ground to the GK

- GK controls the back pass, returns the ball directly back to Server 3 with a **1 or 2 Touch Pass**, once again using proper communication ("Yes & Server 3's name!")
  - o GK can use any combination with the feet
- GK then sprints back into goal & gets into position for a shot from Server 1
- After making the save (or if a goal is scored or if the ball is struck wide by Server), GK quickly moves & gets set again for a 2nd shot from Server 2 & this repeats for a 3rd shot from Server 3
- **All shots by Servers must be a touch/shot – not a still ball shot**
- Rebounds are alive ONLY on the 3rd shot
- If a rebound is given up – Server 1, Server 2 & Server 3 can all go after the rebound
- After the 3rd shot is dead, Server 4 or Server 5 (they can alternate) strikes a long through ball back to the GK
- GK must clear the ball out with a **1X Clearance**
- After the play is dead, GK resets in the middle of the goal
- GK quickly runs to the left & outside of the frame of the goal, asks for the ball from Server 1 using proper communication ("Yes & Server 1's name!")
- Server 1 plays a back pass on the ground to the GK
- GK controls the back pass, returns the ball directly back to Server 1 with a **1 or 2 Touch Pass**, once again using proper communication ("Yes & Server 1's name!")
  - o GK can use any combination with the feet
- GK then sprints back into goal & gets into position for a shot from Server 3
- After making the save (or if a goal is scored or if the ball is struck wide by Server), GK quickly moves & gets set again for a 2nd shot from Server 2 & this repeats for a 3rd shot from Server 1
- **All shots by Servers must be a touch/shot – not a still ball shot**
- Rebounds are alive ONLY on the 3rd shot
- If a rebound is given – Server 1, Server 2 & Server 3 can all go after the rebound
- After the 3rd shot is dead, Server 4 or Server 5 (they can alternate) strikes a long through ball back to the GK
- GK must clear the ball out with a **1X Clearance**
- After the play is dead, GK resets in the middle of the goal
- The activity is repeated for 3X each side
- Rotate GK's & repeat activity

Scoring

- GK passes the ball directly back between the 2 target cones where the Servers are located with a **1 or 2 Touch Pass**: **GK +1pt**
- GK makes the save: **GK +1pt**
- GK sticks the ball cleanly on a catch (cannot use the body & cannot bobble the ball): **GK +2pts**
- GK clears the ball high & far: **GK +1pt**
- GK clears the ball directly to either Server 4/5: **GK +2pts**
- Any Server that scores a goal: **Server +1pt**
- Any Server that scores on a rebound: **Server +1pt**
- Any Server that misses the target on any shot: **Server -1pt** (Servers can go in the hole on scoring)
- Point possibilities stay alive if rebound is given up on 3rd shot until ball is either in the net, out of bounds or out of the 18yd box
- Game is over after competing GK's have completed the same # of back passes & shots

Variations

- Vary the type of service on the back pass (ground-ball, mid-ball or high-ball)

- Points can be adjusted as to how the GK handles & delivers the back pass
- GK receives the ball from Server 3, cleans it up & passes across to the Server 1
    o Server 1 then takes 1st shot; Server 2 takes 2nd shot & Server 3 takes 3rd shot
- The coach may use only 2 Servers if #'s dictate

Coaching Points

- GK's follow the rules of the game
- **GKC (GK Coach)** reinforces all points covered in the session in regard to
    o Handling techniques
    o Kicking/passing techniques
    o Communication
- On all back passes & clearance attempts, GK's feet are in a 2-foot bounce, not flat footed
- GK clearances are high, far & wide
- GK clearances are to a target if possible
- The **GKC** may use only 2 Servers if #'s dictate

Shadow with Multiple Shots

Set Up

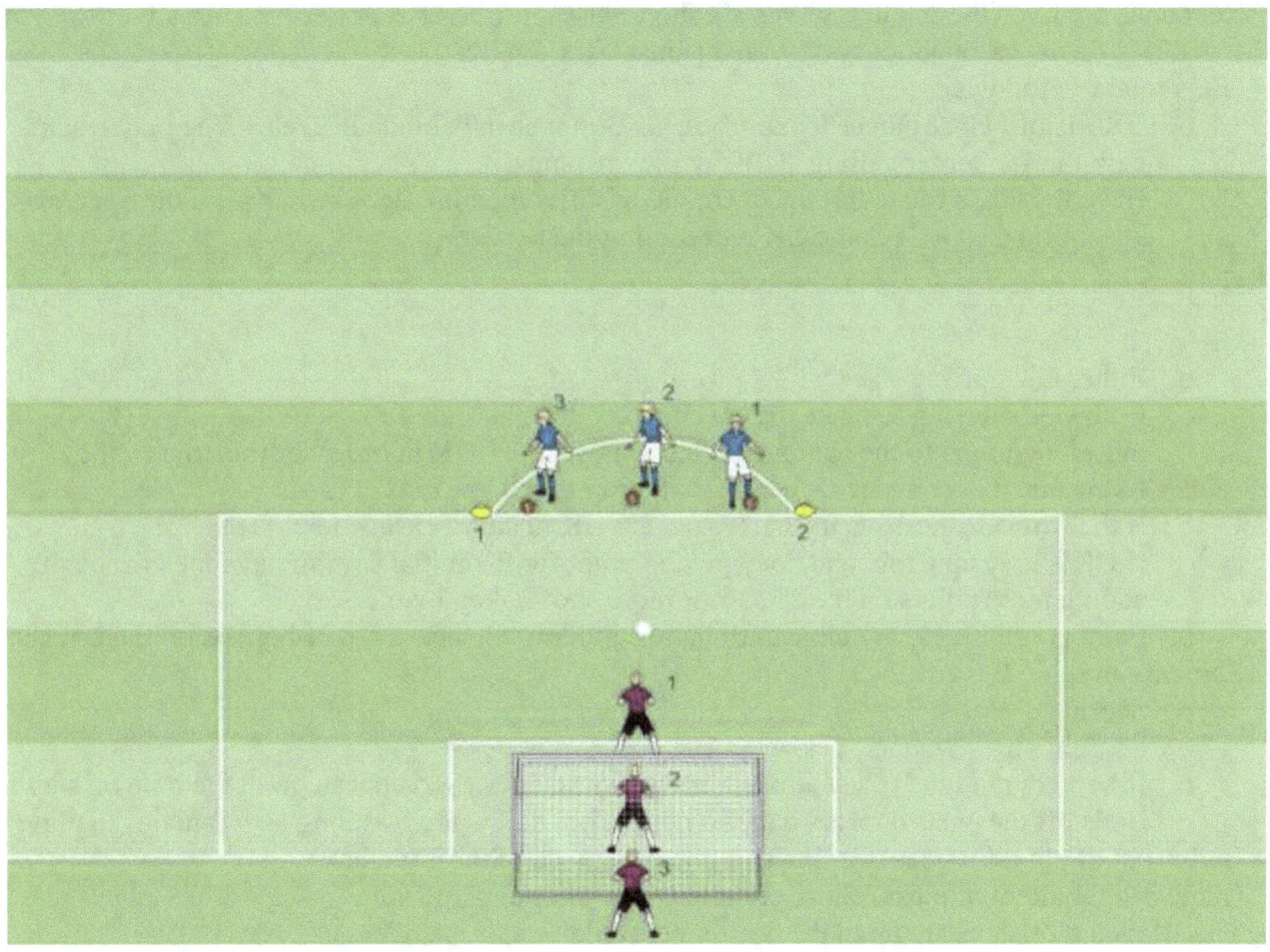

- Place cone 1 & cone 2 on the same line just outside of the 18yd line & just outside the frame of the goal
- Place cone 3 on the 6yd line & out from the center of the goal
- Make up teams between the GK's attending the training
- Servers set up with balls 15yds – 18yds away from goal line & between cone 1 & cone 2
- GK1 lies down on belly with head at cone 1 & feet back towards goal
- GK2 lies down in the same fashion directly behind GK1
- GK3 (if numbers require) stays off to the side of the goal & will rotate in

Activity

- Minimum # of players: 2 – 4 GK's/team
- 2 GK's lie down on their bellies in the center of the goal & one behind the other
- Servers, each with a ball, take positions between cone 1 & cone 2
- The GK's are a team – the Servers are a team
- Server 1 yells "UP!" & both GK's jump up into **Set Positions**
- GK2 must stay directly behind GK1 for the shot (GK2 is the Shadow) – the 2 GK's cannot split the goal in half
- Both GK's try & keep the shot from going into the net (as a team)

- After 1st shot is completed (a goal is scored/a save is made/the shot misses the target), GK's quickly reset & Server 2 takes a shot
- After the 2nd shot is completed (a goal is scored/a save is made/the shot misses the target) GK's reset & Server 3 takes a shot
- Rebounds are live ONLY after Server 3's shot; Server 1, Server 2, & Server 3 are all allowed to work 3V2 on the rebound to try & score against GK1 & GK2
- GK's rotate as follows
  - GK1 Is off; GK2 moves to the front; GK3 moves in behind GK2, etc. The play restarts with the 1st Server yelling "UP!" & play resumes
  - Have the GK's rotate through a couple of times then the sides switch with the Servers becoming the GK's & the GK's becoming the Servers

Scoring

- GK's can score by
  - Either GK making a save: **GK +1pt**
  - Both GK's having to make the save to keep the ball out of the net: **GK +2pts** (the ball must be going into the net on a deflection by the 1st GK in order for this to be valid)
  - If any GK makes a clean stick (no bobbling of the ball): **GK +2pts**
  - If the front GK deflects the ball & the 2nd GK makes a clean stick: **GK +3pts**
  - If GK's give up a rebound, they get the point for the initial save & have the chance of adding more points on the 2nd, 3rd or more shots taken by the Servers
  - Point possibilities stay alive until ball is either in the net or out of bounds on the last shot
- Servers can score by
  - Scoring a goal: **Servers +1pt**
  - Scoring on a rebound: **Servers +1pt**
  - If Servers miss the target altogether: **Servers -2pts** (Servers can go in the hole on scoring)
  - Balls off the posts or cross bar: no points, but ball is alive as long as it remains in play
- Ball is out of play if it goes over the end line or outside of the 18yd box
- Game is over after both teams have completed the allotted # of shots
- The allotted # of shots are up to the discretion of the **GKC (GK Coach)**

Variations

- **GKC** has the discretion of varying the starting positions of the GK's
  - GK's on sides, backs, up/downs, etc.
- **GKC** may change the shooting angle for the servers to be more of angle to the goal

Coaching Points

- GK's compete fairly within the rules of the game
- GK's/teams keep their own score

Soccer Tennis

Set up

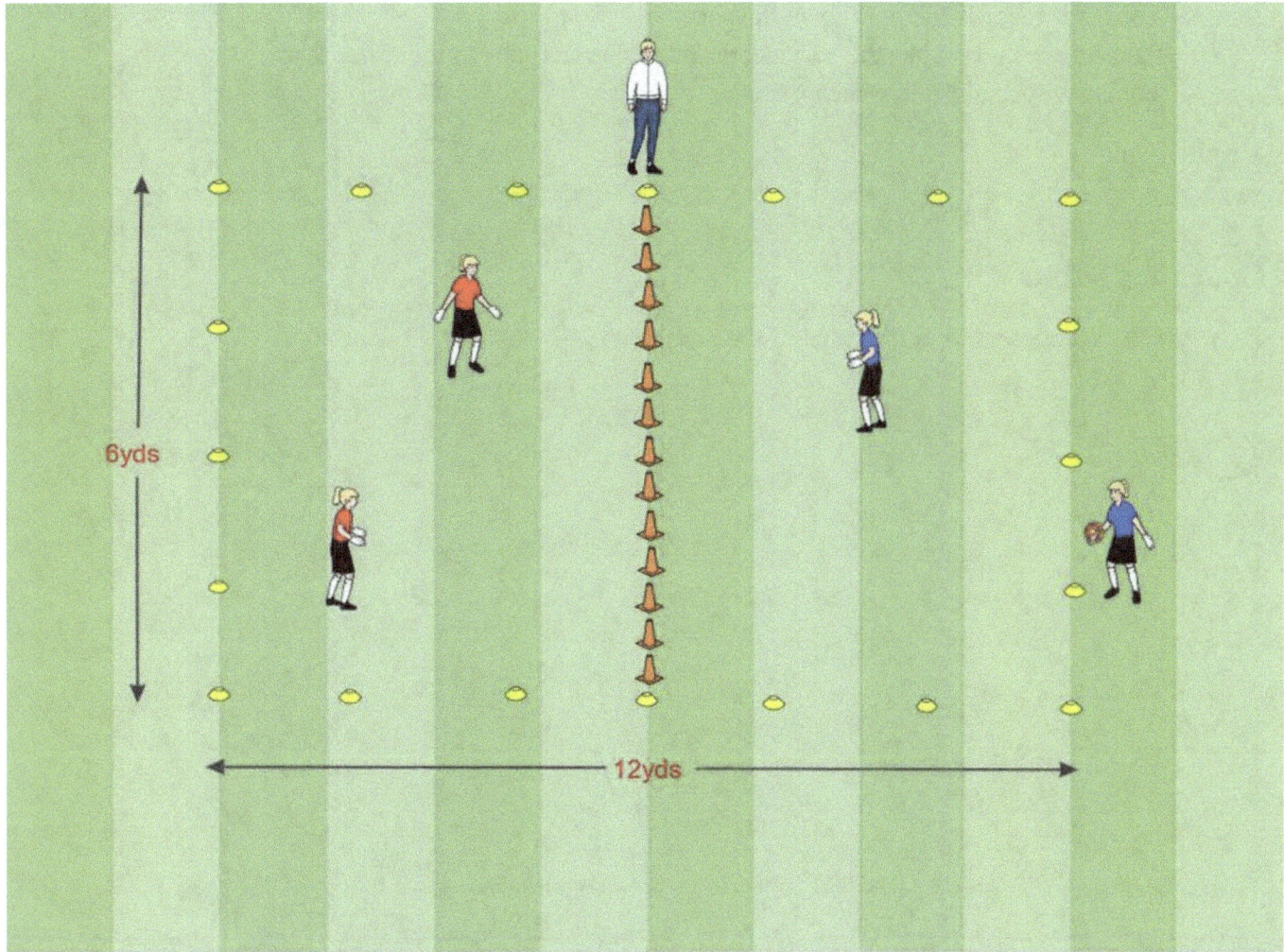

- Create a grid out of cones, 12yds long X 6yds wide
- Place a barrier (net), approximately 3 ft in height across the mid line of the grid

Activity

- Divide GK's into teams of 2 – 3 GK's each
- Determine which side starts with the ball
- Game starts with GK serving from behind the end line
- Service can be a **Throw/Volley**/or drop the ball & **Volley** it over
- Ball must cross over the barrier/net & land in the opposite grid to play
- Receiving team can
    - Bat or catch the ball & toss it back over the barrier
    - Use any part of the body to knock it back over the net
    - Can use the hands or a body part to knock it in the air to partner who then can hit it/toss it over the net
- Ball is allowed to bounce once at anytime
- Maximum of 3 touches amongst teammates before ball has to go back over the barrier
- Points scored

- o   Ball goes out of bounds
- o   Ball cannot be played back over the net
- o   Team takes too many touches
- Play for points or time
- Team that records the point gets the service
- If serving team botches the service, point & service goes to the other team
- Teams switch sides after each game

Variation

- Cannot throw the ball over

Coaching Points

- GK's compete within the rules of the game

Techniques Used in Training Sessions

<u>**Foot-work**</u>

- **Chop Step**

Photos Courtesy of Matt Broomall & Modern Goalkeeper Training Systems, LLC

  - o **Lateral Foot-work** with an up & down pattern
  - o GK's go to the left, the left foot leads (left, right, left, right)
  - o GK's go to the right, the right foot leads (right, left, right, left)
  - o Performed in ladders or through cones
  - o Hands remain in normal **Set Position**
- **Fast Feet (Quick Feet)**
  - o **Foot-work** in which the feet move up & down quickly while the GK is moving forward at a slow pace
  - o Feet remain shoulder width apart and hands remain in normal set position
  - o This same fast up and down **Foot-work** technique may be used while the GK is moving laterally at a slow pace
  - o Hands remain in normal **Set Position**
- **Shuffle Step**
  - o **Lateral Foot-work** in which the feet shuffle to the left (left foot lead) or to the right (right foot lead)
  - o GK's feet should not be clicking during the movement
  - o Movement is clean, balanced, & quiet
  - o GK's should not bounce up & down
  - o Hands remain in normal **Set Position**
- **Shuffle Cut – Change of Direction**
  - o Shuffle laterally in one direction, then a hard-cut back & shuffle in the other direction

- o Hands remain in normal **Set Position**
- **1-2 step between each cone**
  - o **Foot-work** where both feet alternately touch down between each cone (or ladder)
  - o Left/right stepping or right/left stepping
  - o Can be used going forward or laterally
  - o Hands remain in normal **Set Position**
- **Cross Over Step**
  - o **Lateral Foot-work** pattern in which one-foot crosses over in front of the other foot
- **Forward/Backward Weave**
  - o Facing forward in **Set Position**
  - o GK moves forward/backward in a tight weaving motion while moving laterally through cones
  - o Hands remain in normal **Set Position**
- **Forward Foot-work**
  - o **Fast Foot-work** in a forward motion
  - o Hands can move normally
- **Backward Foot-work**
  - o **Fast Foot-work** moving directly backwards
  - o Recommended only over very short distances (1yd – 2yds)
  - o Hands can move normally
- **Drop-Step/diagonal run or Sideways run**
  - o Used when GK's need to get to balls that have been hit over their heads & they must cover a few yards
  - o Involves turning the hips, dropping the first step backward, & then running on a diagonal angle, while maintaining eye contact on the ball the whole time
  - o Drop step turning left – left foot leads
  - o Drop step turning right – right foot leads
  - o Hands move normally
- **Circle Foot-work**
  - o Quick movement of the feet in a clock-wise/counter-clockwise pattern
  - o Hands remain in normal **Set Position**
- **Figure 8 Foot-work**
  - o Can be performed either in a forward/backward pattern or a lateral pattern
  - o Hands remain in normal **Set Position**
- **Carioca**
  - o Another lateral movement pattern
  - o Alternate moving one foot in front of the other & then behind the other while moving laterally, quickly
  - o Arms swing side-to-side quickly

Foot Skills

- **2 Touch Passing**
  - o Receiving/passing using 2 touches with either foot

- **1 Touch Passing**
  - o Receiving/passing using 1 touch with either foot

- **Inside of the Foot Pass (IOF)**

Photo Courtesy of Matt Broomall

  - o Striking the ball to a target with the **Inside of the Foot** (left & right foot)
- **Volley**

Photo Courtesy of Matt Broomall & Modern Goalkeeper Training Systems, LLC

  - o Striking the ball to a target out of the air using the laces of the boot (left & right foot)
  - o Technique
    - ▪ Drop the ball – don't toss it away from the body

- Use both hands to drop the ball or the hand opposite of the foot kicking the ball
- Lock toe down and strike the ball with the laces
- Slight backward lean after striking the ball

- **½ Volley**

Photo Courtesy of Matt Broomall & Modern Goalkeeper Training Systems, LLC

o Striking the ball to a target just after it bounces upwards from the ground using the laces of the boot (left & right foot)
o Technique
  - Drop the ball – don't toss it away from the body
  - Use both hands to drop the ball or the hand opposite of the foot kicking the ball
  - Lock toe down and strike the ball with the laces
  - Strike the ball just after it bounces upwards off the ground

- **Driven Balls**

Photos Courtesy of Matt Broomall & Modern Goalkeeper Training Systems, LLC

- o Striking a ball from the ground to a target using the laces of the boot
- o Ball rises & is directed towards target
- o Technique
  - The ball is approached at a 45-degree angle
  - Plant foot is alongside and a bit in front of the ball, pointed toward the target
  - Lock ankle of the striking foot outwards when striking the ball
  - Contact the ball with the laces of the boot just below center to get the back spin
  - The ball should have a little back spin on it
  - Lean back on the strike to get the ball airborne
  - Follow through toward the target
  - Hip stays locked towards target
  - Body pulls away from the ball & slightly backwards after the strike

- **Laced Ball along the Ground**

Photos Courtesy of Matt Broomall & Modern Goalkeeper Training Systems, LLC

- o Ball is struck from the ground with the laces of the boot
- o Ball skims along the ground
- o Also called a "Worm Burner"
- o Technique
  - The ball is approached at a 45-degree angle
  - Plant foot is alongside and a bit in front of the ball, pointed toward the target
  - Lock ankle of the striking foot outwards when striking the ball
  - Contact the ball with the laces of the boot just below center to get the back spin
  - The ball should have a little back spin on it
  - Stay over the ball & follow through toward the target

- **1X Clearance**

Photo Courtesy of Matt Broomall & Modern Goalkeeper Training Systems, LLC

o   When waiting to clear the ball with the feet, GK is readied by doing a 2-foot bounce, to be prepared for any random bouncing/movement of the ball coming back
o   GK uses inside of the foot or laces to clear the ball
o   GK's eyes watch the foot strike the ball
o   GK uses the pace of the ball as a propellent for the **Clearance** instead of trying to over hit the ball
o   GK attempts to hit a target on all **Clearances**
o   If GK cannot hit a target, **Clearance** should be hit high, far, & wide
o   GK stays composed when striking **Clearance**; does not panic
o   GK – If in doubt, knock it out

Set Positions

- **Basic (Traditional) Set Position**

Photos Courtesy of Erin Guthrie Corsi

- o GK's eyes are on the ball
- o Feet shoulder width apart
- o GK on balls of the feet – not the heels
- o Bend at the ankle, knee, & hip (GK's bum is down & the chest is up; do not lean too far forward)
- o Hand position is inside the body & located at waist height
- o Palms facing inward toward the body
- o Elbows slightly flared
- o GK is balanced

- **Modern Set Position**

Photos Courtesy of Matt Broomall & Modern Goalkeeper Training Systems, LLC

o GK's eyes are on the ball
o Feet shoulder width apart
o GK on balls of the feet – not the heels
o Bend at the ankle, knee & hip
o Hand position is now **extended more forward of the body** & at body's width, or just a bit wider than the body, & positioned at waist height
o Palms open & facing each other
o Elbows no longer flared; elbows now pinched in toward the waist & are slightly in front of the waist
o Elbows & hands are parallel to each other & located approximately the same distance apart
o GK is balanced

- **Close Range Stance/Blocking Stance**

Photos Courtesy of Matt Broomall & Modern Goalkeeper Training Systems, LLC

- o Stance is used for close range shots (4 – 12yds)
- o **Kick Saves** on low balls; **Push or Blocking Saves** with hands on balls hit higher
- o GK's **Set Position** is a little lower & stronger than the regular **Set Position**
- o Foot placement is a little closer; must protect the ball from going through the legs
- o **Hands are at waist height or just above the waist & set just outside of the body; palms facing outward**
- o Most likely a save will result in a rebound; GK needs to recover & prepare for a possible 2nd shot
- o A highly effective save for a shot hit closely to and with pace at the GK
- o An effective save in 1v1 situations

-   **Cut Back Positioning**

Photo Courtesy of Matt Broomall & Modern Goalkeeper Training Systems, LLC

o   Used when attacking player is penetrating along the goal line & is still outside the 6yd box is looking to strike a cut back pass

o   GK needs to protect the near post & be prepared for a ball being passed (cut back) to another attacking player in front of the goal

o   GK sets up on a 45-degree angle approximately 1 – 2 steps inside the near post, as well as, 1 – 2 steps off the goal line itself

o   Set position is a **Close Range Stance/Blocking Stance**

- **Stance/Positioning when attacker is along the endline and is at or inside the 6yd box**

Photo Courtesy of Matt Broomall & Modern Goalkeeper Training Systems, LLC

o GK sets up at the post as shown
o Body square to the attacker
o Heels slightly in front of post
o Body set low
o Feet close together; hands spread
o Be sure to have "holes" around the body/post closed so ball cannot get through
o Stay low & steady anticipating shot
o Be ready to move if attacker performs cut back pass

Low Ball Handling Techniques

- **Hands Low Catch**

Photos Courtesy of Matt Broomall & Modern Goalkeeper Training Systems, LLC

- o A hand-eye coordination catch that is a good introduction to the Chest Down/Basket Catch
- o When making the catch
  - Open stance with knees slightly bent outwards
  - Drop butt down
  - Make a ramp out of the hands & arms
    - Palms facing upwards
    - Pinkies touching
    - Elbows together

- Distance between the wrists and elbows is about the same
  - Bring chest down to the ball (don't bring the ball up to the chest)
  - Catch the ball with the fingertips & hold it there on the ground
  - GK ends up in a low position with knees extending slightly outwards; head is over the ball

- **Chest Down/Basket Catch**

Photos Courtesy Erin Guthrie Corsi

- ○ Rotate palms forward; pinkies touching; ramp made out of the arms
- ○ Bum dropped down; chest brought down to the ball; bring ball into belly
- ○ Knees slightly opened up; NOT pinched in
- ○ Head & body tucked over the ball
- ○ Hold the finish for 1 second to have keeper "feel" the finish

- **Front Smother Catch**

Photos Courtesy Erin Guthrie Corsi

o Step lead foot forward & on a slight angle away from the body
  ▪ Right foot should lead when the ball is coming to the right side of the GK
  ▪ Left foot should lead when the ball is coming to the left side of the GK
o Turn opposite heel in so that it's pointing to the heel of the lead foot (like a fencer's stance)
o Do not point lead foot directly at the ball – let the ball come between the feet
  ▪ GK should move the feet so that the ball is approaching in between the feet
o Rotate hands & arms so that palms face forward, pinkies are touching & make a ramp out of the arms
o Drop the bum down low; scoop the ball into the arms like the chest down/basket catch
o Tuck chin over ball
o Softly fall forward & land on forearms
o Hold the finished catch

- **Controlled Collapse Left/Right**

  o **Collapsing to the left**

Photo Courtesy of Matt Broomall & Modern Goalkeeper Training Systems, LLC

Photo Courtesy of Matt Broomall

- Step with the left foot, pointing the toe directly at the ball to the left
- Drop bum down low as step is taken
- Collapse to the ball landing on left side, leading with the hands & the head
- Pin the ball to the ground
  - Left hand behind the ball; right hand on top of the ball; use the ground as the 3rd hand
- Head behind the ball
- Upper leg (right leg) bent at the knee & hip to protect stomach
- Upper leg (right leg) off the ground
- Lower leg (left leg) is kept slightly extended
- Feel the finish

      o **Collapsing to the right**

Photo Courtesy of Matt Broomall & Modern Goalkeeper Training Systems, LLC

- Step with the right foot, pointing the toe directly at the ball to the right
- Drop bum down low as step is taken
- Collapse to the ball landing on right side, leading with the hands & the head
- Pin the ball to the ground
  - Right hand behind the ball; left hand on top of the ball; use the ground as the 3rd hand
- Head behind the ball
- Upper leg (left leg) bent at the knee & hip to protect stomach
- Upper leg (left leg) off the ground
- Lower leg (right leg) is kept slightly extended
- Feel the finish

- **Low-ball Deflections (1 Hand – 2 Hands)**

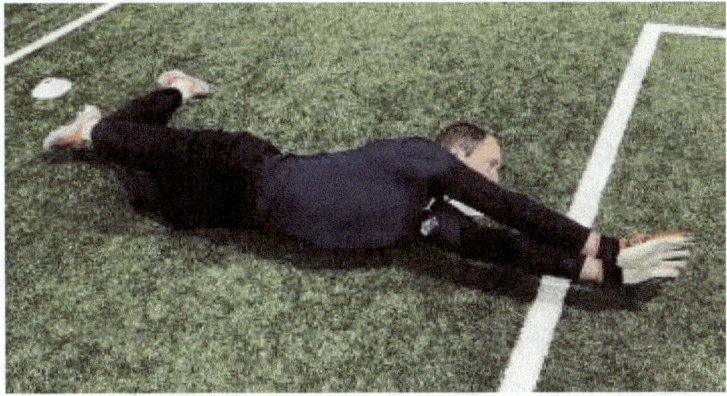

Photos Courtesy of Matt Broomall & Modern Goalkeeper Training Systems, LLC

- o Push off with one foot
    - ▪ If going to the right, push off (step) with the right foot
    - ▪ If going to the left, push off (step) with the left foot
- o Drop bum down low as step is taken
- o Push the core to the ball, don't just reach with the arm
- o If shots are from chest height and lower, deflect with the low hand & land on same side
    - ▪ If deflecting the ball to the right, step with the right foot; push the ball away with the right hand; land on the right side
    - ▪ If deflecting the ball to the left, step with the left foot; push the ball away with the left hand; land on the left side

- o Elbow of the deflecting hand starts in a bent position & then extends towards the ball for contact
- o Palm of hand faces the ball
- o Bottom part of hand (pinky finger) slides along the ground
    - Don't flick at the ball with the fingertips pointing downwards
    - Don't karate chop at the ball
    - Don't swipe hand over the top of the ball
- o Hand comes late to the ball; if GK extends hand/arm too soon, they will lose some power on the ball
- o Best to push the ball away with the heel of the hand, if possible; otherwise, any part of the hand could work
- o Head turns in the direction of the deflected ball; the eyes stay on the ball all the way through the deflection

Mid-ball Handling Techniques

- **Chest Down/Basket Catch**

Photos Courtesy of Erin Guthrie Corsi

- o Rotate palms; pinkies touching; ramp made out of the arms
- o Bum dropped down; chest brought down to the ball; bring ball into belly
- o Knees slightly opened up; NOT pinched in
- o Head and body tucked over the ball
- o Hold the finish for 1 second to have keeper "feel" the finish

- **Front Smother Catch on Mid-ball**

Photos Courtesy of Erin Guthrie Corsi

o Step lead foot forward & on a slight angle away from the body
o Turn opposite heel in so that it's pointing to the heel of the lead foot (like a fencer's stance)
o Do not point lead foot directly at the ball – let the ball come between the feet
   ▪ GK should move the feet so that the ball is approaching between the feet
o Rotate hands & arms so that palms face forward, pinkies are touching & make a ramp out of the arms
o Drop the bum down low; scoop the ball into the arms like the chest down/basket catch
o Tuck chin over ball
o Catch the ball with the Chest Down/Basket Catch Technique
o Softly fall forward & land on forearms in a controlled manner
o Hold the finished catch

- **Mid-ball Controlled Collapse Left/Right**

Photo Courtesy of Matt Broomall

- o **Collapsing to the left**
  - Step with the left foot, pointing the toe directly at the ball to the left
  - Drop bum down low as step is taken
  - Collapse to the ball landing on left side leading with the hands & the head
  - Pin the ball to the ground
    - Left hand behind the ball; right hand on top of the ball; use the ground as the 3rd hand
  - Head behind the ball (head should be at the same level as the ball)
  - Upper leg (right leg) bent at the knee & hip to protect stomach
  - Upper leg (right leg) off the ground
  - Lower leg (left leg) is kept slightly extended
  - Feel the finish
- o **Collapsing to the right**
  - Step with the right foot, pointing the toe directly at the ball to the right
  - Drop bum down low as step is taken
  - Collapse to the ball landing on right side leading with the hands & the head
  - Pin the ball to the ground
    - Right hand behind the ball; left hand on top of the ball; use the ground as the 3rd hand
  - Head behind the ball (head should be at the same level as the ball)
  - Upper leg (left leg) bent at the knee & hip to protect stomach
  - Upper leg (left leg) off the ground
  - Lower leg (right leg) is kept slightly extended
  - Feel the finish

- **Mid-ball Deflections**
  - o Push off with one foot
    - If going to the right, push off (step) with the right foot
    - If going to the left, push off (step) with the left foot
  - o Drop bum down low as step is taken
  - o Drop head down to ball level

- Push the core to the ball, don't just reach with the arm
- Deflect the ball with the low hand & land on same side
  - If deflecting the ball to the right, step with the right foot; push the ball away with the right hand; land on the right side
  - If deflecting the ball to the left, step with the left foot; push the ball away with the left hand; land on the left side
- Elbow of the deflecting hand starts in a bent position & then extends towards the ball for contact
- Palm of hand faces the ball
- As much as possible, deflect the ball with the heel of the hand; fingertips may work, but the attempt to deflect should be made with the heel of the hand
  - Don't flick at the ball with the fingertips pointing downwards
  - Don't karate chop at the ball
  - Don't swipe hand over the top of the ball
- Hand comes late to the ball; if GK's extend hand/arm too soon, they will lose some power on the ball
- Best to push the ball away with the heel of the hand, if possible; otherwise, any part of the hand could work
- Head turns in the direction of the deflected ball; the eyes stay on the ball all the way through the deflection

<u>High Ball Handling Techniques</u>

- **Diamond/Contour Catch (For Ball at Chest to Head Height)**

Photos Courtesy of Matt Broomall

Photos Courtesy of Matt Broomall & Modern Goalkeeper Training Systems, LLC

- o GK reads the flight of the ball, holds ground & does not take off too early
- o GK makes the decision to go for the high ball, feet should be moving in quick, short steps to prepare for a well-timed take off
- o GK yells out **"KEEPER!"** on **decision** to go for the ball
- o When going to the right
    - ▪ GK takes off on left foot & brings right knee up towards right shoulder (for protection, balance, & thrust for the jump)
- o When going to the left
    - ▪ GK takes off on right foot & brings left knee up towards left shoulder (for protection, balance, & thrust for the jump)
- o The catch is made with a diamond, contoured hand shape; hands need to be around the ball
- o Catch the ball on the way up
- o Ball is caught above the GK's head & a little in front of the face (so GK can see the back of the hands)
- o Look into the ball after it is in the hands
- o GK lands on 2 feet
- o Keep the ball up after the catch (bring it in if contact is inevitable)

- **High ball Collapse**

Photo Courtesy of Matt Broomall

o **Collapsing to the left**
  - Step with the left foot, pointing the toe directly at the ball to the left
  - Head is at ball low as step is taken
  - Collapse to the ball landing on left side leading with the hands & the head
  - Pin the ball to the ground
    - Left hand behind the ball; right hand on top of the ball; use the ground as the 3rd hand
  - Head behind the ball (head should be at the same level as the ball)
  - Upper leg (right leg) bent at the knee & hip to protect stomach
  - Upper leg (right leg) off the ground
  - Lower leg (left leg) is kept slightly extended
  - Feel the finish
o **Collapsing to the right**
  - Step with the right foot, pointing the toe directly at the ball to the right
  - Head is at ball low as step is taken
  - Collapse to the ball landing on right side leading with the hands & the head
  - Pin the ball to the ground
    - Right hand behind the ball; left hand on top of the ball; use the ground as the 3rd hand
  - Head behind the ball (head should be at the same level as the ball)
  - Upper leg (left leg) bent at the knee & hip to protect stomach
  - Upper leg (left leg) off the ground
  - Lower leg (right leg) is kept slightly extended
  - Feel the finish

- **High Ball Catching Technique (Diamond/Contour Catch)**

<table>
<tr><td align="center">**Right Knee up – Front**</td><td align="center">**Right Knee Up – Side**</td></tr>
</table>

Photos Courtesy of Matt Broomall & Modern Goalkeeper Training Systems, LLC

- **Two-Hand Fist Punching**

Photos Courtesy of Matt Broomall & Modern Goalkeeper Training Systems, LLC

o Create a fist that is a flat surface from the back knuckles to the middle knuckles
- Bring the two hands together so that the flat surface extends across both hands
- Thumbs are outside of the four fingers (not tucked under the fingers) & along-side the index finger
- Elbows need to be tucked in & close to the sides of the body
- GK's make the fists as the they jump up for the ball
- Strike the ball by extending the arms through the center of the ball
- Hit the ball high and far
- GK yells "**KEEPER**!" when making the **decision** to go for the ball
- Two-fisted punch is good to change the direction of the ball

- **One-Hand Fist Punching**

Photos Courtesy of Matt Broomall & Modern Goalkeeper Training Systems, LLC

o Create a fist that is a flat surface from the back knuckles to the middle knuckles
o When going at the ball with one fist, be sure to start with the punching elbow close to the body; no round-house strike at the ball
o Strike through the ball with the fist
o Strike through the center of the ball
o One-fisted punch is good to keep the ball going in the same direction, or when two hands cannot get to the ball

- **Jump Catch**
  o Jumping, catching the ball with the feet off the ground, tossing the ball back to the server before the feet come back to the ground (much like in the game of taps)
  o Performed with proper **Diamond/Contour Catching Technique**
  o Catch the ball in front of the face
  o Catch the ball on the way up in their jump

o If throwing the ball over the goal: after catching the ball, GK throws the ball back over the crossbar with a two-hand toss to the server **BEFORE** their feet come back to the ground

- **One-Hand Jump Catching**
  o If catching with the right hand
    - Jump off left foot
    - Right hand is above the right elbow (like taking a foul shot in basketball)
    - Right hand is cupped around the ball, not open-handed & flat
    - Catch the ball on the way up
    - Release the ball back like taking a foul shot
    - Follow through to the target
    - Eyes stay engaged with the ball throughout
  o If catching with the left hand
    - Jump off right foot
    - Left hand is above the left elbow (like taking a foul shot in basketball)
    - Left hand is cupped around the ball, not open-handed & flat
    - Catch the ball on the way up
    - Release the ball back like taking a foul shot
    - Follow through to the target
    - Eyes stay engaged with the ball throughout

- **High Ball Deflections/Parrying (over the goal or to the side of the goal)**

Photos Courtesy of Matt Broomall & Modern Goalkeeper Training Systems, LLC

  o Footwork
    - GK runs laterally towards the direction of the ball (Cross-over running step)
    - Hips stay facing forward when running laterally
  o GK takes off with the proper lead foot
    - Moving to the left – left foot take off
    - Moving to the right – right foot take off

- o Eyes stay on the ball the whole time (head does not turn away from the ball)
- o As GK jumps up off the leading leg, the other knee is brought towards the chest
- o Ball is deflected around the post, or over the bar with the top hand
  - ▪ Left hand if moving to the right
  - ▪ Right hand if moving to the left
- o Elbow of the arm deflecting the ball stays tight to the body
- o Elbow then extends towards the ball
- o For the deflection
  - ▪ Use the heel of the hand, if possible
  - ▪ Fingertips may also be used
  - ▪ Fist not recommended (surface too rounded; not enough control)
- o Just redirect the ball away from the goal
- o GK lands on side
- o GK can do a tuck & roll landing on opposite shoulder

1v1 Situation Techniques

- **60/40 1v1 Situation – Collapsing Technique**

Photo Courtesy of Matt Broomall & Modern Goalkeeper Training Systems, LLC

- o Technique used in 1v1 situations where the GK will get to the ball first, just before the attacker does
- o Technique is the same used when going into a **Controlled Collapsing Save**, either to the right or to the left (See below)
- o GK takes off on lead foot early so that the body can get down quickly for protection against the oncoming attacker

- o GK uses the hands & the ball to protect the face
- o GK's head must get down behind the ball
- o Do not go in with the feet/legs 1st; could result in serious injury
- o GK yells **"KEEPER!"** when going for the ball

- **Containment Stance - 40/60 1v1 Situation**

Photo Courtesy of Erin Guthrie Corsi

- o In 1v1 situations & if possible, GK's should close the distance down to the ball to 2 - 3yds; if this can be done, GK gets into the **Containment Stance**
- o The keeper's **Containment Stance** is as follows
    - GK gets into **Containment Stance** approximately **2yds from the ball**
    - Center of gravity is low (GK is not leaning, but is squatting)
    - One foot is generally a bit in front of the other; GK is in an athletic stance (helps to change direction)
    - Feet not too wide apart (so GK can't be nutmegged)
    - The head directed at the ball
    - The hands are placed
        - Palms open towards the ball
        - Just outside of the legs
        - Just in front of the feet
        - Low enough so that a ball can't go underneath them
- o **GK's job at this point is just as it is with a defender – containing the ball**
- o GK remains patient & waits for attacker to make the 1st move
- o GK explodes to the ball when it is off the attacker's foot & is exposed

- **50/50 Saves -Cobra Hand Positioning**

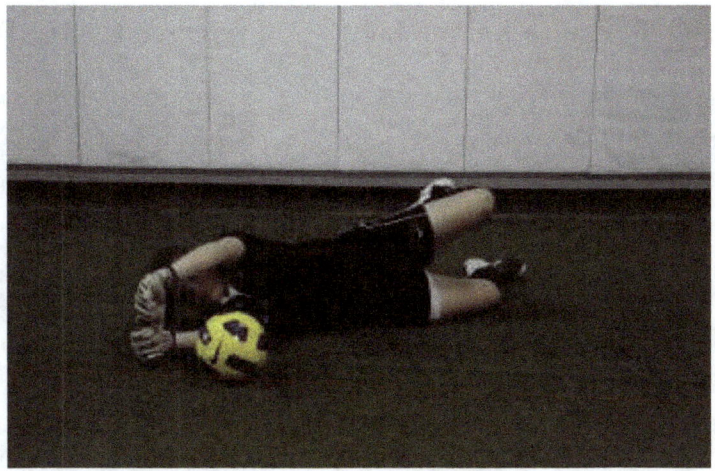

Photo Courtesy of Erin Guthrie Corsi

o Good technique when going for the ball in 50/50 situations
o In these situations, GK's **must** attack the ball with the hands first
o Head is down & behind the hands/arms for protection
o The keeper's hand positioning in the Cobra
  - Hands together, wrists very close together & hands cupped; elbows close together, as well (this guards against the ball coming through the arms & striking the face)
o Performing the Cobra technique
  - GK explodes to the ball as in the **Low-ball Collapsing Technique**
  - If going to the right, lead with the right foot as the butt is lowered
  - If going to the left, lead with the left foot as the butt is lowered
  - As the GK goes to strike the ball, the force comes from the core, upper back & shoulders; do not just swing in with the arms only, could result in an injury
  - Hands stay cupped throughout the technique; wrists stay together
  - GK strikes the ball with the wrists & attempts to direct the ball into the body for possession
  - If hands open up & don't stay cupped, or if GK attempts to stop the force of the ball by striking with the fingers only, force of the striker can bend wrists/fingers backward resulting in lost possession & possible injury
  - Eyes must remain open throughout the strike so GK can maintain constant visual contact with the ball throughout the technique

- **K-Save Stance**

Preferred K-save Technique Left   **Preferred K-save Technique Right**

Alternate K-save Technique (upper-hand in a higher position)

Photos Courtesy of Matt Broomall & Modern Goalkeeper Training Systems, LLC

o A 1v1 save technique
o **K-Save Stance** only used for close range/point blank shots
o GK drops knee to the ground as the ball is being struck from the 1 – 2yd distance
   ▪ If GK is moving to the left, the right knee goes down
   ▪ If GK is moving to the right, the left knee goes down
o Other knee is bent at approximately 90 degrees & the foot is planted right next to the dropped knee (so the ball cannot pass through the gap between the knee & foot)
o The lead foot & the dropped knee are on the same plane
o The dropped knee is to the ground
o Space between heel of the lead foot & dropped knee in the **K-Save** is smaller than the diameter of the ball
o Arms are spread low; both the arms and body are curved forward to surround the ball (See Preferred K-save photos above)
o The hand/arm on the side of the dropped knee is extended on a downward angle (approximate 45-degree angle) over the back foot with palm open towards the ball
o The hand/arm on the side of the knee that's above the planted foot is extended forwards

- Alternate form (see Alternate K-save Technique photo): The hand/arm on the side of the knee that's above the planted foot is extended upwards (approximate 45-degree angle) with palm open towards the ball
  - Chest is squared to the shooter, not angled
  - This shot will result in a rebound so the keeper needs to recover & prepare for a possible 2nd shot

- **Kick Save**

Photo Courtesy of Matt Broomall & Modern Goalkeeper Training Systems, LLC

- The feet are fairly close together in the **Starting Position** (close enough so a ball cannot pass through them)
- GK's body stays low through the **Kick Save**, does not pop up
- This technique involves the core, so breath out when making the **Kick Save**
- **Do not attempt to go down in a K-save type of Technique – the speed of the shot will not give the GK time to do so**
- This save replicates the **Kick Save Technique** used by a hocky goaltender
- Understand that this save will result in a rebound so GK is alert, finds the ball and resets for possible 2nd shot
- A highly effective save for a shot hit closely to and with pace at the GK
- An effective save in 1v1 situations

Distribution Techniques with the Hands

- **Bowling**

Photo Courtesy of Matt Broomall

- o One hand rolling of the ball to a team-mate that simulates the technique used in bowling
- o The ball is released with either hand as close to the ground as possible
- o If right-handed release, left foot should lead & vice-versa
- o Core is lowered as step is taken
- o Ball is released smoothly off hand; hand follows through to target
- o Ball rolls on the ground to the target; does not bounce

- **Overhand (Windmill) Throw**

Photos Courtesy of Matt Broomall & Modern Goalkeeper Training Systems, LLC

- o Throwing the ball over hand to a target in a wind mill motion; throwing the ball over the head while keeping the elbow straight
- o Keeper's starting position
  - Body sideways
  - Athletic stance
  - Non-throwing hand pointing straight at target
  - Throwing hand behind body & pointing in opposite direction (away from target)
- o Start by stepping forward with the lead foot (opposite foot of throwing hand)
- o Non-throwing hand pulls down towards the ground
- o Throwing hand pulls over the head keeping the elbow straight
- o The ball is released straight forward or downward into the ground (depending upon distance to the target)
- o Throwing hand follows through to the target
- o Body releases towards the target; back leg follows through by coming forward
- o GK communicates with the player receiving the ball
- o GK should throw the ball towards the feet of the target, so that it arrives on the 2nd or 3rd bounce (easier for target to handle)
  - If leading the target, throwing higher is okay
- o Do not throw the ball using the baseball technique – puts a lot of stress on the shoulder muscles

Recovery Techniques

When the GK is not able to catch a shot cleanly & deflects the ball, they need to recover to the feet & get ready for a possible rebound shot. This skill requires a strong core.

- **To a Ball Deflected in the Same Direction**
  - o Kick upper leg backwards and tighten core; at the same time, drive upper shoulder forward and use hand(s) to scramble to feet
  - o Or, just pop up to the feet using core muscles only
- **To a Ball Deflected in the Opposite Direction**
  - o Spin Recovery
    - Drive upper knee into chest initiating the spin
    - Spin from hip to hip; (if on right side, spin so that the left hip is on the ground before scrambling up)
    - Eyes stay on the ball
    - Do not rotate back onto buttocks; the spin is centered on the lower spine (like a breakdance move)
    - Spin needs to be completed so that the body is angled forward before getting up
      - If a keeper is facing backwards on a save, the spin is an excellent recovery method

Additional Influences and Coaching Experiences (Alphabetically)

Author's Note: After close to 50 years of coaching and teaching in the game of soccer, it is impossible to include everyone who has been an influence in my journey; that would be a whole other book in itself. I do want everyone to know, that if our paths have crossed through the game or otherwise, you have been influential in me becoming the man that I am today. You are a part of my being and I am thankful.

Kris Cherry – Kris was a former 2nd Division goalkeeper in Holland, a former staff member of Paul Blodgett Goalkeeper Training School, LLC (PBGKTS, LLC), and presently is a GK Coach with Player Development Academy (PDA) Girls. Kris was a part of a very talented group of professional and international goalkeepers whom I trained at one point in my career (Karina LeBlanc, Lubos Ancin, Ryan Hayward and Kris).

Glenn Crooks – Glenn is a successful TV and radio personality, as well as, a journalist and podcast host. His coaching experience includes the collegiate, scholastic and club team levels. I met Glenn while he was the Head Women's Coach at Rutgers and we have a strong and lasting friendship. Glenn has been very supportive of my goalkeeping interests and has given me a sounding platform on his radio show over several occasions.

"I cherish my friendship with Blodge but also cherish his knowledge of the position. I've never had any formal keeper coach training but through informal interactions whether in a training session or out for a coffee, he has helped me understand the position. I've always been hard on my keeper coaches (probably in an unfair way). Blodge has helped calm me down and fully appreciate the challenges for the keeper coach and the goalkeepers themselves."

GLENN CROOKS

Ashley Denti – I trained Ashley for many years starting as a youth soccer keeper and then throughout her stellar career at Centenary College in Hackettstown, NJ. She went on to become an outstanding coach (goalkeeper and youth development).

Chris Duggan – Chris, who is now the Assistant Coach/Goalkeeper Coach for Princeton Women's Soccer, helped me greatly when I was getting the project off the ground. At the time he was the Director of Goalkeeping for Cedar Stars Girls Academy in Tinton Falls, NJ. Chris provided me with his detailed curriculum for the development of his goalkeepers at the Academy, which greatly assisted me in writing mine.

Annie George – Annie was a staff member of PBGKTS and had a stellar career playing for FDU-Florham Park in NJ where she was captain and an All-MAC Freedom Conference Goalkeeper. She is presently representing the United States as a member of the US Marine Corp.

Kristin Giotta (Spohner) – Spohner is one of my closest associates in the game and a dear friend. We worked together over many years at NJYS/ODP and in other collaborations. I have become a much better coach and mentor to keepers because of her. Her impressive resume includes: Co-Interim Director of

Athletics for Compliance, Head Women's Soccer Coach and Senior Woman Administrator at FDU-Florham Park in NJ. She is also the Girls Director of Goalkeeping at Match Fit Academy.

Robyn Jones Horner – Robyn is another longtime friend and confidant. Her impressive career now has her as the Head Coach for Charlotte Independence of the W League. She is also Girls GK Coaching Director for the Charlotte Independence Soccer Club. Robyn had a successful collegiate/professional playing career and also collegiate coaching career. Even though her career has her as a Head Coach, she maintains her strong roots to the position and its advancements. We have worked and grown together in our passion for the position.

Charlie Inverso – Charlie is a true legend in the game as has been a major influencer in the growth and development of goalkeeping in the US. History shows his incredible coaching career at the collegiate and National Team levels. Charlie is a constant in the analytics of goalkeeping, in its history and in its innovations.

Ian Joyce – Ian played professionally in England and the MLS before turning his expertise to a coaching and successful business career. Ian is a staff coach for the USWNT. Ian has been valuable in my continuing education of the position.

TJ Mack – TJ has been a good friend for many years; he worked for PBGKTS and other clubs and organizations. TJ is a great student of the game, as well as the position; He is an excellent motivator and one of the better teachers of the GK position that I have worked with.

Konrad Madej – Konrad is a former student of mine who has become a close and trusted friend. He has a great soccer mind and an incredible passion for the game. He has helped me to learn and understand the many facets of the game at all levels. Konrad is a successful coach who keeps climbing the coaching ladder and is advancing to be a professional coach.

Sam Maira – Sam was the goalkeeper at Rutgers the year prior to our arrival at The Banks. I didn't have the chance to coach him but we struck a lasting and close friendship. Sam helped me in my early Rutgers Camp days and we worked together during his camps when he was the successful Head Coach at Seneca High School. Sam's love of the game and the position has led him to becoming the Assistant/Goalkeeper Coach at the highly regarded Princeton Men's Program under Legendary Head Coach, Jimmy Barlow.

Jillian McVicker – I worked with Jillian for over a decade and watched her develop from a fledgling GK to a very successful D1 level keeper at Ohio State. She then went onto play professionally in Romania where she competed in the UEFA Women's Champions League, making it to the round of 16; she then played in the Finnish League. Jillian was one of the most dedicated keepers with whom I ever worked. A genuinely wonderful and joyous human being, Jillian is one of those special people in my life. She endured two horrific, potentially career ending injuries but fought back in both instances to continue her career.

Rick Meana – Rick is the Director of Coaching for New Jersey Youth Soccer. He was very influential in me becoming a better teacher of the position through my presentations to prospective coaches in the State Licensing Programs in NJ. Rick also became a student of the position and we had many meaningful discussions about goalkeeping.

Kevin McMullen – Kevin had a successful collegiate playing career at SMU and then Rutgers, He is the owner and founder of his own goalkeeper company, The Science of Goalkeeping. Kevin is a trusted friend; we worked together on several goalkeeping projects.

Hannah Mitchell – I worked with Hannah from the time she was 9 years old throughout her collegiate career (UCLA & U of Arizona). Hannah was one of the hardest working and most dedicated GK's that I have had the privilege of working with. Our player/mentor relationship developed into a valued friendship that will last a lifetime. She is a reminder of why I do what I do.

Jack Mulder – Jack came aboard the Rutgers Men's Soccer Staff at the same time I did when Bob Reasso took over as the Head Coach. A highly successful coach in soccer and track and field at the scholastic level at Willingboro High School in NJ, Bob knew Jack's value as a coach and mentor; Jack was one of the major factors in our successful years at Rutgers. He is a great friend, a positive influence in my life, and someone who always supported and believed in me.

Rob Nydick – I started working with Rob when he was at Burlington City High School coached by good friend Scott Shirk. I mentored Rob through his college career and also when he became an Assistant Coach at Rutgers. He went on to become the Senior Associate Athletic Director and Head Men's Coach at Arcadia University and presently is the Athletic Director at Lansdale Catholic in PA. A dear friend, Rob continues to grow and have influence in the field of athletics.

Josh Osit – Josh is a former staff coach for PBGKTS and a keeper that I trained during his standout collegiate career at NJIT. He is presently the Head Women's Soccer Coach at Seton Hall and formerly an Assistant Coach with Columbia Women's Soccer, as well as, with Rutgers Women's Soccer. Josh is a Head Coach who understands the importance of a goalkeeping culture and its value to the overall picture of a successful soccer program.

Dave Pekarek – Dave is a former staff member of PBGKTS, LLC, who went on to develop his own successful GK company.

Auke Wiersma – I work with Auke through NJYS/ODP. He is a successful coach who wears many hats: Professional Coach, Club USSF & NJYS Coaching Educator and Owner of Soccer Alliance, LLC. He has helped me to become a better teacher of the position, not only because of his passion for the game but mostly because of his intent interest in goalkeeping. An avid learner, he has help promote the goalkeeping out of his sheer interest in the position and its role in the game.

Amanda Wong – Amanda is presently with CBS/Paramount+ as an Associate Producer for UEFA Champions League, CONCACAF, and Serie A. I trained Amanda for years through her collegiate years at Muhlenberg College. Her dedication to her craft is the reason for her success. Amanda's friendship is one of those special relationships that come along in one's lifetime, something which the game has provided me and for which I am very thankful.

Clubs and Organizations

UGKA, United Goalkeeping Alliance – The UGKA is an ever-growing network of goalkeeper coaches from around the world with agreed upon goals of educating generations of goalkeepers. It emphasizes a goalkeeper culture while supporting goalkeepers through every stage of their development via a virtual education platform and other offerings.

It is an honor for me to be on the Board of Directors of this organization. If you are a goalkeeper or a goalkeeper coach, I highly urge you to join this Alliance and become a part of its ever-growing influence on goalkeeper development and education.

(Some of the verbiage about the UGKA is taken directly from its website with permission from its founder, Erik Eisenhut.)

(https://www.unitedgkalliance.com)

Inside the 18 Podcast – Inside the 18 is the best podcast in the world on everything dealing with goalkeeping. It is hosted by Michael Magid, Saskia Webber and Omar Zeenni, three incredibly knowledgeable people about the world of goalkeeping. Every broadcast is a very entertaining presentation.

Each episode covers current issues and, as stated on its website: "The show is a must listen for the goalkeeping enthusiasts."

(www.insidethe18media.com)

NJYS/ODP, New Jersey Youth Soccer/Olympic Development Program – Technical Director of Goalkeeping for Boys/Girls with the NJYS/ODP. This has afforded Paul the opportunity to develop/oversee the training and assessment of the boy and girl goalkeepers for the State Program in NJ. It has also provided him with a platform to help instill a Goalkeeper Culture within the state organization.

PDA, Players Development Association Girls, NJ – a nationally renowned ECNL program which has given Paul the opportunity of working with many of the top female goalkeepers in NJ, as well as, in the country. This includes PDA North, PDA Shore and PDA South.

SPFSC, Scotch Plains Fanwood Soccer Club – Coach Mike Walch, Coach Cristine Davis and Paul have been working together with the SPFSC goalkeepers for over 18 years. This is one of the longest associations that Paul has had with any club organization in NJ. Their introductory programs to goalkeeping are exceptional, resulting in the position becoming a cornerstone of the club and high school programs.

Following are notable goalkeepers whom I trained at Rutgers University (Men's and Women's Programs), TCNJ Women's Soccer Program, as well as, those who were professional and World Class keepers. All of these keepers were part of an impressive group of athletes who helped develop the tradition of goalkeeping in New Jersey.

Notable Goalkeepers During Tenure at Rutgers Men's Soccer

Andy Kruczek

Andy was the 1st GK I worked with at Rutgers; he started the tradition of goalkeeper excellence in the modern soccer era at Rutgers; Co-Captain; Alfred B. Sasser Award Winner.

Dave Yeager

Dave had an outstanding career at Rutgers; Co-Captain; great presence in goal.

Steve Erdman

Steve was a very technical keeper; NJ product.

Joe DeMorat

Arguably the best athlete to play the position at Rutgers, Joe was the Bob McNulty MVP Award Winner; he went on to work with the DEA and FBI.

Pictured from left to right: Dave Barrueta (RU HOF). Blodge. JD Martin

Dave Barrueta

Tim Mulqueen stated that Dave was "The best big-game keeper to come through Rutgers"; he is a Rutgers Athletic Hall of Fame inductee, a Bob McNulty MVP Award Winner and he also played professionally in the MLS; Dave is a coach at the professional level – Chattanooga Red Wolves SC.

Billy Andracki

Billy, a Co-Captain at Rutgers, was the 1st All-American in the Men's program. He did not give up a goal in the 1990 Final Four. Billy went on to play professionally and to coach in the Rochester, NY area. He was honored as a member of the Rutgers Men's Soccer 75th Anniversary Team. Billy is also an inductee into the Rutgers Athletic Hall of Fame.

Tony Faticoni

Tony is the Head Men's Soccer Coach at Pfeiffer University in North Carolina.

Cory Hunter

Cori was one of the purest athletes to play at Rutgers; he played professionally.

Steve Widdowson

Steve had an exceptional goalkeeper career at Rutgers where he was a Co-Captain. He played professionally and is now a successful Head Coach at Millersville University in PA.

Jon Conway

Jon was our 2nd All-American goalkeeper at Rutgers. He was a Co-Captain, a Bob McNulty MVP Award Winner and was honored as a member of the Rutgers Men's Soccer 75th Anniversary Team. Jon had an extensive MLS playing career and is presently the Goalkeeper Coach for Toronto FC in the MLS.

Ricky Zinter

A goalkeeper from the Rochester, NY area, Ricky's playing career included an outstanding game in shutting out National Champion UCONN. Ricky, unfortunately passed away in a whitewater rafting accident in Utah. See the **Dedications** section for more on Ricky.

JD Martin

JD was a two-time Co-Captain at Rutgers. He played his graduate year at Northwestern where he established the single season shut out record. He earned All-Big Ten Honors and played Professionally with the Chicago Fire before pursuing a highly successful career in Financials.

Scott Conway

Scott was a Co-Captain at Rutgers. His play earned him a Soccer American Team of the Week selection.

Lubos Ancin

After playing at Rutgers, Lubos went on to play professionally in the Czech Republic. One of the best goalkeeper coaches in the country, Lubos is now the Associate Head Coach/Goalkeeper Coach for Rutgers Women Soccer, producing multiple, outstanding goalkeepers.

Matt Van Oekel

After a successful playing career at Rutgers, Matt went on to play professionally, and is still playing and coaching at that level at this writing.

Notable Goalkeepers for Rutgers Women's Soccer Program

Robin Copperthwaite

Robin was the first woman goalkeeper I ever worked with. She never played the position until her freshmen year at Rutgers; in one year, Robin developed into a D1 level goalkeeper – an amazing accomplishment in itself! She was one of two, 1st 4-year letter winners of the program, and she was a two-time captain. After playing a short stint as a semi-professional, Robin went on to coach at the collegiate level at Rutgers, George Washington and Yale.

Saskia Webber

Unquestionably, the most decorated women's goalkeeper to play at Rutgers University in the program's history, Saskia etched her name in the record books and established a level of goalkeeping at Rutgers that became a standard. Her career was ground breaking in women's soccer and it elevated her to the highest level of women's soccer in playing for the USWNT.

Saskia was a member of the legendary 1999 Woman's World Cup championship team and she also won a Gold Medal in the 1996 Olympic games.

While at Rutgers, she was a four-year starter and established multiple records while in goal. In 1992, she was selected as the Missouri Athletic Club Goalkeeper of the Year, was a finalist for the Hermann Player of the Year and received All-American honors. She received the prestigious Sony Werblin Award and was the first female soccer player to be inducted into the Rutgers Athletic Hall of Fame in 1988.

After playing professionally and coaching at the collegiate level, Saskia is now a founding investor of Angel City FC and is a NWSL Broadcaster/ Analyst, and Owner of The Union Sports App.

I had the privilege of working with Saskia as she trained along-side the Rutgers men soccer keepers and she had no problem holding her own at that level. A tremendous athlete and competitor, Saskia was a joy to work with. I value our relationship greatly to this day.

Erin Guthrie Corsi

Erin had a stellar career at Rutgers. Erin was kind enough to let me use some pictures of her in this book that we took while she was training with me. Please read more about Erin in the **Notables** section of this book.

Jess Janosz

An imposing figure in the goal, Jess was named the 2014 Rutgers Female Athlete of the Year the and also made the Rutgers 2014 Team of the Year. In 2013, she was a 2013 American Athletic Conference Finalist and was the American Athletic Conference Championship Most Outstanding Defensive Player in the same year.

We diligently worked together and her hard work and dedication lofted her to a new standard at Rutgers. Jess is the perfect example of setting a lofty goal for herself then working incredibly hard to achieve that goal. I have the upmost respect for her.

Casey Murphy

Casey Murphy has developed into one of the top women goalkeepers in the world. At this publication, she is currently with the USWNT preparing for the World Cup. Her accolades include: 2017, Big Ten Goalkeeper of the Year; Rutgers all-time career shutout leader; earned multiple Defender/Goalkeeper of the Week honors in the Big Ten and nationally; 1st Team United Soccer Coaches All-American; scholar athlete; played professionally in France and is currently in the NWSL with the North Carolina Courage.

I always looked forward to the opportunity of working with Casey; she is a tremendous athlete who has an incredible work ethic and is destined for greatness. What I enjoy mostly about Casey, however, is her character and spirit; she is as genuine and warm-hearted person as I have ever met. Casey is an excellent example of the model that a goalkeeper should achieve.

Notable Goalkeepers During Tenure at TCNJ Women's Soccer

The goalkeepers of The College of New Jersey Women's Soccer Program were a major reason for the team's perennial success. Following are the keepers who started for TCNJ during my tenure there as the Goalkeeper Coach/Assistant Coach. TCNJ Goalkeepers achieved the distinction of All-American Honors five times in succession.

Jessica Clarke

Jess was my first goalkeeper when I started at TCNJ. She was a phenomenal big game keeper advancing TCNJWS to 3 Final Fours in her career; she took the team to the National Championship match in her freshmen year. She started as a freshman, led the team to two NJAC Conference Championships and was NJAC Goalkeeper of the Year in her sophomore year. Jess was Captain in her senior year and still holds the career shutout record with 48 clean sheets. She now is Director of Sports & Entertainment at Audacy in NYC.

Kendra Griffith

Kendra Griffith was a four-year starter in goal at TCNJ. She was the NJAC Rookie of the Year in 2010 and All NJAC Conference Team selection multiple times. A team Captain, she became my first keeper at TCNJWS to be selected as United Soccer Coaches All-American (1st Team).

Jessica Weeder

I started working with Jess when she was around 11-12 years old and was very fortunate to have continued coaching her at TCNJ Women's Soccer. Jess was a two-time Captain. She achieved the high honor of being selected as a United Soccer Coaches Scholar All-American. Jess was selected to the All NJAC Conference Team in her senior year. Jess just recently achieved her degree as Doctor of Veterinary Medicine (DVM) from Auburn University.

A United Soccer Coaches Scholar All-American, Jess was selected to the All NJAC Conference Team in her senior year. She was also a team Captain.

Nicole DiPasquale

Nicole received the distinct honor of being a Two-time United Soccer Coaches All-American! Being named All-American is a great honor, but to have achieved the honor two-times in her collegiate career is very admirable. In her senior year, she was named United Soccer Coaches First Team All-Region, NJAC Goalkeeper of the Year, was a First-team All-NJAC selection. She was also a two-time team Captain and led TCNJWS to a Final Four.

Alex Panasuk

Alex waited her time to play at TCNJ due to the fact that she was behind two previous All-Americans. A two-time Captain, who had to miss a year due to Covid, she came back and led the team to the Final Four. She was named United Soccer Coaches All-American after having a stellar senior year, 2021.

Additional Professional/World Class Goalkeepers

In addition to world class keepers, Saskia Webber and Karina LeBlanc, Paul has had the opportunity of working with Karen Bardsley, England's Women's National Team and Manchester City's keeper and Jillian Loyden, of the USWNT and founder of The Keeper Institute. Paul also helped professional goalkeepers Billy Gaudette, Bryan Meredith, Ian Joyce and Neal Kitson in preparations for their careers. Adelaide Gay, another keeper Paul started working with at a young age, is still playing professionally in Iceland after having won a D1 National Championship at the famed UNC and playing in Sweden.